C++
for Java Programmers

Mark Allen Weiss
Florida International University

PEARSON

Prentice
Hall

Upper Saddle River, NJ 07458

Library of Congress Cataloging-in-Publication Data on file.

Vice President and Editorial Director, ECS: *Marcia J. Horton*
Publisher: *Alan R. Apt*
Associate Editor: *Toni Dianne Holm*
Editorial Assistant: *Patrick Lindner*
Vice President and Director of Production and Manufacturing, ESM: *David W. Riccardi*
Executive Managing Editor: *Vince O'Brien*
Managing Editor: *Camille Trentacoste*
Production Editor: *Geri Mattson*
Director of Creative Services: *Paul Belfanti*
Creative Director: *Carole Anson*
Art Director and Cover Manager: *Maureen Eide*
Cover Designer: *Kenny Beck*
Managing Editor, AV Management and Production: *Patricia Burns*
Art Editor: *Gregory Dulles*
Manufacturing Manager: *Trudy Pisciotti*
Manufacturing Buyer: *Lisa McDowell*
Marketing Manager: *Pamela Shaffer*

© 2004 Pearson Eduction, Inc.
Pearson Prentice Hall
Pearson Education, Inc.
Upper Saddle River, NJ 07458

Pearson Prentice Hall® is a trademark of Pearson Education, Inc.

Printed in the United States of America

10 9 8 7 6 5 4 3 2 1

ISBN: 0-13-919424-X

Pearson Education Ltd., *London*
Pearson Education Australia Pty. Ltd., *Sydney*
Pearson Education Singapore, Pte. Ltd.
Pearson Education North Asia Ltd., *Hong Kong*
Pearson Education Canada, Inc., *Toronto*
Pearson Educación de Mexico, S.A. de C.V.
Pearson Education—Japan, *Tokyo*
Pearson Education Malaysia, Pte. Ltd.
Pearson Education, Inc., *Upper Saddle River, New Jersey*

To my wife and best friend for life, Jill

Contents

3   Pointers and Reference Variables   35

4   Object-Based Programming: Classes   51

6   Object-Oriented Programming: Inheritance   112

7   Templates   136

8   **Abnormal Control Flow**   **155**

Preface

For many years, C++ was the *defacto* language of choice in introductory Computer Science courses, due largely to its support for object-oriented programming, as well as its wide adoption in industy. However, because C++ is arguably the most complex language ever to be widely-used, Java, which also supports object-oriented programming, recently has emerged as the preferred introductory language. Nonetheless, demand for C++ skill is still high in industry and most universities require C++ programming at some point in the Computer Science curriculum. Although Java and C++ look similar, programming in C++ is somewhat more challenging and filled with subtle details. While there are many books that thoroughly describe C++ (see the Bibliography), the vast majority exceed 1,000 pages and, for the most part, are written for either experienced industry programmers or novices.

This book is designed as a quick start guide for students who are knowledgeable in an object-oriented language (most likely Java) and would like to learn C++. Throughout the text, we compare and contrast Java and C++, and show C++ substitutes for Java equivalents. We do not describe in detail basic concepts (such as inheritance) that are common in both C++ and Java; rather, we describe how the concepts are implemented in C++. This helps achieve one of the important goals of this book, which is to keep the page count reasonably low. Consequently, this book is not appropriate for students who have limited or no prior programming experience.

Organization

The book begins with a brief overview of C++ in Chapter 0. In Chapter 1, we describe some of the basic expressions and statements in C++, which mostly mirror simple Java syntax. Functions, arrays, strings, and parameter passing are discussed in Chapter 2. We use the modern alternative of introducing and using the standard `vector` and `string` classes in the C++ library, rather than the older-style built-in array constructs.

Chapter 3 describes pointers and reference variables, paying particular attention to the host of pitfalls that await a C++ programmer. Chapter 4 is a long chapter that describes the basics of classes.

Two C++ features that are not part of Java are operator overloading and templates. Operator overloading is discussed in Chapter 5 and templates are discussed in Chapter 7. In between, we cover inheritance in Chapter 6. In Chapter 8, we examine exceptions in C++, as well as older library routines such as `abort`.

The next two chapters discuss some C++ libraries. Chapter 9 deals with I/O and Chapter 10 introduces the Standard Template Library, which is the C++ equivalent of the Collections API. Both libraries are complex enough to require an entire book: We provide the most important highlights, rather than attempting to list every detail.

Many courses will require C programming in addition to C++ programming. Because C++ builds on C, many C programming techniques are also found in C++, although in C++ they are not always the preferred way to do things. Chapter 11 covers primitive arrays and strings. As we mentioned earlier, modern C++ uses library classes as an alternative. Nonetheless, primitive arrays and strings will almost certainly be encountered by any C++ programmer, and the techniques are essentially the same in C++ and C. Chapter 12 covers C idioms that are occasionally used in C++, but probably should be avoided. Finally, in Chapter 13, we describe the Java Native Interface (again a whole book can be written on this one topic), which allows Java programmers to implement their methods in C++ or C.

Acknowledgments

As usual, many people were crucial in bringing the book to fruition.

First, at Pearson Education, I'd like to thank the Publisher, Alan R. Apt, Associate Editor, Toni D. Holm, Editorial Assistant, Patrick Linder, and Freelance Review/Supplement Editor, Jake Warde.

The reviewers provided valuable comments, many of which have been incorporated into the text, Alphabetically, they are:

Roger Hartley, New Mexico State University;

Ralph Hooper, University of Alabama; and

Sakke Karstu, Michigan Tech University.

Production of the text was handled smoothly thanks to my Copy Editor Cheryl Kranz, my Project Manager Geri Mattson and Proofreader Patrick Kelly. Camille Trentacoste did a wonderful job with the interior book design and providing Framemaker templates. The beautiful cover was done by Maureen Eide.

Some of the material in this text (especially Chapters 1, 2, 3, 11, and 12) is adapted from my textbook *Efficient C Programming: A Practical Approach* (Prentice-Hall, 1995).

My World Wide Web page, `http://www.cs.fiu.edu/~weiss`, will contain updated source code, an errata list, and a link for receiving bug reports.

M.A.W
Miami, Florida
July, 2003

Introduction

0

Chapter Outline

C++® and Java™ look similar syntactically. Many of the basic constructs in Java, such as basic expressions, conditionals, and loop constructs are indeed identical except for minor technical differences. Other Java features, such as support for object-based programming via classes, have a similar look and feel in C++, as does much of the syntax related to inheritance. One could (more or less) mechanically translate Java code into C++ code without great difficulty, since most Java constructs have at least one corresponding C++ construct. Some people have even renamed Java as C++-lite. Yet, as we will see, while there are many similarities, the languages have significant differences.

In this chapter, we begin by discussing the progression of languages from C to C++ to Java. Then we discuss some of the major high-level differences between C++ and Java.

1

🐚 0.1   A History Lesson

In 1972, Dennis Ritchie designed C and implemented it on a PDP-11. The initial design of C reflected the fact that it was used to implement an operating system. Until then, all operating systems were written in an assembly language because compiler technology did not generate sufficiently efficient code from higher-level languages. C provided constructs, such as pointer arithmetic, direct memory access, increment operators, bit operations, and hexadecimal constants that mimicked the PDP-11's instruction set, while at the same time keeping the language small but high level. Consequently, the compiler was able to generate reasonably efficient code. Eventually, Unix® was written mostly in C, with only a few parts requiring assembly language.

By early 2002, a top-of-the-line home computer selling for less than $2,000 could execute several hundred million instructions per second. Home computers could be purchased with 1 Gigabyte of main memory and 120 Gigabytes of hard drive space. By the time you read this, the computer just described may well be a relic.

On the other hand, a PDP-11/45, which I actually used as a college undergraduate, sold for well over $10,000 (in 1970 dollars). Our model had 128 kilobytes of main memory and executed only several thousand instructions per second. The PDP-11/45 was a 16 bit machine, so not surprisingly, the `int` type was 16 bits; other PDP models had 12, 18, or even 36 bits. The C compiler on the PDP-11/45 typically took about 30 seconds to compile a trivial 100 line program, but since it used 32K of memory to do so, compilations were queued, like printer jobs, to avoid compiling two programs at once and crashing the system! Our PDP-11/45 supported over 20 simultaneous users, all connected via old-style "dumb" terminals. Most of the terminals operated at 110 baud, although there were a few fast ones that ran at 300 baud. At 110 baud, approximately 10 characters per second are transmitted, so screen editors were not widely used. Instead editing was done a line at a time, using the Unix editor `ed` (which still exists!). C thus provided rather terse syntax to minimize typing and, more importantly, displaying.

In this environment, it is not surprising that the number one goal of the compiler was to compile correct programs as fast as possible into code that was as fast as possible, and since the main users were typically experts, dealing with incorrect programs was left to the programmer rather than the compiler (or runtime system). No checks were performed to ensure that a variable was assigned a value prior to use of its value. After all, who wanted to wait any longer for the program to compile? Arrays were implemented in the same manner as in an assembly language, with no bounds checking to consume precious CPU cycles. A host of programming practices that involved the use of pointers to achieve performance benefits emerged. There was even a reserved word, `register`, that was used to suggest to the compiler that a particular local variable should be stored in a machine register, rather than on the runtime stack, to make the program run faster, since the compiler would not try to do any flow analysis on its own.

Soon, Unix became popular in the academic community, and with it, the C language grew. At one point, C was known as the great portable language, suitable for systems use on many machines. Unix itself was ported to a host of platforms. Eventually a host of software vendors started producing C compilers and adding their own extra features, but in so doing, they made the language less portable, in part because the language specification was vague in places, which allowed competing interpretations. Also, a host of clever but nonetheless unacceptable and unportable programming tricks had emerged; it became clear that these tricks should be disallowed. Since compiler technology had become better and computers had become faster, it also became feasible to add helpful features to the language in the hopes of enhancing portability and reducing the chances of undetected errors. Eventually, in 1989, this resulted in ANSI C, which is now the gold standard of C to which most programmers adhere. In 1999, C99 was adopted, adding some new features, but since C99 is not yet widely implemented in compilers, few programmers find a need to use those features.

In parallel with the standardization of C was an effort by Bjarne Stroustrup to create a more object-oriented approach to using C. Eventually C++ emerged and then ultimately underwent a standardization process.

C++ should be viewed as a completely new language, based largely on C. It includes modern constructs to support object-oriented programming. Several design issues have greatly influenced C++.

First and foremost, C++ was intended to be upward compatible with C as much as possible. Thus legal C programs should be legal C++ programs, although this is not 100% true. (Obvious exceptions include C programs that use as identifiers any reserved word that was added to C++, such as `class`.) As a result, numerous constructs from C that perhaps we could live without are part of C++, as is the entire idea of using pointers to do arrays. Additionally, because each new reserved word breaks existing code, the C++ community is reluctant to add new reserved words, preferring instead to overuse existing words, such as `const` and `static`. So whereas Java has `throw` and `throws`, in C++ we simply use `throw` both to throw an exception and to list exceptions.

The second crucial philosophy of C++ was in part political: C++ programs should be as fast as C programs if they do the same thing. Otherwise, it was thought, nobody would want to learn a more complicated language just to write slower code. As part of this philosophy, in C++, if you do not use a feature, you should not have to pay a cost at runtime. Among other things, this still means, no runtime bounds checks, no dynamic dispatch by default, and no garbage collection.

The third thing to know about C++ is that it has continually evolved. The first widely used version of C++ supported classes and inheritance. *Templates*, discussed in Chapter 7, were added later. Exceptions were added even later. At another time came *namespaces*. The templates got fancier, with templates inside of templates. This has lead to compilers being perennially behind the official specification, buggy with new features, and especially bug-prone when several new features are used at the same time, much to the chagrin of programmers and textbook authors. Fortunately, C++ has more or less stabilized and the latest compilers are quite good at meeting (and in some cases doing more than required by) the language specification.

Java was developed by Sun Microsystems and marketed as a modern alternative to C++. Thus, cosmetically, there are many similarities. However, the designers of Java had (at least) two main goals. First, they attempted to allow the programmer to write the same set of programs that C++ allows, using simpler syntax. In cases where C++ has several ways to do the same thing, Java attempts to pick the idiom most widely endorsed by the C++ community and support it with a language feature. In cases where C++ features are abused, Java does not allow the feature. Thus some C++ features are not found in Java. Second, the designers attempted to make it harder for incorrect code to run, requiring the compiler to detect many sets of errors when it first compiles the program and then requiring the Virtual Machine to throw an exception when bad things happen at runtime. By detecting most occurrences of bad behavior, not only are honest programming errors avoided, but system security against hacking is enhanced, since hacking generally works by having the system do something it is not designed to do.

The Java designers have several advantages. First, in designing the language, they can expect the compiler to work hard. We no longer use PDP-11s, and compiler research has advanced greatly to the point that modern optimizing compilers can do a terrific job of creating code without requiring the programmer to resort to various tricks common in the good old days. Second, Java designers specified most of the language (classes, inheritance, exceptions) at once, adding only a second minor revision (inner classes); most changes after Java 1.1 dealt with the library. In doing so, they were able to have language features that don't clash.

Although Java is the new kid on the block (unless C# becomes the next new kid) and has lots of nice features, it is certainly not true that Java is better than C++, neither would we say that C++ is better than Java. Instead, a modern programmer should be able to use both languages, as each language has applications that can make it the logical choice.

0.2   High Level Differences

As we just described, Java and C++ have different views of the world. C++'s main priority is getting correct programs to run as fast as they can; incorrect programs are on their own. Java's main priority is not allowing incorrect programs to run; hopefully correct programs run reasonably fast, and the language makes it easier to generate correct programs by restricting some bad programming constructs.

0.2.1   Compiled vs. Interpreted Code

Java consists of both a compiler and a Virtual Machine. The compiler generates Java bytecode, and the bytecode is then interpreted at runtime. As a result, not only is Java code portable, the compiled bytecode is portable and in theory can be run on any platform.

On the other hand, a C++ compiler generates native code. The C++ language specification provides no guidance on the specifics of what the native code looks like, so not only is the result of the compilation not transferable to a different type of computer, but parts of a single program that are compiled on the same computer by different compilers are almost always not compatible with each other.

Originally, the difference between compiled code and interpreted code meant that C++ was as much as 50 times faster than Java. Recent improvements in the Java compiler and, more importantly, the Virtual Machine have dramatically closed the gap. In some cases, Java code may actually be faster than C++, but generally speaking, one would expect that since C++ does less runtime checks than Java, equally skilled compiler writers should be able to generate somewhat faster C++ code than Java code, assuming similar coding styles.

0.2.2   Security and Robustness

We have already seen that Java is very concerned with not allowing unsafe code to compile and with throwing exceptions at the first sign of trouble. C++ is, unfortunately, somewhat lax in this regard. C++ suffers from several problems that can never occur in pure Java code. Four that stand out are the following:

1. It is possible in C++ to have a pointer or reference to an object that has been returned to the memory heap, which is a sure disaster. This is because standard C++ does not do garbage collection; instead the programmers must manage memory themselves and programmers are surprisingly bad at doing so. However, some C++ systems include garbage collection and add runtime checks to avoid using stale pointers. These systems are quite close to the Java standard of avoiding memory problems.

2. Standard C++ does not check array indexes, and a common hacker attack is to find an input routine that reads a string, but doesn't check that there is enough space for a very very long string. By judiciously passing a huge string, the hacker can overflow the buffer and write replacement values onto variables that are stored in memory adjacent to the buffer. Although this could never happen in Java, since the C++ specification does not disallow bounds checks, there is no reason that a safe C++ system couldn't check array bounds. It would simply be slower (but safer) than a competitor and so it is not widely done by default.

3. Old C++ typecasts allow type confusion, in which a type is cast to an unrelated type. This can never happen in Java, but is allowed in C++.

4. In Java, all variables have a definite assigned value prior to use of their value. This is because variables that are not local to a method by default are initialized to zero for primitives and to `null` for references. For local variables, an entire chapter of the Java Language Specification is devoted to *definite assignment*, whereby the compiler is required to perform a flow analysis and produce an error message if a local variable cannot be proven (under a long set of rules) to have been definitely assigned to through all flows of the method. In C++, this behavior is not required. Rather, a program that uses an uninitialized variable is said to be incorrect, but the compiler is not required to take any particular action. Most C++ compilers will print warning messages if uninitialized variables are detected, but the program will still compile. A similar story occurs in the case of a flow that fails to return a value in a non-`void` function.

0.2.3   Multithreading

C++ does not support multithreading as part of the language. Instead, one must use a set of library routines that are native to the particular platform. Although Java supports multithreading, the Java memory model and threading specification has been discovered to be inadequate and is undergoing revision.

0.2.4   API Differences

The Java API is huge. The core library includes, among other things, the Swing package `javax.swing` for designing (mostly) portable GUIs, a networking package in `java.net`, database connectivity in `java.sql`, built-in compression, serialization, and other I/O in `java.util.zip` and `java.io`, reflection in `java.lang.reflect`, and even support for remote methods, servlets, and XML.

Standard C++ has a very small API, containing little more than some I/O support, a complex number package, and a Collections API, known as the *Standard Template Library* (STL). Of course, compiler vendors augment Standard C++ with huge libraries, but each vendor has different versions rather than implementing a single standard.

0.3   Ten Reasons to Use C++

The preceding section might leave you to conclude that C++ has little to offer. This is not true; there are lots of reasons why you would want to learn and use C++. In this section we list 10 advantages of using C++, including features found in C++ that are not found in Java. Figure 0-1 summarizes the differences described in both Section 0.2 and this section, as well as a few differences that are described later in this text, but not otherwise mentioned in this chapter.

0.3.1   C++ Is Still Widely Used

Perhaps the most important reason to learn C++ is that it is still very widely used, and since it is a more complex and difficult language than C++, it is likely that there will always be a strong market for knowledgeable C++ programmers.

0.3.2   Templates

Perhaps the most requested missing feature in Java is the equivalent of the C++ *template*. In C++, templates allow the writing of generic type-independent code, such as sorting algorithms and generic data structures that work for any type. In Java, this is done by using inheritance, but the downside is that many errors are not detected at compile time and instead linger until run time. Further, using templates in C++ seems to lead to faster code than the inheritance-based alternative in Java. Generics are under consideration for Java 1.5. Templates are discussed in Chapter 7.

Feature	Java	C++
Compiler output	Virtual Machine bytecode	Native code
Portability	High	Moderate
Garbage collection	Yes	No
Checks array indices	Yes	No
Multithreading	Yes	Platform specific
API	Huge	Small
Security checks	Yes	No
Compiler checks	Numerous	Some
Operator overloading	No	Yes
Templates	No	Yes
Multiple inheritance	Interface only	Yes
Standard GUI library	Yes	No
Data structures	Collections API	STL
Exception handling	Yes	Yes, but poorly integrated
Conditional compilation	No	Yes
Global functions	No	Yes
Class grouping	Packages	Namespaces
Pointer variables	No	Yes
Class documentation	Javadoc	Not in standard
Reflection	Yes	No
Space efficient	Not really	Yes

Figure 0-1   Differences between Java and C++

0.3.3   Operator Overloading

Java does not allow the user to define operators for class types. C++ does, and this is known as *operator overloading*. We discuss operator overloading in Chapter 5.

0.3.4   Standard Template Library

C++ provides a large library, known as the Standard Template Library (STL) for data structures and generic algorithms. The STL has several advantages compared to the Java Collections API and we discuss these differences in Chapter 10.

0.3.5   Automatic Reclamation of Resources

Although Java provides garbage collection, which is a fantastic feature, it is hard to control the management of other resources. For instance, in Java, the programmer must remember to close files and database connections when they are no longer in use, dispose of graphics contexts, and so on. Although many (nonmemory) resources are released by object finalization, relying on object finalization in Java is a poor idea, since objects need not be reclaimed if the garbage collector deems that memory is not low.

In C++, each class can provide a special method known as the *destructor*, which will automatically be invoked when an object is no longer active. Careful C++ programmers need not remember to release nonmemory resources, and memory resources can often be released by layering the memory allocations inside of classes. Many Java programmers who have prior C++ experience lament the lack of destructors. We describe destructors in Section 4.6.

0.3.6   Conditional Compilation

In C++, it is possible to write code that is compiled only if certain conditions are met at compile time. This is achieved by use of the preprocessor and is a useful feature during debugging. Java has only a limited way of doing this. The preprocessor is described in Section 12.1.

0.3.7   Distinctions between Accessor and Mutator

In Java, when a reference variable is marked as `final`, it simply means that the reference variable cannot change; there is no easy way to signal that the state of the object being referenced cannot be changed (i.e., that the object is immutable). C++ provides syntax to distinguish between methods that are accessors and mutators, and marking an object as `const` (the equivalent of `final`) allows only the accessors of the object to be invoked. Many Java programmers who have prior C++ experience lament the difficulty of enforcing immutability. We describe accessors and mutators in Section 4.2.

0.3.8   Multiple Implementation Inheritance

Java does not allow multiple implementation inheritance because it is notoriously difficult to use generally. However, there are always some cases when it is very useful, and C++ does allow multiple implementation inheritance. We discuss this in Section 6.8.

0.3.9   Space Efficiency

Java programs are notoriously space inefficient. For instance, a `String` of length 16 uses roughly 76 bytes under Sun's Java 1.3 compiler. C++ programs are often more space efficient than Java programs.

0.3.10 Private Inheritance

Java supports only public inheritance, via the `extends` clause. C++ supports private inheritance, which is occasionally useful for changing visible interfaces and implementing adapter patterns. Private inheritance is discussed in Section 6.10.2.

Key Points

- C++ is based on C.
- The most important consideration in the design of C++ is to make correct programs run as fast as possible.
- Compile-time checks in C++ are not as rigid as in Java, but now many compilers perform some of the same checks as a Java compiler and yield warning messages.
- Runtime checks in C++ are not as rigid in Java. In C++, bad array indexes, bad typecasts, and bad pointers do not automatically cause a runtime error. Some compilers will do more than the minimum and issue runtime errors for you, but this behavior cannot be relied on.
- Compiled units are not compatible across different types of machines, nor are they compatible on the same machine when generated by different compilers.
- Although the STL in C++ is excellent, the remainder of the Standard C++ Library pales in comparison to Java, but many nonstandard additions are available.

Exercises

1. Compare and contrast the basic design goals of C++ and Java.
2. What are the different versions of C++?
3. What are the basic differences between compiled and interpreted languages?
4. What is a buffer overflow problem?
5. List features of Java that are not part of Standard C++ and result in C++ being a less safe language.
   Describe some features of C++ that make it more attractive than Java.

Basic Types and Control Structures

1

Chapter Outline

Many Java constructs have direct analogs in C++. In both languages, execution starts at `main`, basic control flow constructs are mostly identical, and both languages have similar support for basic object-based concepts of encapsulation and information hiding via the class. Object-oriented programming is supported in both languages via inheritance. Both languages support strings as a library class type, provide primitive array support, and provide a growable array as part of the standard library. Both languages have library support for data structures collections. However, there are some organizational differences even in the simplest part of the language.

In this chapter, we look at the basics of compiling the first C++ program, and discuss the basic types and control structures that are common in both languages.

1.1   First Program

The typical first C++ program is shown in Figure 1-1. By way of comparison, the equivalent Java code is shown in Figure 1-2. The C++ program should be placed in a file that has an appropriate suffix. C++ does not specify a particular suffix, but most compilers recognize `.cpp`.

1.1.1   `main` Function

Like Java, control starts at `main`. Unlike Java, `main` is not part of any class; instead, it is a non-class method. In C++, methods are called *member functions*. We will adopt the convention that a function that is not declared as part of a class is simply a *function* (with the adjective *member* conveniently omitted). C++ also allows global variables.

  `main` must always be declared in global scope and it must have return type `int`, which by convention will be 0 unless a nonzero error code is to be transmitted back to the invoking process in a manner that is similar to calling `System.exit` (we will always return 0). Although some programmers prefer to use a `void` return type, the language specification is clear that the return type of `main` should be `int`.

  `main` can take additional parameters for command-line arguments (we discuss this in Section 11.5). Because `main` is in global scope, there can be only one version of `main`. This contrasts with Java, which allows one `main` per class.

1.1.2   The Preprocessor

Line 1 is an *include directive* that reads the declarations for the standard I/O routines. The include directive has the effect of having the compiler logically insert the source code taken from another file. Specifically, the filename that resides in between < and > refers to a system file. Alternatively, a pair of double quotes can be used to specify a user-defined (nonsystem) file. Thus in our example, the entire contents of the file `iostream`, which resides in a system-dependent location, is substituted for line 1. In Section 2.1.7 we discuss how the include directive is typically used to enable faster compilations.

  In C++, lines that begin with the # are preprocessor directives. We will see an important use of preprocessor directives in Section 4.12.

```
1   #include <iostream>
2   using namespace std;
3
4   int main( )
5   {
6       cout << "Hello world" << endl;
7       return 0;
8   }
```

Figure 1-1   First C++ program

```
1   public class FirstProgram
2   {
3       public static void main( String [ ] args )
4       {
5           System.out.println( "Hello world" );
6       }
7   }
```

Figure 1-2   First Java program

1.1.3   The **using** Directive

The declaration at line 2 is a *using directive* and is the moral equivalent of an import directive in Java. Whereas in Java, classes in package `java.lang` are automatically known without requiring the full class name that includes their package, in C++, classes in the equivalent namespace, `std`, require a full class name unless the using directive is supplied. Thus this using directive is the C++ equivalent of

```
import java.lang.*;
```

We discuss the using directive and the C++ equivalent of packages in Section 4.15.

1.1.4   Output

Ignoring the return statement, the simple program in Figure 1-1 consists of a single statement. This statement, shown at line 6, is the output mechanism in C++. Here a constant string is placed on the standard output stream `cout`. Simple terminal input is similar to output, with `cin` replacing `cout` and >> replacing <<. As an example,

```
int x;
cout << "Enter a value of x: ";
cin >> x;
```

reads the next series of characters (skipping white space) and interprets them as an integer. Of course, this example fails to discuss handling input errors, which is crucial in any serious application. Input and output is discussed in more detail in Chapter 9.

 ## 1.2   Primitive Types

While Java has only eight primitive types and these types have precise sets of possible values on all platforms, C++ has a host of primitive types with unspecified ranges.

1.2.1   Integer Types

The basic integer type in C++, like Java, is `int`. However, whereas Java specifies the precise range of `int`, C++ makes no such guarantees; an `int` can be 16, 32, or 64 bits, depending on the platform. Even for 32 bit `int`s, the precise range can vary from machine to machine.

The `int` type can be augmented with the reserved words `short` or `long`. Alternatively `short` and `long` can be used by themselves without `int`. Once again, the language specification makes few guarantees about how large `short` and `long` are except to state that an `int` is never shorter than a `short`, and never longer than a `long`. Historically, a `short` has been 16 bits, a `long` has been 32 bits, and an `int` has been whatever fits best on the machine (currently 32 bits). A long constant includes an L at the end, as in 1000L (the L is never needed if the constant is larger than what could be stored in an `int`).

Two modifiers to the `int` type are `signed` and `unsigned`. These modifiers can be applied to any of the integer types (or `char`). An `unsigned int` will never be negative and in effect instructs the compiler to interpret what would normally be the sign bit as an extra bit. Thus, whereas a `short` might store values in the range −32,768 to 32,767, an `unsigned short` could store values in the range 0 to 65,535. This use of `unsigned` to double the set of range of positive integers carries the significant danger that mixing unsigned and signed values can produce surprising results, so it is best to use unsigned types judiciously. An unsigned constant includes a U at the end, as in 1000UL. By default, the integer types are signed.

C++ does not define an equivalent to the byte data type. Historically, C++ programmers have used `signed char`, which in C++ is simply 8 bits, for this purpose.

1.2.2   Floating Point Types

Floating point types in C++ are represented with `float` and `double`. Like Java, `double` provides more significant digits than a `float` and its use is preferred to minimize roundoff errors. Java specifies constants for "not a number" and both positive and negative infinity. Though the C++ standard does not require it, some C++ implementations are able to store and print such values when they occur.

1.2.3   Character Type

The `char` type, as in Java, is used to store characters. However, unlike Java, where a character is a 16 bit Unicode©, the C++ standard does not specify a size, so C++ compilers generally use only 8 bits and store ASCII characters. Additionally, whether a `char` is signed or unsigned by default is unspecified.

A character constant is represented in a pair of single quotes, as is done in Java. Additionally, there is a rich set of escape sequences that can be used to express unprintable characters, quotes, backslashes, and so forth. The Java escape sequences are part of C++, as are some addition sequences, including \a for the bell, \? for the question mark, and \v for the vertical tab. The escape sequence that allows up to three octal characters is also part of C++. The escape sequence that uses four hexadecimal characters is not part of Standard C++.

The standard header file `cctype` contains routines such as `isupper`, `islower`, and `isalpha` that determine if a character has a certain property. Also present are `toupper` and `tolower` that return upper- and lowercase versions of a character or the character itself, if it is not a lowercase letter. In effect these routines are versions of the static methods in `java.lang.Character`.

Recent C++ compilers have adopted the Java style of supporting Unicode characters with the addition of the `wchar_t` type and the wide-character literal. Wide-character literals begin with an L prior to the opening quote, as in `L'x'` or `L"hello"`. As you may expect by now, the specific behavior of the `wchar_t` type is implementation dependent.

1.2.4   Boolean Type

Like Java, C++ has a Boolean type. In C++, this type is `bool` and it has values `true` or `false`. However, unlike Java, this Boolean type was not originally part of C++ and can result in erroneous code that is legal. We discuss this in Section 1.3.2.

1.3   Syntactic Differences

Many of the basic operators, expressions, and statements are identical in C++ and Java, with only minor differences.

1.3.1   Operators and Expressions

Operators in C++ are for the most part identical to their Java counterparts, although in many cases, dubious Java code has well-defined semantics, whereas the same code in C++ can be implementation dependent. Classic examples of this include the overuse of the ++ operator, as in

```
int x = 5;
x = x++;
```

In Java this code will set x to be 5 (since the ++ is executed prior to the assignment of the original value of x). In C++, the result of this code is implementation dependent. In both languages the code is poor style. More generally, Java specifies that arguments to methods and operands of an operator (except for assignment operators) are evaluated in left-to-right order, whereas C++ makes no such guarantees. Thus, if function `readInt` is intended to read one integer from standard input, the result of `readInt()-readInt()` when 4 and 3 are placed on standard input is guaranteed to be 1 in Java, but can be 1 or −1 in C++.

In Java, integer division rounds down, so `8/-5` is always −1. In C++, the result is implementation dependent and can be −1 or −2, depending on whether the division truncates or rounds to the nearest integer.

C++ adds the comma operator, but the only good use is the use allowed in Java in the expressions that are part of a for loop. The comma operator takes two expressions, evaluates the first, and then the second, and the result of the comma operator is the second expression. This is more trouble than it's worth, as illustrated by the fact that mistyping `3.14` as `3,14` does not generate a compiler error (it simply evaluates to 14). Similarly, the call `pow(3,4)` returns 81 (three to the fourth power), whereas `pow((3,4))` does not compile because `(3,4)` evaluates to 4 and then `pow` is short a parameter. Yuk!

Java has the >>> shift operator, which does bit shifting (to the right), filling in high bits with 0s. The >> shift operator in Java fills in high bits with whatever the high bit of the left operand was originally. In C++, only the >> shift operator is available, and its semantics depend on whether the left operand is signed or unsigned. If it is unsigned, high bits are filled with 0; if it is signed, high bits are filled in with the high bit of the left operand.

1.3.2   Conditionals

The if statement in C++ is identical to Java, except that in C++ the condition of the if statement can be either an `int` or a `bool`. This stems from the fact that, historically, early implementations of C++ did not have a `bool` type, but instead interpreted 0 as false and anything nonzero as true. The unfortunate consequence of this decision is that code such as

```
if( x = 0 )
```

which uses = instead of the intended == is not flagged as a compiler error, but instead sets x to zero and evaluates the condition to false. This is possibly the most common trivial C++ programming error.

Occasionally, especially when reading old C++ code, shorthands that make use of the fact that nonzero evaluates to true are placed in the conditional expression. Thus it is not uncommon to see tests that should be

```
if( i != 0 )
```

rewritten as

```
if( i )
```

Newly written code should avoid these types of shortcuts, since they tend to make the code less readable and no more efficient.

1.3.3   Loops

Like Java, C++ has the for loop, the while loop, and the do loop, along with break and continue statements. However, in C++, the use of the labelled break and labelled continue to affect flow of an outer loop is not allowed.

C++ allows the goto, but its use is strongly discouraged.

1.3.4   Definite Assignment

An entire section of the Java Language Specification deals with errors that a Java compiler is required to detect; such errors cause the compilation to fail. For instance, a Java compiler must apply a conservative flow analysis to ensure that every local variable has been definitely assigned a value, regardless of the flow of control. Although occasionally this forces the programmer to rewrite valid code, much more often it finds programming errors at compilation time. A Java compiler is required to verify that all flows of control return a value in a nonvoid method. C++ compilers are not required to perform such analyses, although many do by request when suitable compilation options are specified. It won't take long until you will write a C++ program that compiles and uses an uninitialized variable, causing you runtime grief; so pay attention to warning messages and turn on the compiler's ability to generate extra warnings.

1.4   Additional Syntax

This section discusses the relatively straightforward issues of primitive typecasts, labels, and the `typedef` statement.

1.4.1   Primitive Typecasts

In Java, the typecast operator has two basic uses: downcasting a reference variable to a subclass reference type and interpreting a primitive type as a different type (for instance, casting an `int` to a `byte`). C++ has several different typecasts. In this section we discuss the typecasts that are used for primitive types.

First, let us mention that C++ is more liberal than Java in accepting code without a cast. In Java,

```
double x = 6.0;
int y;
y = x;
```

does not compile, but the code does compile (possibly with a warning about losing precision) in C++. In some cases, typecasting is essential to produce a correct answer, as in

```
double quotient;
int x = 6;
int y = 10;
quotient = x / y;
```

In this example, in both Java and C++, quotient evaluates to 0.0 rather than 0.6, because the operands are both of type `int` and so division is performed with truncation to an `int`. There are several syntactical ways to handle the typecast. The Java style, which also works in C++,

```
quotient = (double) x / (double) y;
```

in which we cast both operands, is easy to read. Since only one operand needs to be a `double`,

```
quotient = (double) x / y;
```

also works. However, this code is hard to read because one must be aware that the precedence of the typecast operator is higher than the precedence of division, which is why the typecast applies to x, and not x/y. An alternative in C++ is preferred:

```
quotient = double( x ) / y;
```

Here, the parentheses surround the expression to be cast, rather than the new type. (Note that this does not work for complex types such as `unsigned int`.)

Although this second style is preferable, it is hard to find the typecasts that are being used in a program, since the syntax does not stand out. A third form, a late addition to C++, is to use the *static cast*

```
quotient = static_cast<double>( x ) / y;
```

Although this is more typing, it is easy to find the casts mechanically.

A different type of typecast, useful for downcasting in inheritance hierarchies, is the `dynamic_cast`. We discuss this in Section 6.7.

1.4.2   Labels

C++ allows labels prior to virtually any statement, for use with the goto statement. Since gotos typically are symptomatic of poorly designed code, one would rarely expect to see labels in C++ code.

1.4.3   typedef Statement

The *typedef statement* is provided by C++ to allow the programmer to assign meaningful names to existing types. As an example, suppose that we need to declare objects of type 32 bit unsigned integer. On some machines this might be `unsigned long`, while on other, perhaps an `unsigned int` is the most appropriate type. On the first machine, we would use

```
typedef unsigned long uint32,
```

whereas on the second machine, we would use

```
typedef unsigned int uint32;
```

Now, in the rest of the code, either machine can declare variables of type `uint32`,

```
uint32 x, y, z;
```

meaning that the nonportable aspect of the code is confined to one line.

Key Points

- In C++, methods are known as member functions.
- In C++, functions can be written outside of any class.
- Flow in C++ begins at `main`. Function `main` returns an `int`. Each program can have only one `main`.
- Lines that begin with # are preprocessor directives. The include (preprocessor) directive causes the contents of the file referenced by the directive to be logically placed in the source code in place of the include directive.
- Simple output is performed by using `cout` and the `<<` operator.
- Simple input is performed by using `cin` and the `>>` operator.
- The C++ primitive types include `short`, `int`, `long`. These types may be `signed` or `unsigned`. The `byte` type in Java can be simulated with `signed char`.
- The C++ `char` is typically only 8 bits and is used to store ASCII characters. The newly introduced `wchar_t` type is 16 bits and can be used to store Unicode characters.

- The standard header file `cctype` contains routines that are similar to the static methods in `java.lang.Character`.
- The `bool` type is a late addition to C++. Conditions in C++ use the C-style convention of zero for false and nonzero for true, leading to programming errors when = is used instead of ==.
- C++ adds the comma operator, which is best avoided except in the typical Java use in for loop expressions.
- C++ does not support the labelled break or labelled continue.
- C++ does not precisely define the semantics of some operations that can be reasonably implemented in different ways on various machines.
- A C++ compiler is not required to check that variables are definitely assigned values prior to their use nor that all flows return a value in functions that have nonvoid return types. Many compilers do so, but only when requested.
- C++ has three forms of typecast, one of which looks like the Java style. For casting between primitive types, the `static_cast` is recommended.
- The `typedef` statement allows the programmer to assign meaningful names to existing types.

Exercises

1. Compile, link, and run the program in Figure 1-1.
2. Write a program to print out the values of the largest and smallest `int` on your system by printing the appropriate values in the standard header file `<climits>`.
3. What is the result of

```
if( x = y )
   cout << x << endl;
else
   cout << y << endl;
```

4. What is the result of

```
if( x < y < z )
   cout << "Sorted" << endl;
else
   cout << "Not sorted" << endl;
```

5. How does C++ handle uninitialized variables?
6. What does the `typedef` statement do?

Functions, Arrays, Strings, and Parameter Passing 2

Chapter Outline

In this continuation of the discussion in Chapter 1, we examine how nonclass methods are written, discuss the library string and growable array types, and see several parameter passing mechanisms that are available in C++.

2.1 Functions

In Section 1.1.1 we mentioned that C++ allows methods that are not members of a class. Typically we refer to these as *functions*. This section discusses functions; member functions are discussed in Chapter 4.

2.1.1 Function Definition

Functions, not being part of a class, simply consist of a return type, function name, parameter list, and body. This complete set, in which the function body is included, is often called a function

19

definition. A function can be invoked from any other function simply by providing an appropriate set of parameters. Figure 2-1 illustrates a function definition of max2 that looks similar to Java code except that both a visibility modifier and the static reserved word are omitted. (We use max2 to avoid an accidental match with a Standard Library routine named max.)

2.1.2   Function Invocation

A function is invoked by simply providing arguments of types that are compatible with the formal parameters. In C++, there is more latitude granted when the arguments are not of the exact types required. For instance, a long can be an acceptable argument (possibly with a warning) even if the formal parameter is an int. When parameters are passed as in Figure 2-1, call-by-value is used. Thus the formal parameters become copies of the actual arguments and, as in Java, the values of the actual arguments cannot be changed as a result of the function invocation. C++ also provides additional ways to pass parameters, including call-by-reference, which does allow changes to the values of the actual arguments. This is discussed in Section 2.3.

2.1.3   Function Overloading

C++ allows function overloading along the same lines as Java. Several functions can have the same name as long as they have different signatures. As with Java, the signature of a function includes the function name and the number and types of the parameters. (It also includes the parameter passing mechanism, which we discuss in Section 2.3.) Like Java, the signature does not include the return type. C++ has a complicated set of rules that are used to resolve an over-loaded call in the case where there are several candidates.

```
1   #include <iostream>
2   using namespace std;
3
4   int max2( int a, int b )
5   {
6       return a > b ? a : b;
7   }
8
9   int main( )
10  {
11      int x = 37;
12      int y = 52;
13
14      cout << "Max is " << max2( x, y ) << endl;
15      return 0;
16  }
```

Figure 2-1   Invoking an already-defined method

2.1.4   Function Declarations

When a function is invoked, the C++ compiler checks actual parameters against the signatures of all the functions that it has seen thus far so as to resolve overloading. However, because historically a C++ compiler processes the source code from top to bottom, if a function definition has not already been seen, a compiler would not include its signature in the list of candidates. As a specific example, the code in Figure 2-2, in which the max2 method is defined after the invocation is attempted, does not compile.

To resolve this, the programmer would have to ensure that every function is defined prior to its invocation. This is tedious at best and perhaps impossible in the case of mutual recursion (in which two functions call each other). Thus C++ introduced the notion of the *function prototype*.

The syntax of the function prototype is, for all intents and purposes, identical to the listing of a method in a Java interface. For instance, the prototype for max2 is

```
int max2( int a, int b );
```

The prototype does not include the body, but instead terminates the declaration with a semicolon. The prototype, which is also known as a function declaration, allows the max2 function, which is presumed to be defined elsewhere, to be a candidate when max2 is invoked. Typical strategy would thus involve listing all the prototypes prior to the first function definition, thus assuring that all functions can call all other functions. Figure 2-3 illustrates the use of the function prototype.

```
1   #include <iostream>
2   using namespace std;
3
4   int main( )
5   {
6       int x = 37;
7       int y = 52;
8
9       cout << "Max is " << max2( x, y ) << endl;
10      return 0;
11  }
12
13  int max2( int a, int b )
14  {
15      return a > b ? a : b;
16  }
```

Figure 2-2   Invoking an unseen method does not compile

```
1   #include <iostream>
2   using namespace std;
3
4   int max2( int a, int b );
5
6   int main( )
7   {
8       int x = 37;
9       int y = 52;
10
11      cout << "Max is " << max2( x, y ) << endl;
12      return 0;
13  }
14
15  int max2( int a, int b )
16  {
17      return a > b ? a : b;
18  }
```

Figure 2-3   Invoking a method after function prototype

2.1.5   Default Parameters

C++ allows the user to specify default values for formal parameters. Typically the default values are included in the function declaration. As an example, the following declaration for `printInt` specifies that, by default, integers should be printed in decimal:

```
void printInt( int n, int base = 10 );
```

Given this declaration, both of the following invocations are legal:

```
printInt( 50 );         // Outputs 50
printInt( 50, 8 );      // Outputs 62 (50 in octal)
```

If a default value is specified for a formal parameter, all subsequent formal parameters must have default values too. In the example above, for instance, we could not specify

```
void printInt( int base = 10, int n );
```

Consequently, parameters that might be omitted are arranged so that the most likely to assume default values will go last.

A default value cannot be specified in both the function declaration and function definition. A default value can be specified in the function definition instead of the declaration, but this is considered bad practice because it requires that the function definition be placed prior to the function invocation so that the signature that does not include parameters that have defaults is considered as a candidate during overload resolution.

Overuse of default values can lead to ambiguities. For instance,

```
void printInt( int n, int base = 10 );
void printInt( int n );
```

is ambiguous if `printInt` is invoked with one parameter.

2.1.6 Inline Functions

In some situations, the overhead of making a function call can be significant. For instance, the max2 routine is trivial, and so one might be tempted to simply replace the function invocation in main with the code that max2 is logically performing:

```
cout << "Max is " << ( x > y ? x : y ) << endl;
```

Of course, this would be sacrificing good programming practice for speed. To avoid this one can use the inline directive.

The *inline directive* suggests to the compiler that it should generate code that avoids the overhead of a function call but is nonetheless semantically equivalent. The inline directive can appear in either a function declaration or a function definition; however, the function definition must be available at the point of invocation. Its use is illustrated in Figure 2-4.

Modern compilers have very sophisticated techniques that are used to decide if honoring the directive produces better code. The compiler may well refuse to perform the optimization for functions that are too long. Additionally, the directive is likely to be ignored for recursive functions.

2.1.7 Separate Compilation

Often we would like to split a program up into several source files. In such a case, we expect to be able to invoke a function that is defined in one file from a point that is not in the same file. This is acceptable as long as a prototype is visible.

The typical scenario to allow this is that instead of having each file list its function declarations at the top, each file creates a corresponding .h file with the function declarations. Then, any file that needs these declarations can provide an appropriate include directive.

```
1    #include <iostream>
2    using namespace std;
3
4    inline int max2( int a, int b )
5    {
6        return a > b ? a : b;
7    }
8
9    int main( )
10   {
11       int x = 37;
12       int y = 52;
13
14       cout << "Max is " << max2( x, y ) << endl;
15       return 0;
16   }
```

Figure 2-4   The inline method definition must be visible prior to a call to be expanded

In our example this gives three files, all of which are shown in Figure 2-5. The file max2.h simply lists the function declarations for all functions defined in max2.cpp. The main program is defined in a separate file and provides the include directive. Recall that this directive replaces line 5 with the contents of the file max2.h. Finally, max2.cpp provides an include directive also. This include directive is not needed, but would be typical in the case in which max2.cpp had several functions that were calling each other. Section 4.12 discusses one other issue that is common with this technique.

Compiling this program depends on the platform. Most IDEs perform two steps: compilation and linking. The compilation stage verifies the syntax and generates object code for each of the files. The linking stage is used to resolve the function invocations with the actual definitions (sometimes this occurs at runtime).

In a typical IDE, the .cpp files would be made part of the project; the .h files would not. Since the contents of the .h files are logically copied into the .cpp files by the include directives, the .h files should not define any functions or global variables, since this would result in an error message concerning multiple definitions during the linking stage. One exception to this rule is that inline functions should be placed in the .h files; the compiler will make arrangements to avoid the multiple definition error message, even if the inline directive is not honored.

```
1   // Source file: max2.h
2   int max2( int a, int b );
```

```
1   // Source file: main.cpp
2   #include <iostream>
3   using namespace std;
4
5   #include "max2.h"
6
7   int main( )
8   {
9       int x = 37;
10      int y = 52;
11
12      cout << "Max is " << max2( x, y ) << endl;
13
14      return 0;
15  }
```

```
1   // Source file: max2.cpp
2   #include "max2.h"
3
4   int max2( int a, int b )
5   {
6       return a > b ? a : b;
7   }
```

Figure 2-5   Separate compilation: max2.h, main.cpp, and max2.cpp are shown

If a function is declared and it is invoked, but there is no definition available anywhere, then during the linking stage an error will occur, stating that the function is undefined. Often this means either that your function declaration is not the same as the function definition or that your project does not include the file that contains the missing function definition. Most compilers will tell you not only the name, but the signature of the function that is either undefined or multiply defined.

 ## 2.2   Arrays and Strings

In C++, we can declare and use arrays in two basic ways. The primitive method is to use the built-in array. The alternative is to use a `vector`. The differences between the two is somewhat comparable to the difference between Java's built-in array type and `ArrayList` library type. Actually, this is probably an understatement, because using built-in arrays in C++ is much more difficult than using the Java counterpart, whereas `vector` and `ArrayList` are, for all intents and purposes, identical. The reason is that using C++ built-in arrays may require you to independently maintain the array size and also provide additional code to reclaim memory. `vector` has neither of these problems. The built-in C++ array type is discussed in Chapter 11. If you would like to keep your blood pressure low, it's a good idea to stick with the `vector` type as much as possible.

Similarly, strings in C++ come in two basic flavors. The primitive string is simply a built-in array of characters, and is exasperating and dangerous to use; see Chapter 11. The library type, `string`, is a full-fledged string class and is easy to use.

2.2.1   Using the `vector` Library Type

To use the standard `vector`, your program must include the standard header file `vector`, as in

```
#include <vector>
```

A using directive may be needed if one has not already been provided.

As we will discuss in more detail in Chapter 3, C++ deals with objects differently than Java. Specifically, in Java, objects are accessed by reference variables and are treated, by design, differently from primitive types. In C++, objects are meant to look just like primitive types. Thus, they can be declared as local variables on the runtime stack, rather than allocated from the memory heap by calling `new`.

A `vector` is created by giving it a name, telling the compiler what type the elements are, and optionally providing a size (that defaults to zero). The `vector` maintains its current size and current capacity in the same manner as an `ArrayList`. If additions to the `vector` cause its size to exceed capacity, than internally the capacity is expanded. Thus in

```
vector<int> arr1( 3 );
vector<int> arr2;
```

`arr1` is a `vector` that stores `int`s; the valid indices are currently 0, 1, 2 and an attempt to use any other index is incorrect. `arr2` is a `vector` that also stores `int`s. There are no valid indices. A `vector` is indexed by using `[]`.

```
1   #include <iostream>
2   #include <vector>
3   using namespace std;
4
5   int main( )
6   {
7       vector<int> squares;
8
9       for( int i = 0; i < 100; i++ )
10          squares.push_back( i * i );
11
12      for( int j = 0; j < squares.size( ); j++ )
13          cout << j << " squared is " << squares[ j ] << endl;
14
15      return 0;
16  }
```

Figure 2-6   Using the `vector` class

The size of a `vector` can always be obtained by invoking member function `size`. A `vector` can be resized by invoking member function `resize`.

The `add` method in `ArrayList`, which adds to the end of the collection of objects is renamed as `push_back` in the `vector`. Thus, the result of `arr1.push_back(2)` is that `arr1.size()` now returns 4 and `arr1[3]` is now 2.

Figure 2-6 shows a `vector` that is used to store the first 100 perfect squares. In this code, replacing line 10 with `squares[i]=i*i` does not work; the array index would be out of bounds. Unfortunately, unlike Java, this does not cause an exception; rather, the program runs and some part of the memory gets unintentionally overwritten.

Java programmers might be tempted to create a `vector` of size 0 by using code such as

```
vector<int> arr3( );
```

thinking that the default parameter would use size 0. Unfortunately this is wrong! The declaration above does not create a `vector`; instead, it states that `arr3` is a function that takes no parameters and returns a `vector<int>`. Ouch! The result would almost certainly be a bizarre string of unintelligible error messages when `arr3` was used later.

2.2.2   Using the `string` Library Type

To use the `string` library type, you must have the include directive (and possibly the usual `using namespace std` directive if it is not already present)

```
#include <string>
```

Because objects in Java are meant to look like primitive types, `string`s in C++ are also easier to use than in Java. Most importantly, the normal equality and relational operators `==`, `!=`, `<`, `<=`, `>`, `>=` all work for the C++ `string` type. No more bugs because you forgot to use the equals method for `String`s. When = is applied to a `string`, a copy is made; changes to the original do not affect the copy. The length of a `string` can always be obtained by calling the `length` member function.

Java strings are *immutable*: once created a Java string's state cannot be changed. In contrast, the C++ `string` is mutable. This has two consequences. First, using the array indexing operator [], not only can individual characters be accessed, but they easily can be changed (however, as in `vector`, no bounds checking is performed). Second, the += operator is efficient; no more `StringBuffer`s! Figure 2-7 illustrates the use of string concatenation; `makeLongString` takes quadratic time in Java, but is linear in C++.

Two member functions deserve special attention. First, the member function to get substrings is `substr`. However, unlike Java, the parameters in C++ represent the starting position and length of the substring, rather than the starting position and first nonincluded position. Thus in

```
string s = "hello";
string sub = s.substr( 2, 2 ); // gives "ll"
```

sub is a `string` of length 2, whose first character is `s[2]`.

```
1   #include <iostream>
2   #include <string>
3   using namespace std;
4
5   // return a string that contains n As
6   // In Java this code takes forever
7   string makeLongString( int n )
8   {
9       string result = "";
10
11      for( int i = 0; i < n; i++ )
12          result += "A";
13
14      return result;
15  }
16
17  int main( )
18  {
19      string manyAs = makeLongString( 250000 );
20
21      cout << "Short string is " << makeLongString( 20 ) << endl;
22      cout << "Length is " << manyAs.length( ) << endl;
23
24      return 0;
25  }
```

Figure 2-7   String concatenation is efficient in C++ because strings are mutable

Second, some legacy code (and C++ libraries) expect primitive strings, not the `string` library type. Resist the temptation to use primitive strings. Instead, do all your dirty work with the `string` library type, and when a primitive string is required, use the `c_str` string member function that is part of `string` to obtain the primitive equivalent.

2.2.3   Arrays of Objects

In Java, there is no such thing as an array of objects. Instead, what you have is an array of references; when the array is created, by default, all the references are `null`. In C++, when you create an array of objects, either using a primitive array or a `vector`, you really get an array of objects. Specifically, all the items in the array are objects that have been created by calling an appropriate zero-parameter constructor. In C++, this does not work well when the objects are different types (for instance, they are related via inheritance), but if they are the same type (e.g., `string`), it works fine and no special syntax is required.

2.2.4   Primitive Arrays of Constants

Occasionally, we revert to primitive arrays when we have global constants. The reason is the convenient array initialization that is similar to Java and is illustrated by

```
const int DAYS_IN_MONTH[ ] = { 31, 28, 31, 30, 31, 30,
                               31, 31, 30, 31, 30, 31 };
```

Unlike Java, the [] follows the identifier. However, like Java, this creates an array of 12 items. The number of items can be determined by

```
const int NUM_MONTHS = sizeof( DAYS_IN_MONTH ) /
                       sizeof( DAYS_IN_MONTH[0] );
```

2.2.5   Multidimensional Arrays

The primitive implementation of multidimensional arrays is truly exasperating to use and is discussed briefly in Section 11.6. There is no library type available, but it is fairly trivial to write one and we do so in Section 7.3.

 ## 2.3   Parameter Passing

In Java, all parameters are passed using call-by-value: that is, the values of the actual arguments are copied into the formal parameters. Parameter passing in C++ is also call-by-value by default. Although this is often desirable, there are two separate situations where an alternative is useful.

2.3.1   Call-by-Reference

Figure 2-8 illustrates a function, `swap2`, that attempts to swap the values of its parameters. However, if `main` is run, the values of x and y are not swapped because of call-by-value. The code

```
1    #include <iostream>
2    using namespace std;
3
4    // Incorrect implementation of swap2
5    void swap2( int val1, int val2 )
6    {
7        int tmp = val1;
8        val1 = val2;
9        val2 = tmp;
10   }
11
12   int main( )
13   {
14       int x = 37;
15       int y = 52;
16
17       swap2( x, y );
18
19       cout << x << " " << y << endl;
20
21       return 0;
22   }
```

Figure 2-8   Swap function that does not work because of call-by-value

swaps val1 and val2, but since these are simply copies of x and y, it is not possible to write a swap routine that changes x and y when x and y are passed using call-by-value.

C++ allows call-by-reference. To pass a parameter using call-by-reference, we simply place an & prior to each of the parameters that are to be passed using this mechanism. Thus, some parameters can be passed using call-by-value and others using call-by-reference. The modified version of swap2, which is now correct, is shown in Figure 2-9. Observe that main is unchanged and no special syntax is used to invoke the method.

Because formal arguments that are passed using call-by-reference are modifiable in the invoked function, it is illegal to pass a constant using call-by-reference. Thus the code swap2(x,3) would not compile.

Actual arguments must be type-compatible with the formal arguments, without the use of a typecast. This is required because a typecast generates a temporary variable and that temporary variable would become the actual argument. Then changes to the formal parameter in the invoked function would change the temporary variable (instead of the original), leading to hard-to-find bugs.

Finally, we mention that the parameter-passing mechanism is part of the signature of the method and must be included in function declarations.

```
1   #include <iostream>
2   using namespace std;
3
4   // Correct implementation of swap2
5   void swap2( int & a, int & b )
6   {
7       int tmp = a;
8       a = b;
9       b = tmp;
10  }
11
12  int main( )
13  {
14      int x = 37;
15      int y = 52;
16
17      swap2( x, y );
18
19      cout << x << " " << y << endl;
20
21      return 0;
22  }
```

Figure 2-9   Swap function that works using call-by-reference

2.3.2   Call-by-Constant Reference

Figure 2-10 illustrates a second problem with call-by-value. Here we have a binary search algorithm that returns the index of an item in a sorted `vector` and a `main` that repeatedly calls binary search. In theory, binary search is an efficient algorithm, requiring only a logarithmic number of steps, so on a modern machine, 5,000 binary searches in a 30,000 item array should execute in less than a millisecond. However, this code takes noticeably longer, using up seconds of CPU time. Here the problem is not the binary search, but the parameter passing: because we are using call-by-value, each call to `binarySearch` makes a complete copy of `vector v`.

Needless to say, 5,000 copies of a 30,000 element `vector` doesn't come cheap. This problem never occurs in Java because all objects (nonprimitive entities) are accessed using Java reference variables, so objects are always shared and never copied by using =.

In C++, a variable of type `vector<int>` stores the entire state of the object and = copies an entire object to another object. Similarly call-by-value copies the entire state of the actual argument to the formal parameter.

Certainly one way to avoid this problem would be to use call-by-reference. Then the formal parameter is just another name for the actual argument; no copy is made. Although this would significantly increase the speed of the program and solve the problem, there are two serious drawbacks. First, using call-by-reference changes the semantics of the function in that the caller no longer knows that the actual argument will be unchanged after the call. Second, as we mentioned

```
1   #include <iostream>
2   #include <vector>
3   using namespace std;
4
5   // Broken binarySearch because of call-by-value
6   int binarySearch( vector<int> arr, int x )
7   {
8       int low = 0, high = arr.size( ) - 1;
9
10      while( low <= high )
11      {
12          int mid = ( low + high ) / 2;
13          if( arr[ mid ] == x )
14              return mid;
15          else if( x < arr[ mid ] )
16              high = mid - 1;
17          else
18              low = mid + 1;
19      }
20
21      return -1; // not found
22  }
23
24  int main( )
25  {
26      vector<int> v;
27
28      for( int i = 0; i < 30000; i++ )
29          v.push_back( i * i );
30
31      for( int j = 100000; j < 105000; j++ )
32          if( binarySearch( v, j ) >= 0 )
33              cout << j << " is a perfect square" << endl;
34
35      return 0;
36  }
```

Figure 2-10   Binary search method slowed because of call-by-value

in Section 2.3.1, constants or actual arguments that require typecasts would no longer be acceptable parameters.

The solution, shown in Figure 2-11, is to augment the call-by-reference with the reserved word const, which signifies that the parameters are to be passed by reference, but that the function promises not to make any changes to the formal parameter. Thus the actual argument is protected from being changed. If the function implementation attempts to make a change to a const formal parameter, the compiler will complain and the function will not compile (it is possible to cast away the const-ness and subvert this rule, but that's life with C++). We denote

```
1   #include <iostream>
2   #include <vector>
3   using namespace std;
4
5   // Fixed binarySearch uses call-by-constant reference
6   int binarySearch( const vector<int> & arr, int x )
7   {
8       int low = 0, high = arr.size( ) - 1;
9
10      while( low <= high )
11      {
12          int mid = ( low + high ) / 2;
13          if( arr[ mid ] == x )
14              return mid;
15          else if( x < arr[ mid ] )
16              high = mid - 1;
17          else
18              low = mid + 1;
19      }
20
21      return -1; // not found
22  }
23
24  int main( )
25  {
26      vector<int> v;
27
28      for( int i = 0; i < 30000; i++ )
29          v.push_back( i * i );
30
31      for( int j = 100000; j < 105000; j++ )
32          if( binarySearch( v, j ) >= 0 )
33              cout << j << " is a perfect square" << endl;
34
35      return 0;
36  }
```

Figure 2-11   Correct binary search method using call-by-constant reference

this parameter-passing mechanism as *call-by-constant reference* (even though the more verbose *call-by-reference to a constant* is more accurate)

When a parameter is passed using call-by-constant reference, it is acceptable to supply a constant or an actual argument that requires a typecast. In effect, as far as the caller is concerned, call-by-constant reference has the same semantics as call-by-value except that copying is avoided.

2.3.3   Parameter-Passing Summary

In C++, choosing a parameter-passing mechanism is an easily overlooked programming chore that can affect correctness and efficiency. The rules are actually relatively simple:

- Call-by-reference is required for any object that may be altered by the function.
- Call-by-value is appropriate for small objects that should not be altered by the function. This generally includes primitive types and also function objects (Section 7.6.3).
- Call-by-constant reference is appropriate for large objects that should not be altered by the function. This generally includes library containers such as `vector`, general class types, and even `string`.

Key Points

- A function declaration consists of the function minus the body and looks like a method declaration in a Java interface. A function definition includes the body.
- When invoking a function, only those functions whose declarations or definitions have already been seen are eligible to be candidates.
- C++ allows default parameters. The default parameters must be the last parameters.
- In C++, objects can be created without calling `new`, and can be accessed and copied as if they were primitive entities. See Chapter 3 for more information.
- C++ supports arrays using both a primitive array and a `vector` library type. Similarly, strings can be supported using both primitive arrays of `char` and a `string` library type.
- The `vector` in C++ has functionality that is similar to the `ArrayList` class in Java.
- The `string` class in C++ has functionality that is similar to the `String` class in Java. The `+=` operator is efficient, the substring function `substr` takes a different second parameter, and all the relational operators work, so methods such as `equals` and `compareTo` are not required.
- C++ supports three modes of parameter passing: call-by-value, call-by-reference, and call-by-constant reference.

Exercises

1. Grab the most recent tax table. Write a function that takes an *adjusted gross income* and *filing status* (married, single, etc.) and returns the amount of tax owed. Write a test program to verify that your function behaves correctly.

2. Write a function to compute X^N for nonnegative integers N. Assume that $X^0 = 1$.

3. What is the difference between a function declaration and a function definition?

4. Describe default parameters in C++.

5. What is an inline directive in C++?

6. Describe how C++ supports separate compilation.

7. Write a function that accepts a vector of strings and returns a vector containing the strings in the vector parameter that have the longest length (in other words, if there are 10 strings that are tied for being the longest length, the return value is a vector of size 10 containing those strings). Then write a test program that reads an arbitrary number of strings, invokes the function, and outputs the strings returned by the vector.

8. What are the basic differences between the C++ `string` and the Java `String` classes?

9. What are the different parameter-passing mechanisms in C++ and when are they used?

Pointers and Reference Variables

3

Chapter Outline

Possibly the most significant difference between Java and C++ concerns how objects are managed by the system. Java has a simple model that guarantees, among other things, that once an object has been created, the Virtual Machine will never attempt to destroy the object's memory as long as the object is being actively referenced, either directly or indirectly. C++, on the other hand, allows objects to be accessed in many different ways, making coding very tricky, and leading to many subtle and hard-to-find runtime errors.

In this chapter, we review the Java typing system, briefly describe the C++ object model, and introduce the C++ concepts of pointer variables and reference variables. We will also describe how the C++ programmer destroys objects that are no longer needed.

3.1   Java vs. C++ Memory Model

In Java, life is relatively simple. Except for instances of the eight primitive types, everything in Java is an object. Furthermore, objects in Java can only be created on the memory heap. This is typically done by calling new (the Reflection API allows an alternative, but the object still resides on the memory heap). Such objects are always accessed by reference variables. The Java programmer cannot force the Virtual Machine to reclaim an unused object. Instead, if an object no longer has any references to it, either directly or indirectly, the Virtual Machine may, at its discretion, declare the object inactive and reclaim the object. This process is known as *garbage collection*. The Virtual Machine furthermore guarantees that it will never attempt to reclaim an active object.

In Java, primitive entities can never be accessed by reference variables and can never be created by invoking new. Thus when a local variable in Java is a primitive type, it is allocated on the runtime stack and the local primitive variable is automatically invalidated when the block that it was created in ends.

The C++ memory model is significantly more complicated. As we have already seen, local variables, including objects in C++ (such as vectors and strings) can be created without calling new. In such a case, these local objects are allocated on the runtime stack and have the same semantics as primitive types. Two important consequences of this are as follows:

First, when = is applied to objects, the state of one object is copied. This contrasts to Java, where objects are accessed indirectly by reference variables and an = copies the value of the reference variable, rather than the state of the object.

Second, when the block in which a local object is created ends, the object will automatically be reclaimed by the system. Thus in the code

```
void silly( )
{
    vector<int> arr1;
    vector<int> arr2;
        ...      // other code not shown
    arr2 = arr1;
        ...      // other code not shown
}
```

arr1 and arr2 are separate vector<int> objects. The statement arr2=arr1 copies the entire contents of vector<int> arr1 into vector<int> arr2. When silly returns, arr1 and arr2 will be destroyed and their memory will be reclaimed as part of the function return sequence.

This example illustrates a significant difference between Java and C++. In Java, objects are shared by several reference variables and are rarely copied. C++ encourages, by default, the copying of objects. However, copying objects can take time and often we need to avoid this expense. For instance, we have already seen in Section 2.3 additional syntax to allow copies to be avoided.

In a more general setting inherited from C, C++ allows the programmer to obtain a variable that stores the memory address where the object is being kept. Such a variable is called a *pointer variable* in C++. Pointer variables in C++ have many of the semantics of reference variables in Java, with extra flexibility (that implies extra dangers). C++ also has another type of variable called the *reference variable*, which despite its name is not similar to the reference variable in Java. In the remainder of this chapter, we will discuss both types of variables and several tricky C++ issues that are associated with their use.

 ## 3.2 Pointers

A *pointer variable* in C++ is a variable that stores the memory address of any other entity. The entity can be a primitive type or a class type; however, using pointer variables for primitive types in good C++ code is rarely needed. Since it does simplify our examples, we will make use of pointers to integers in this section.

To have a pointer point at an object, we need to know the memory address of the target objects (i.e., where it is stored). For object `obj`, its memory address is given by applying the *unary address-of operator* &. Thus &obj is the memory location that stores `obj`.

We can declare that an object `ptr` points at an `int` object by saying

```
int *ptr;
```

The value represented by `ptr` is an address. As with integer objects, this declaration does not initialize `ptr` to any particular value, so using `ptr` before assigning to it invariably produces bad results (such as a program crash). Suppose we also have the declarations

```
int x = 5;
int y = 7;
```

We can make `ptr` point at x by assigning to `ptr` the memory location where x is stored. Thus

```
ptr = &x;              // LEGAL
```

sets `ptr` to point at x. Figure 3-1 illustrates this in two ways. On the left, a memory model shows where each object is stored. The figure on the right uses an arrow to indicate pointing.

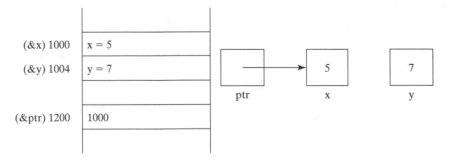

Figure 3-1   Pointer illustration

The data being pointed at are obtained by the *unary dereferencing operator* *. In Figure 3-1, *ptr will evaluate to 5, which is the value of the pointed-at variable x. It is illegal to dereference something that is not a pointer. The * operator is the inverse of & (for example, *&x=5 is the same as x=5 as long as &x is legal). Dereferencing works not only for reading values from an object, but also for writing new values to the object. Thus, if we say

```
*ptr = 10;              // LEGAL
```

we have changed the value of x to 10. Figure 3-2 shows the changes that result. This shows the problem with pointers: Unrestricted alterations are possible, and a runaway pointer can over-write all sorts of variables unintentionally.

We could also have initialized ptr at declaration time by having it point to x:

```
int x = 5;
int y = 7;
int *ptr = &x;          // LEGAL
```

The declaration says that x is an int initialized to 5, y is an int initialized to 7, and ptr is a pointer to an int and is initialized to point at x. Let us look at what could have gone wrong. The following declaration sequence is incorrect:

```
int *ptr = &x;          // ILLEGAL: x is not declared yet
int x = 5;
int y = 7;
```

Here we are using x before it has been declared, so the compiler will complain. Here is another common error:

```
int x = 5;
int y = 7;
int *ptr = x;           // ILLEGAL: x is not an address
```

In this case we are trying to have ptr point at x, but we have forgotten that a pointer holds an address. Thus we need an address on the right side of the assignment. The compiler will complain that we have forgotten the &, but its error message may initially appear cryptic.

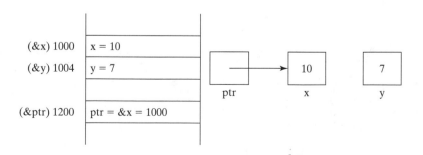

Figure 3-2   Result of *ptr=10

Continuing with this example, suppose that we have the correct declaration but with `ptr` uninitialized:

```
int x = 5;
int y = 7;
int *ptr;                  // LEGAL but ptr is uninitialized
```

What is the value of `ptr`? As Figure 3-3 shows, the value is undefined because it was never initialized. Thus the value of `*ptr` is also undefined. However, using `*ptr` when `ptr` is undefined is worse, because `ptr` could hold an address that makes absolutely no sense at all, thus causing a program crash if it is dereferenced. Even worse, `ptr` could be pointing at an address that is accessible, in which case the program will not immediately crash but will be erroneous. If `*ptr` is the target of an assignment, then we would be accidentally changing some other data, which could result in a crash at a later point. This is a tough error to detect because the cause and symptom may be widely separated in time.

We have already seen the correct syntax for the assignment:

```
ptr = &x;                  // LEGAL
```

Suppose that we forget the address-of operator. Then the assignment

```
ptr = x;                   // ILLEGAL: x is not an address
```

rightly generates a compiler error. There are two ways to make the compiler shut up. One is to take the address on the right side, as in the correct syntax. The other method is erroneous:

```
*ptr = x;                  // Semantically incorrect
```

The compiler is quiet because the statement says that the `int` to which `ptr` is pointing should get the value of x. For instance, if `ptr` is &y, then y is assigned the value of x. This assignment is perfectly legal, but it does not make `ptr` point at x. Moreover, if `ptr` is uninitialized, dereferencing it is likely to cause a runtime error, as discussed above. This error is obvious from Figure 3-3. The moral is to always draw a picture at the first sign of pointer trouble.

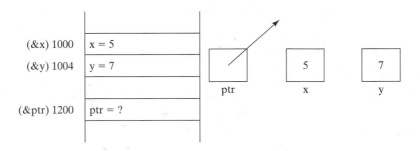

Figure 3-3   Uninitialized pointer

Using *ptr=x instead of ptr=&x is a common error for two reasons. First, since it makes the compiler quiet, programmers feel comfortable about using the incorrect semantics. Second, it looks somewhat like the syntax used for initialization at declaration time. The difference is that the * at declaration time is not a dereferencing *, but rather just an indication that the object is a pointer type.

Some final words before we get to some substantive uses: First, sometimes we want to state explicitly that a pointer is pointing nowhere, as opposed to an undefined location. The NULL pointer points at a memory location that is guaranteed to be incapable of holding anything. Consequently, a NULL pointer cannot be dereferenced. The symbolic constant NULL was prevalent in C, but is being phased out in favor of an explicit 0. However, many users still feel that NULL is more readable, so we use NULL, assuming that the following declaration exists:

```
const int NULL = 0;
```

Pointers are best initialized to the NULL pointer because in many cases they have no default initial values (these rules apply to other predefined types as well).

Second, a dereferenced pointer behaves just like the object at which it is pointing at. Thus, after the following three statements, the value stored in x is 15:

```
x = 5;
ptr = &x;
*ptr += 10;
```

However, we must be cognizant of precedence rules because (as we discuss in Section 11.3) it is possible to perform arithmetic not only on the dereferenced values but also on the (un-dereferenced) pointers themselves.[1] As an example, the following two statements are very different:

```
*ptr += 1;
*ptr++;
```

In the first statement, the += operator is applied to *ptr; in the second statement, the ++ operator is applied to ptr. The result of applying the ++ operator to ptr is that ptr will be changed to point at a memory location one memory unit larger than it used to. (We discuss why this might be useful in Section 11.3.)

Third, if ptr1 and ptr2 are pointers to the same type, then

```
ptr1 = ptr2;
```

sets ptr1 to point to the same location as ptr2, while

```
*ptr1 = *ptr2;
```

assigns the dereferenced ptr1 the value of the dereferenced ptr2. Figure 3-4 shows that these statements are quite different. Moreover, when the wrong form is used mistakenly, the

---

1. This is an unfortunate consequence of C++'s very liberal rules that allow arithmetic on pointers, making use of the fact that pointers are internally stored as integers. We discuss the reasoning for this in Section 11.3.

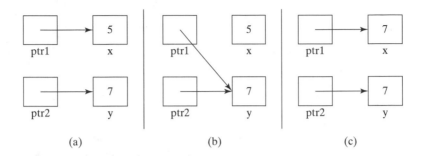

Figure 3-4   (a) Initial state; (b) `ptr1=ptr2` starting from the initial state; (c) `*ptr1=*ptr2` starting from initial state

consequences might not be obvious immediately. In the previous examples, after the assignment, `*ptr1` and `*ptr2` are both 7. Similarly, the expression

    ptr1 == ptr2

is true if the two pointers are pointing at the same memory location, while

    *ptr1 == *ptr2

is true if the values stored at the two indicated addresses are equal. It is a common mistake to use the wrong form.

The requirement that `ptr1` and `ptr2` point to the same type is a consequence of the fact that C++ is strongly typed: We cannot mix different types of pointers without an explicit type conversion, unless the user has provided an implicit type conversion.

If several pointers are declared in one statement, the `*` must precede each variable:

```
int *ptr1, *ptr2;  // Correct ptr1 and ptr2 are both pointer to int
int *ptr1, ptr2;   // Wrong!! ptr2 is an int
```

Finally, when pointers are declared, the white space that surrounds the `*` is unimportant to the compiler. Pick a style that you like.

3.3   Memory Heap Management

Often in C++, local variables can be allocated on the runtime stack. We know that stack-allocated local variables are created when they are reached in the function and are destroyed when they are no longer in scope (for instance, when the function returns). Like Java, C++ allows entities to be created from the memory heap. In C++ this introduces several complications.

3.3.1 The new Operator

Like Java, objects can be created from the memory heap by calling new. The result of new is a pointer to the newly created object, allocated from the memory heap, rather than the runtime stack. new behaves the same in C++ and Java, and parameters can be provided to control initialization of the newly created object.

```
1    #include <iostream>
2    #include <string>
3    using namespace std;
4
5    int main( )
6    {
7        string *strPtr;
8
9        strPtr = new string( "hello" );
10       cout << "The string is: " << *strPtr << endl;
11       cout << "Its length is: " << (*strPtr).length( ) << endl;
12
13       *strPtr += " world";
14       cout << "Now the string is " << *strPtr << endl;
15
16       delete strPtr;
17
18       return 0;
19   }
```

Figure 3-5   Illustration of dynamic memory allocation

Figure 3-5 illustrates the issues involved in memory heap allocation, which is often called *dynamic memory allocation* in C++. It must be emphasized that this example is a poor use of dynamic memory and we do it only to illustrate dynamic memory allocation in a simple context: An automatic string should be used instead.

In Figure 3-5, line 9 creates a new `string` object dynamically. Note that `strPtr` is a pointer to a `string`, so the `string` itself is accessed by `*strPtr`, as shown in lines 10 to 14. The parentheses are needed in line 11 because of precedence rules.

3.3.2 Garbage Collection and `delete` Operator

In Java, when an object is no longer referenced, it is subject to automatic garbage collection. The programmer does not have to worry about it. C++ does not have garbage collection. When an object that is allocated by `new` is no longer referenced, the `delete` operator must be applied to the object (through a pointer). Otherwise, the memory that it consumes is lost (until the program terminates). This is known as a *memory leak*. Memory leaks are, unfortunately, common occurrences in many C++ programs. The `delete` operator is illustrated in line 16.

An example of a memory leak is shown in Figure 3-6, in which we return at line 9 without calling `delete`. Fortunately, many sources of memory leaks can be automatically removed with care. One important rule is to not use `new` when a stack-allocated variable can be used instead. A stack-allocated variable is automatically cleaned up (hence it is also known as an *automatic variable* in C++). Thus in this code, it would make sense to allocate the vector on the runtime stack (and avoid the pointer) instead of using `new` to create it on the heap.

```
1   #include <iostream>
2   #include <vector>
3   using namespace std;
4
5   void leak( int i )
6   {
7       vector<int> *ptrToVector = new vector<int>( i );
8       if( i % 2 == 1 )
9           return;
10         // some other code not shown ...
11      delete ptrToVector;
12  }
```

Figure 3-6   Illustration of memory leak in a program that does nothing useful

3.3.3 Stale Pointers

One reason that programmers can get in trouble when using pointers is that it is possible, and generally expected, that one object may have several pointers pointing at it. Consider the following code:

```
string *s = new string( "hello" ); // s points at new string
string *t = s;                     // t points there, too
delete t;                          // The object is gone
```

Nobody would deliberately write these three lines of code next to each other; instead, assume that they are scattered in a complex function. Prior to the call to delete, we have one dynamically allocated object that has two pointers pointing to it.

After the call to delete, the values of s and t (that is, where they are pointing) are unchanged. However, as illustrated in Figure 3-7, they are now stale. A stale pointer is a pointer whose value no longer refers to a valid object. Dereferencing s and t can lead to unpredictable results. What makes things especially difficult is that although it is obvious that t is stale, the fact that s is stale is much less obvious, if, as assumed, these statements are scattered in a complex function. Furthermore, it is possible that in some situations, the memory that was occupied by the object is unchanged until a later call to new claims the memory, which can give the illusion that there is no problem.

Figure 3-7   Stale pointers: because of the call to delete t, pointers s and t are now pointing at an object that no longer exists; a call to delete s would now be an illegal double-deletion

3.3.4 Double-delete

A second problem is the so-called double-delete. A *double-delete* occurs when we attempt to call delete on the same object more than once. This would occur if we now made the call

```
delete s;                              // Oops -- double delete
```

Since s is stale, the object that it points to is no longer valid. Trouble in the form of a runtime error is likely to result.

Thus, we see the perils of dynamic memory allocation. We must be certain never to call delete more than once on an object, and then only after we no longer need it. If we don't call delete at all, we get a memory leak, and if we have a pointer variable and intend to call delete, we must be certain that the object being pointed at was created by a call to new. When we have functions calling functions calling other functions, it is hard to keep track of everything.

3.3.5 Functions That Return Pointers

If we allocate a large object as a local variable and then return it, we incur the overhead of large copy. For this reason, it is not uncommon to see functions that return pointers instead of objects themselves. Returning pointers is also common in the implementation of linked data structures (in this case, we are returning pointers to nodes). However, when the return type of a function is a pointer, extreme care must be taken to avoid stale pointers, memory leaks, and invalid deletes.

Pointers can go stale even if no dynamic allocation is performed. Consider the code in Figure 3-8. For no good reason (except to illustrate the error), function dup returns a pointer to a string. If dup calls new to create a string, then the caller will be responsible for calling delete. Rather than burdening the caller, the programmer has mistakenly decided to have dup use a stack-allocated string and return its address. The program compiles, but may or may not

```
1   string * dup( const string & str )
2   {
3       string ret = str + str;
4       return &ret;
5   }
6
7   int main( )
8   {
9       string *result = dup( "call" )
10      cout << *result << endl;
11      cout << "Now the string is " << *result << endl;
12      return 0;
13  }
```

Figure 3-8   A stale pointer: the pointee, ret, does not exist after dup return

```
1   string * dup( const string & str )
2   {
3       string *ret = new string( str + str );
4       return ret;
5   }
```

Figure 3-9   Safer code, but the caller must call `delete` or there may be a memory leak

work. It has an error. The problem is that the value that dup returns is a pointer, but the pointer is pointing at `ret`, which no longer exists, because it is a stack-allocated variable and dup has returned. One possible scenario, is that the first print at line 10 works, but in invoking the print routine, the runtime stack overwrites the part of the runtime stack where the local variable `ret` was being stored. If so, the second print at line 11 fails to produce the same answer, which can be quite shocking. Another possibility is that the code works fine and you have a latent bug. When returning pointers, make sure that you have something to point to and that the something exists after the return is complete.

Suppose that it is important for dup to return a pointer to a `string`. How can we fix the stale pointer problem? The easiest way would appear to be to create the new string at line 3 on the memory heap, as shown in Figure 3-9. However, by doing so, we now force the caller to clean up memory by calling `delete` when the caller is done using the return value. If the caller doesn't do so, a memory leak has been created. In this situation, we would expect to see comments accompanying the dup method instructing callers of their obligations.

A third option that is sometimes used frees the caller from reclaiming memory. Here, we return a pointer to a variable that is not allocated from the heap, yet is not allocated on the runtime stack. Two such entities qualify: a global variable or a static local variable. A *static local variable* is essentially the same as global variable except that it is only visible inside the function in which it was declared. The static local variable is created once (the first time the function is invoked) and the variable retains its values between calls to the same function. Thus like a static class variable in Java, a static local variable could be used to keep track of the number of times a function has been invoked. Figure 3-10 illustrates this version of dup.

When a function returns a pointer to a static local variable, the caller no longer has to manage memory. However, now the caller must use the return value and, in particular, the object being pointed at by the return value, prior to making another call to the function. Otherwise, in the code fragment

```
string *s1 = dup( "hello" );
string *s2 = dup( "world" );
cout << *s1 << " " << *s2 << endl;
```

the string `worldworld` is printed twice, because both `s1` and `s2` are pointing at the same static object (`ret`), which is storing the result of the last call to dup. Thus once again, it is incumbent on the programmer to document that the return value is a pointer to a static variable and that the return value must be quickly used.

```
1  string * dup( const string & str )
2  {
3      static string ret;
4      ret = str + str;
5      return &ret;
6  }
```

Figure 3-10 Using `static` local variable frees the caller from having to call `delete`

You should never use `delete` on an object that was not created by `new`. If you do, runtime havoc is likely to result. For instance, an attempt to call `delete` on `s1` or `s2` in the last example may lead to a disaster on some C++ implementations. This shows the largest problem with pointers in C++: When you receive a pointer variable, if the implementation of the function that is sending you the pointer is hidden (which we would typically expect), unless there are comments, you have no way of knowing if you are responsible for calling `delete` or if you should not call `delete`, and making the wrong decision results in either a memory leak or, perhaps, an invalid `delete`. Furthermore, if you have an array of pointers and the objects being pointed at were allocated from the memory heap, then you may need to call `delete` on these objects when you are done with the array. If any object is being pointed at twice, the programmer must write extra code to avoid double-deletions.

 ## 3.4   The -> Operator

In Figure 3-5, at line 11, we see that if `strPtr` is a pointer to a `string`, then `*strPtr` is a `string` and thus the length of the `string` is `(*strPtr).length()`. The (leading) parentheses are needed because of precedence rules. However, this use of parentheses is annoying. To avoid typing the parentheses, C++ provides the `->` operator, which accesses members of a pointed-at class type. Thus `strPtr->length()` is equivalent to `(*strPtr).length()`, but is easier to read and write. In this shorthand, `strPtr->length()` is the length of the object at which `strPtr` is pointing.

 ## 3.5   Reference Variables

In addition to pointer types, C++ has reference types. A reference type is a pointer constant that is always dereferenced implicitly. A reference type can be viewed as an alias for another object. For instance, in the following code, `count` becomes a synonym for a longer, hard-to-type variable:

```
int longVariableName = 0;
int & count = longVariableName;

count += 3;
```

Reference variables must be initialized when they are declared and cannot be changed to reference another variable. This is because an attempted reassignment via

```
count = someOtherObject;
```

assigns to the object `longVariableName` the value of `someOtherObject`. This example is a poor use of reference variables, but accurately reflects how they are used in a more general setting in which the scope of the reference variable is different from that of the object being referenced. One important case is that a reference variable can be used as a formal parameter, which acts as an alias for an actual argument. We have previously discussed this in the context of using call-by-reference and call-by-constant reference to pass vectors (Section 2.3).

Reference variables are like pointer constants in that the value they store is the address of the object to which they refer. They are different in that an automatic invisible dereference operator is applied to the reference variable.

Many C++ libraries are based on functions that were written in C, where reference variables are not available. In C, pointer variables are used to achieve call-by-reference, and C++ programs are likely to run into older code that uses this technique. We discuss the use of pointers to simulate call-by-reference semantics in Section 12.3.

Using C++ reference variables instead of pointer variables translates into a notational convenience, especially because it allows parameters to be passed by reference without the excess baggage of the & operator on the actual arguments and the * operator that tends to clutter up C programs.

By the way, pointers can be passed by reference. This is used to allow a function to change where a pointer, passed as a parameter, is pointing. A pointer that is passed using call-by-value cannot be changed to point to a new location (because the formal parameter stores only a copy of the where value).

Because a reference variable must be initialized at the moment it is declared, it is illegal to have an array of reference variables.

Finally, we mention that a function can return by reference (or constant reference) to possibly avoid the overhead of a copy. In such a case, the expression in the return statement must be an object whose lifetime extends past the end of the function. In other words, an object allocated on the runtime stack should not be returned by reference. We will discuss returning by reference in Chapter 4. Returning by reference (or constant reference) can sometimes make the program more efficient by avoiding the overhead of a copy, but doing so is fairly tricky and modern optimizing C++ compilers have ways to avoid the overhead of a copy anyway. As a result, except for a few standard places where the return by reference idiom is used, we do not recommend it.

3.6   Uses and Abuses of Pointer Variables

Pointer variables are present in much C++ code, and since the vast majority of C++ problems can be traced to memory management issues, it is worth avoiding their use whenever possible. This section describes some of the typical occurrences of pointer variables, mentioning a few instances in which reasonable alternatives exist.

3.6.1 Parameter Passing: Simulating Call-by-Reference

As we have mentioned, libraries that are written to be compatible with C use pointer variables to achieve either call-by-reference or call-by-constant reference. The idiom is discussed in Section 12.3. In newly written C++ code, you should not need to use pointers for this purpose.

3.6.2 Arrays and Strings

Primitive arrays and primitive strings in C++ are implemented using pointer variables. This implementation is a remnant of C that and has been made obsolete by `vector` and `string` library types.

For strings, the primitive variable type that you will often see is `char *` (or `const char *`, for strings that are not to be changed). Here the pointer variable points at the first character in the string and the characters are all stored in an array, with a special character `'\0'` to signify the end of the string (this character would not be included in determining the string length). If you need a primitive string (e.g., as a filename to perform I/O), use the `string` class to construct the `string` and then invoke the `c_str` member function from the `string` class to obtain the primitive string.

Other than this and command line-arguments (Chapter 12), you should not need to use pointer variables for arrays and strings, but if you must interact with legacy code, see Chapter 11.

3.6.3 Avoiding Large Data Movements

When presented with an array of objects that need to be rearranged often, you may find it better to follow the Java style and store an array of pointers to objects, rather than the array of objects. You may be able to avoid using `new`, depending on the particular situation, by allocating the objects in a permanent array and then using the addresses of those objects. If you cannot guarantee the lifetime of your objects, then you will need to allocate them from the memory heap using `new`.

3.6.4 Linked Data Structures

Classic linked data structures, such as linked lists and binary search trees, use pointer variables. Since these data structures are typically implemented as a class, with proper design we can lessen the chances of memory problems with reasonable care. We will discuss implementation of linked data structures later in the text in the context of classes and class templates.

3.6.5 Inheritance

Any serious use of inheritance will require pointer variables and heap memory allocation. The code will look much like Java code except that the programmer will have the significant burden of reclaiming inactive objects. This issue is unavoidable and is a major reason why many people claim Java is an easier-to-use language for object-oriented programming than C++. We will discuss this in more detail in Chapter 6.

Key Points

- In C++, objects can be allocated both on the runtime stack and on the memory heap.
- Objects allocated from the runtime stack are automatically reclaimed when the block in which they were allocated terminates.
- A pointer variable stores the address where another variable resides. A C++ pointer variable has semantics (especially =, ==, !=, and NULL) similar to the Java reference variable.
- Objects allocated from the memory heap must eventually be returned to the memory heap when they are no longer needed. Otherwise, it is possible to create memory leaks that may eventually cause your program to run out of memory. An object is returned to the memory heap by calling `delete` with the address of the object.
- Never call `delete` on an object that was not allocated by `new`.
- After calling `delete` on an object, all pointers to that object become stale and should not be used.
- Never attempt to `delete` an object twice.
- A static local variable is created once per program, but the variable is only visible from inside the function in which it is declared. Each invocation of the function reuses the same variable and its value is retained between function invocations.
- The `->` operator is used to access members of a pointed-at class type.
- A reference variable in C++ is a pointer constant that is always dereferenced implicitly. One can view it as another name for an object. Reference variables must be initialized when they are declared and cannot be changed to reference other variables. Arrays of reference variables are illegal.
- Using pointer variables to simulate call-by-reference or to implement arrays or strings should be avoided when possible.
- Pointer variables will be used to avoid large data moves, to implement linked data structures, and especially in inheritance.

Exercises

1. How is the C++ memory model different from the Java memory model?
2. What is a pointer variable?
3. What is a stale pointer?

4. What is a memory leak?
5. Which objects have their memory automatically reclaimed?
6. What does the `delete` operator do?
7. What happens if `delete` is invoked twice on the same object?
8. What happens if `delete` is invoked on an object that is not heap-allocated?
9. If a function returns a pointer to an object, why can't the object be a stack-based local variable?
10. If a function returns a pointer to static data, what must the user be sure to do?
11. If a function returns a pointer to heap-allocated data, what must the user be sure to do?
12. What does the `->` operator do?
13. What is a reference variable in C++?
14. Why must C++ reference variables be initialized when declared?
15. Consider

```
int a, b;
int *ptr;
int *ptrptr;

ptr = &a;
ptrptr = &ptr;
```

   a. Is this legal?
   b. What are the values of `*ptr` and `**ptrptr`?
   c. Is `ptrptr=ptr` legal?

16. Is `*&x` always equal to `x`? If not, give an example.
17. Is `&*x` always equal to `x`? If not, give an example.
18. For the declaration

```
int a = 5;
int *ptr = &a;
```

   what are the values of the following?

   a. `ptr`
   b. `*ptr`
   c. `ptr == a`
   d. `ptr == &a`
   e. `&ptr`
   f. `*a`
   g. `*&a`
   h. `**&ptr`

Object-Based Programming: Classes

4

Chapter Outline

Like Java, C++ uses the class to support object-based programming and uses inheritance to support object-oriented programming. Classes in C++ operate in much the same way as in Java except that there is significant additional syntax because of C++'s attempt to make class types look exactly like primitive types.

In this chapter, we begin by examining the similarities. Then we look at a host of important syntactic constructs found in the implementation of classes in C++. This chapter does not discuss two interesting topics: operator overloading (Chapter 5) and inheritance (Chapter 6).

4.1   Similarities, Modulo Syntax

We begin by rewriting the Java class shown in Figure 4-1. This class wraps an `int` variable and allows access to the wrapped `int` via `getValue` and `setValue`. The C++ equivalent of this class is shown in Figure 4-2.

In C++, top-level classes cannot be declared with any visibility specifier. Also notice that the class declaration in C++ ends with a semicolon. Forgetting the semicolon is a common error that almost always produces an error message, but the message can be hard to decipher, and if the class is declared in a `.h` file, the error might point to the `.cpp` file that includes this `.h` file.

Two other difference are immediate. First, instead of supplying a visibility modifier for each member, we simply provide visibility modifiers for sections of the class. Thus in Figure 4-2, the constructors and methods are public, while the data are private. There is no package visible specifier in C++. In a C++ class, visibility is private until a `public` modifier is seen.

```
1   public class IntCell
2   {
3       public IntCell( )
4         { this( 0 ); }
5
6       public IntCell( int initialValue )
7         { storedValue = initialValue; }
8
9       public int getValue( )
10        { return storedValue; }
11
12      public void setValue( int val )
13        { storedValue = val; }
14
15      private int storedValue;
16  }
```

Figure 4-1   Java class that stores an `int` value

```
1   class IntCell
2   {
3     public:
4       IntCell( int initialValue = 0 )
5         { storedValue = initialValue; }
6
7       int getValue( )
8         { return storedValue; }
9
10      void setValue( int val )
11        { storedValue = val; }
12
13    private:
14      int storedValue;
15  };
```

Figure 4-2   Initial version of C++ class that stores an `int` value (needs more work)

Second, in Java, constructors can invoke each other using a call to `this`. In C++, this is not allowed. Instead, there are two typical alternatives. The first alternative, shown in Figure 4-2, is to use default parameters in the constructor. Thus an `IntCell` can be constructed with either an `int` or no parameters. The default parameter of 0 signals that if no parameter is provided, the parameter defaults to 0. Default parameters must be compile-time constants. Another alternative that works if the constructors are too different to be expressed with default parameters is to declare a private member function that can be invoked by all the constructors. (Although the initialization routine can be a public member function, like Java, it is best to avoid doing so, because of considerations that come into play with inheritance.)

Figure 4-3 illustrates the use of the `IntCell` class. The class declaration of `IntCell` must be placed prior to using the `IntCell` type name. Typically, one would place it in a `.h` file, and the

```
1   int main( )
2   {
3       IntCell m1;
4       IntCell m2 = 37;
5       IntCell m3( 55 );
6
7       cout << m1.getValue( ) << " " << m2.getValue( )
8                               << " " << m3.getValue( ) << endl;
9       m1 = m2;
10      m2.setValue( 40 );
11
12      cout << m1.getValue( ) << " " << m2.getValue( ) << endl;
13
14      return 0
15  }
```

Figure 4-3   Example showing the use of `IntCell`

main program would use an include directive. Observe that in `main` we create `IntCell` objects on the runtime stack, using both no parameters and one-parameter constructors. Also observe that if the constructor accepts parameters, they can be placed in parentheses (if there are two or more parameters, they must be placed in parentheses). Line 9 shows that objects can be copied. As a result of this statement, the contents of the `IntCell` object m2 are copied into `IntCell` object m1. This is the equivalent of cloning in Java. Thus the second output statement prints 37 and then 40.

4.2   Accessors vs. Mutators

The `IntCell` example in Figure 4-2 is relatively simple, yet by itself it shows some complications. For instance, suppose we have a `vector` of `IntCell` objects and we want to count how many of these objects are storing the value 0. The code shown in Figure 4-4, which should be straightforward, does not compile.

This code does not compile because `arr` is supposed to be constant and the compiler is unsure whether invoking the `getValue` method on one of the array elements will cause a change to one of the array elements and thus the array. Although the compiler could look at the implementation of `getValue` and see that no changes are made to the `IntCell`, typically this implementation might not be available in C++ form (in the most general case, it may be invoking other member functions that are already compiled into a library). Thus we need some syntax to tell the compiler that `getValue` is not going to change the state of the `IntCell`.

A member function that looks at an object but promises not to changed the state of the object is known as an *accessor*. A member function that might change the state of the object is known as a *mutator*. In the `IntCell` class, `getValue` is logically an accessor and `setValue` is logically a mutator.

In C++, a member function is assumed to be a mutator unless it is explicitly marked as an accessor. To mark a member function as an accessor, we place a `const` at the end of its signature as shown:

```
int getValue( ) const
  { return storedValue; }
```

```
1   bool containsZero( const vector<IntCell> & arr )
2   {
3       for( int i = 0; i < arr.size( ); i++ )
4           if( arr[ i ].getValue( ) == 0 )
5               return true;
6
7       return false;
8   }
```

Figure 4-4   Routine to return true if a `vector` of `IntCell`s contains at least one zero. Not compatible with original version of `IntCell`

Whether a member function is an accessor or a mutator is considered part of its signature. When invoking a member function on a constant object, only the accessors are candidates; as we've already seen, attempts to invoke the mutator fail.

Many less-experienced C++ programmers view the const as an annoyance or little more than a comment. In fact, deciding whether a member function is an accessor or a mutator is an important part of the class design: The const that signifies an accessor should never be omitted. If it is, you wind up having to remove the const in other places, making your code less readable and less robust. The ability to mark an object as constant and expect that this object's state will not change (at least in the context of a method) allows the compiler to perform aggressive optimization and avoids the need to lock in a multithreaded environment in which several threads access the object simultaneously. Experienced C++ programmers who move to Java often find the lack of Java support for immutability (the ability to mark the state of an object as unchangeable) to be a liability.

If a member function is marked as an accessor, then the compiler will not allow the member function to compile if it attempts to make any changes to the values of its data members. This disallowance includes assignment to the data members as well as invoking other mutators of the class (since invoking the mutator could change the data members).

Occasionally an accessor needs to change the values of one of its data members. For instance, if a data member is being used to count the number of calls to getValue, we might want to adjust it. This would not normally be allowed if getValue is an accessor, but a data member can be marked as mutable to exempt it from the normal restrictions.

 ## 4.3   The explicit Keyword

To see the second problem with the IntCell class, consider the code in Figure 4-5. Here at line 5, we see an assignment statement that would never be allowed in Java and that looks a bit dubious: We are copying an int into an IntCell, in spite of the fact that they have different types.

However, this code does compile. The reason for this is that C++'s type compatibility rules are somewhat lenient in places. The thinking of the compiler is that since m is an IntCell, it should (by default) expect to see an IntCell on the right-hand side of the assignment operator. What it sees is not an IntCell. However, the compiler is willing to do a type conversion. So the question it must answer is whether it can fabricate a temporary variable of type IntCell in place of the 3. That requires constructing the temporary, and since there is an IntCell constructor that takes an int, the compiler will use that constructor to fabricate the temporary and then copy that value into m. Whether this is a good idea or not depends on the application. For instance, in a class RationalNumber, if there is a constructor that takes a single int, then a statement such as r=0, where r is of type RationalNumber, would be convenient and would, in fact, compile.

```
1   int main( )
2   {
3       IntCell m;
4
5       m = 3;
6       cout << m.getValue( ) << endl;
7
8       return 0;
9   }
```

Figure 4-5   Example of implicit type conversion, which may or may not be desirable depending on context

On the other hand, since the `vector` type has a one-parameter constructor, this would open the door to allow

```
vector<double> arr(20);
...
arr = 5;
```

which would create a temporary vector of size 5, copy its contents into `arr`, and then free up the temporary instead of doing the sensible thing and reporting an error.

Faced with this dilemma, C++ adopts the following rule: A one-parameter constructor automatically implies the ability to perform a type conversion. Furthermore, by default the compiler will apply the type conversion if needed, even if not requested, to satisfy assignments and parameter matches (but not call-by-reference, which requires exact matches). This is known as an *implicit type conversion*. The reason for this is that C++ is trying to treat objects in the same fashion as it treats primitives. To disallow implicit type conversions, the programmer can mark the constructor as `explicit`.

The explicit directive is meaningless for constructors that do not take one parameter. If a constructor is marked as `explicit`, then it will not be considered in object creations in which the initialization uses =; instead you must explicitly place the one parameter in parentheses. What this means is that if `IntCell` is marked `explicit`, then in Figure 4-3, the declarations of `m1` and `m3` are acceptable, but the declaration of `m2` is in error.

As a general rule, one-parameter constructors should be marked `explicit` unless it makes sense to allow implicit type conversions. Thus in the `vector` type, the single parameter constructor has been marked `explicit`. In the `string` type, in which a `const char *` (primitive string constant) can be passed as a parameter, the constructor is not marked as `explicit` to facilitate the mixing of `const char *` and `string` library types.

The revised version of `IntCell`, with the changes made to signify that `getValue` is an accessor and the constructor is marked `explicit` is shown in Figure 4-6.

```
1   class IntCell
2   {
3     public:
4       explicit IntCell( int initialValue = 0 )
5         { storedValue = initialValue; }
6
7       int getValue( ) const
8         { return storedValue; }
9
10      void setValue( int val )
11        { storedValue = val; }
12
13    private:
14      int storedValue;
15  };
```

Figure 4-6   Second version of C++ class that stores an `int` value (still needs more work)

4.4   Why C++ Needs More Syntax Than Java

Already we have seen two examples where C++ adds syntax that is not needed at all in Java. Both examples are similar in that the syntax is added to allow C++ class types to behave like primitive types, which is in marked contrast to the design decisions in Java.

In Java, primitive entities can be marked `final` and certain operations are not allowed on them (assignments, autoincrement, etc.). However, it is impossible to mark an object as final. Only the reference can be marked `final`, but that does not prohibit changes to the state of the object. The only way to enforce object immutability in Java is to declare data private and provide no mutators. Thus Java is not concerned with extending the immutability concept from primitive entities to objects. C++ is, but this adds syntax.

In Java, a typecast for reference variables does not create a new object; instead it simply allows the object to be accessed by a different, yet compatible, reference variable. Since objects are accessed by reference variables, creating new objects implicitly is never needed for non-primitive entities.

When a class includes data members that are not primitive entities, a whole new set of considerations is introduced. For example, the code in Figure 4-7 shows a Java class with three private data members, the syntactically similar C++ class (which has different semantics), and a second C++ class whose semantics more closely mirror the Java class.

Figure 4-8 shows the layout in the Virtual Machine for Java objects of type `Student`. Since `name` and `birthDate` are objects, they are accessed by reference variables. The intent of the picture is that the data fields that are stored as part of a `Student` instance are simply pointer variables.

```
1    // Java version: see Figure 4-8
2    class Student
3    {
4        private String name;
5        private Date    birthDate;
6        private double gpa;
7    }
8
9    // C++ version: see Figure 4-9
10   class Student
11   {
12     private:
13       string name;
14       Date    birthDate;
15       double gpa;
16   };
17
18   // C++ version with non-primitive members accessed by pointers
19   // Same memory layout as Java version: see Figure 4-8
20   class Student
21   {
22     private:
23       string * name;
24       Date    * birthDate;
25       double   gpa;
26   };
```

Figure 4-7   Data members in a Java class and two C++ classes

Figure 4-9 shows the layout in C++ for the first declaration of type `Student`. The declaration is cosmetically identical to the Java declaration, but as is evident from Figure 4-9, complete instances of the data members are stored as part of the `Student` entity. We can expect that a copy of `Student` objects copies all the data members, and this looks good in C++, except of course, that the copy can be expensive if the data members are large. Recall also that, by default,

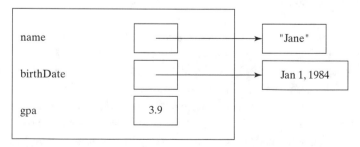

Figure 4-8   Memory layout in Java and also in C++ when data members include pointers

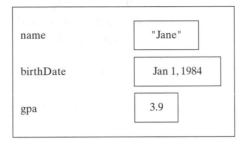

Figure 4-9   Memory layout in C++ when objects are declared as nonpointer data members

parameter passing and returning makes copies, which is why it can be important to pass objects using call-by-constant reference instead of call-by-value.

Figure 4-9 shows one new issue that C++ must deal with. In Java, in the constructor, each of the reference data members is initialized to null and then assigned to reference an object of the appropriate type. In C++, the first step of initializing members to null does not work. The alternative, initializing each member with a default constructor, might work, but there are limitations. For instance, there might not be a zero-parameter constructor for type Date. Thus, we need some syntax to specify how each of the data members is initialized. We discuss this in Section 4.5.

Although the first piece of C++ in Figure 4-7 looks similar to Java code, we have seen that it is quite different semantically. Furthermore, often it is the case that the data members are pointer variables; as we mentioned in Section 3.6, this may be needed in linked data structures and programs that involve inheritance. The last piece of code in Figure 4-7 shows the data members declared as pointer variables. With this declaration, the memory layout mirrors the Java layout. However, this layout creates numerous subtleties.

First, a copy is no longer a real copy; when data members are copied, the result is that the birthDate and name are shared amongst two instances of Student. This is known as a *shallow copy*. Typically with C++, we expect a *deep copy*. Certainly the visible semantics of C++ should not depend on the implementation details, and the default visible semantics that we would expect to see should be a deep copy. Thus when data members are pointer variables, if we expect deep copy semantics, we must redefine the assignment operation to ensure correct behavior. We discuss this in Section 4.6.

A related problem concerns how objects of type Student are returned. By default, a copy is made, but the copy creates a new temporary object. This is not an assignment operator, but instead a different kind of constructor, known as the *copy constructor*. We discuss this in Section 4.6. The default can be time-consuming, so in some cases it is worth trying to avoid it by returning using constant reference. We discuss this in Section 4.10.

Another related problem is that in the first implementation, when objects of type Student are created and destroyed, all of the constituent components which are part of

Student are automatically destroyed too. In the second implementation, this is no longer true by default because name and birthDate are simply pointer variables. The objects they are pointing at are not reclaimed unless delete is applied to them, and whereas these are private variables, it is difficult for the user to do so. Instead we need to provide a routine, called the *destructor*, that ensures that private heap objects allocated by the Student class are reclaimed when the Student is itself reclaimed. We discuss this in Section 4.6.

Another complication deals with the fact that in Java, the language consists of both the Java Language Specification and the Java Virtual Machine Specification. Specifically, a Java compiler can look at Java bytecode to decide the valid methods for a class. The C++ setup places the class declaration in a .h file, whose contents are logically copied into all source files that provide an appropriate include directive. This can make compilation slow. In C++, we can specify the declaration of the class, which lists its member functions and memory layout, and provide an implementation separately, thus reducing the size of the .h file. We discuss this in Sections 4.11 and 4.12.

4.5   Initializer Lists

The *initializer list* is the C++ construct that is used to specify nondefault initialization of each data member in an object. As an example, the initializer list can be used to rewrite the IntCell constructor in Figure 4-6 as

```
explicit IntCell( int initialValue = 0 )
  : storedValue( initialValue )
  { }
```

Syntactically, the initializer list is part of the constructor and appears prior to the opening brace that signifies the body of the constructor. Although the behavior appears the same, the revised constructor shown above is different from the original.

In the new form, in which an initializer list is used, the storedValue data member is immediately initialized to using initialValue when the memory for it is set aside in the newly constructed IntCell object. Because the body of the constructor is empty, no further operations are performed.

The original form behaves slightly differently. When the memory for storedValue is set aside for the newly constructed IntCell object, storedValue is initialized by using the default initialization for int. Then in the body of the constructor, initialValue is copied into storedValue using the copy assignment operator (for int).

The difference between these two is minor when data members are primitives. However, when data members are not primitives, failing to use initializer lists can cause inferior performance and may even cause code to not compile.

Consider, for instance, two alternatives for a Student class constructor. The first version is shown in Figure 4-10 without an initializer list, while an improved version is shown in Figure 4-11 with an initializer list.

```
1    // Inferior constructor: uses copy assignment
2    class Student
3    {
4      public:
5        Student( const string & n, const Date & b, double g )
6        {
7            name = n;
8            birthDate = b;
9            gpa = g;
10       }
11
12     private:
13       string name;
14       Date   birthDate;
15       double gpa;
16   };
```

Figure 4-10   Inferior constructor uses copy assignment

Consider the initialization of the birthDate data member. In this instance, using an initializer list allows us to initialize the Date data member directly. Without an initializer list, we must first create a default Date. Since a default Date must represent a valid Date, this Date may well be initialized to the current Date (today); it certainly will not be some random memory values. Then in the body of the constructor, the intended Date must be copied into the Date data member, overwriting the initialized state. Obviously this means that we have wasted CPU cycles to initialize the Date to today's date. Depending on how complex the Date class itself is and how often Student objects are constructed, this could be nontrivial, because it could involve creation of strings to store months and so on.

```
1    // Better version: uses initializer lists
2    class Student
3    {
4      public:
5        Student( const string & n, const Date & b, double g )
6          : name( n ), birthDate( b ), gpa( g )
7        {
8        }
9
10     private:
11       string name;
12       Date   birthDate;
13       double gpa;
14   };
```

Figure 4-11   Constructor uses initializer list

Because initialization of each class member should usually be done with its own constructor, when possible you should use explicit initializer lists. Note, however, that this form is intended for relatively simple cases only. If the initialization is not simple (e.g., if error checks are needed or the initialization of one data member depends on another), perhaps the body of the constructor should be used for more complex logic.

It is important to note that the order of evaluation of the initializer list is given by the order in which class members are listed. This is one reason why it is bad style to have the initialization of a data member depend on another data member. If your code depends on the order of initialization, it's probably dubious code and should be avoided; if this is impossible, at least comment the fact that there is an order dependency, so a future programmer does not change the order of the data members.

An initializer list is required in four common situations.

1. If any data member does not have a zero-parameter constructor, the data member must be initialized in the initializer list.
2. If a superclass does not have a constructor, the subclass must use an initializer list to initialize the inherited component (Chapter 6). One can view this as being the same as the first situation.
3. Constant data members must be initialized in the initializer list. A constant data member can never be altered after the data member is constructed. This means you cannot apply the copy assignment operator in the body of the class constructor to set the value of the constant data member. An example of a constant data member is the identification number in a `Student` class. Each `Student` has his or her own unique identification number, but presumably the identification number never changes. This is similar to final data members in Java, except that in Java, it is the reference variable that is final, not the object being referenced. In C++ it is the dereferenced object.
4. A data member that is a reference variable (for instance, an `ostream &`) must be initialized in the constructor.

4.6   The Big Three: Destructor, Copy Constructor, and `operator=`

In C++, classes come with three special functions that are already written for you. These are destructor, copy constructor, and `operator=`, collectively known as the *Big Three*. In many cases, you can accept the default behavior provided by the compiler; sometimes you cannot.

4.6.1   Destructor

The *destructor* is called whenever an object goes out of scope or is subjected to a `delete`. Typically, the only responsibility of the destructor is to free up any resources that were allocated during the use of the object. This includes calling `delete` for any corresponding `new`s, closing any files that were opened, and so on. The default applies the destructor on each data member.

4.6.2 Copy Constructor

There is a special constructor that is required to construct a new object that is initialized to a copy of the same type of object. This is the *copy constructor*. For any object, such as an `IntCell` object, a copy constructor is called in the following instances:

- A declaration with initialization, such as

```
IntCell copy = original;
IntCell copy( original );
```

  but not

```
copy = original; // Assignment operator, discussed later
```

- An object passed using call-by-value (instead of by & or `const` &), which, as mentioned in Section 2.3, should usually not be done anyway for large objects.
- An object returned by value (instead of by & or `const` &)

The first case is the simplest to understand because the constructed objects were explicitly requested. The second and third cases construct temporary objects that are never seen by the user. In both cases we are constructing new objects as copies of existing objects, so certainly the copy constructor is applicable.

By default the copy constructor is implemented by applying copy constructors to each data member in turn. For data members that are primitive types (for instance, `int`, `double`, or pointers), simple assignment is done. This would be the case for the `storedValue` data member in our `IntCell` class. For data members that are themselves class objects, the copy constructor for each data member's class is applied to that data member.

4.6.3 `operator=`

The *copy assignment operator*, `operator=`, is called when = is applied to two **already-constructed** objects. `lhs=rhs` is intended to copy the state of `rhs` into `lhs`. By default `operator=` is implemented by applying `operator=` to each data member in turn.

4.6.4 Issues Concerning the Defaults

If we examine the `IntCell` class, we see that the defaults are perfectly acceptable, so we do not have to do anything. This is often the case. If a class consists of data members that are exclusively primitive types and objects for which the defaults make sense, the class defaults will usually make sense. Thus a class whose data members are `int`, `double`, `vector<int>`, `string`, and even `vector<string>` can accept the defaults.

The main problem occurs in a class that contains a data member that is a pointer. Suppose the class contains a single data member that is a pointer. This pointer points at a heap-allocated object. The default destructor for pointers does nothing (recall that we must `delete` ourselves), so there may be a memory leak if the default is used. Furthermore, the copy constructor and `operator=` both copy not the objects being pointed at, but simply the value of the pointer. Thus we will simply have two class instances that contain pointers that point to the same object. As discussed in Section 4.4, this is a so-called shallow copy. Typically, we would expect a deep copy, in which a clone of the entire object is made. Thus, when a class contains pointers as data members and when deep semantics are important, we typically must implement the destructor, operator=, and copy constructor (in other words, the Big Three) ourselves.

For IntCell, the signatures of these operations are

```
~IntCell( );                        // destructor
IntCell( const IntCell & rhs );     // copy constructor
const IntCell & operator=( const IntCell & rhs );
```

Although the defaults for IntCell are acceptable, we can write the implementations anyway as shown in Figure 4-12. For the destructor, after the body is executed, the destructors are called for the data members; so the default is an empty body. For the copy constructor, the default is an initializer list of copy constructors, followed by execution of the body.

operator= is the most interesting. Line 18 is an alias test to make sure we are not copying to ourselves. Assuming we are not, we apply operator= to each data member (at line 19).

```
1    class IntCell
2    {
3      public:
4        ~IntCell( )
5        {
6            // Does nothing since IntCell contains only an int data
7            // member. If IntCell contained any class objects their
8            // destructors would be called.
9        }
10
11       IntCell( const IntCell & rhs )
12         : storedValue( rhs.storedValue )
13       {
14       }
15
16       Const IntCell & IntCell::operator=( const IntCell & rhs )
17       {
18           if( this != &rhs )   // Standard alias test
19               storedValue = rhs.storedValue;
20           return *this;
21       }
22
23       ...
24
25     private:
26        int storedValue;
27   };
```

Figure 4-12   The defaults that are generated automatically by the compiler

We then return a reference to the current object at line 20, so assignments can be chained, as in a=b=c. [The return is actually a constant reference, so that the nonsensical (a=b)=c is disallowed by the compiler. However, it seems that returning a reference instead of a constant reference is more common and is the default.]

　　　Let us look at the uses of the keyword this in more detail. In C++, the pointer this is defined to point at the current object in exactly the same way as this references the current object in Java. Consequently, *this is the current object, and returning *this achieves the desired result. As in Java, under no circumstances will the compiler knowingly allow you to modify this. As we see, the return at line 20 uses *this. The other use of this is at line 18.

　　　The expression a=a is logically a nonoperation (no-op). In some cases, although not here, failing to treat this as a special case can result in the destruction of a. As an example, consider a program that copies one file to another. A normal algorithm begins by truncating the target file to zero length. If no check is performed to make sure the source and target file are indeed different, then the source file will be truncated, hardly a desirable feature. When performing copies, the first thing we should do is check for this special case, which is known as *aliasing*.

　　　In the routines that we write, if the defaults make sense, we will always accept them. However, if the defaults do not make sense, we will need to implement the destructor, operator=, and the copy constructor. When the default does not work, the copy constructor can generally be implemented by mimicking normal construction and then calling operator=. Another often-used option is to give a reasonable working implementation of the copy constructor, but then place it in the private section to disallow call-by-value.

4.6.5　When the Defaults Do Not Work

The most common situation in which the defaults do not work occurs when a data member is a pointer type and the pointee is heap-allocated by some object member function (such as the constructor). As an example, suppose we implement the IntCell by dynamically allocating an int as shown in Figure 4-13.

```
1   class IntCell
2   {
3     public:
4       explicit IntCell( int initialValue = 0 )
5         { storedValue = new int( initialValue ); }
6       int getValue( ) const
7         { return *storedValue; }
8       void setValue( int val )
9         { *storedValue = val; }
10
11    private:
12        int *storedValue;
13  };
```

Figure 4-13　Data member is a pointer; defaults are no good

```
1   int f( )
2   {
3       IntCell a( 2 );
4       IntCell b = a;
5       IntCell c;
6
7       c = b;
8       a.setValue( 4 );
9       cout << a.getValue( ) << endl << b.getValue( ) << endl
10              << c.getValue( ) << endl;
11
12      return 0;
13  }
```

Figure 4-14   Simple function that exposes problems in Figure 4-13

There are now numerous problems, which are exposed in Figure 4-14. First, the output is three 4s, even though logically only a should be 4. The problem is that the default copy constructor and `operator=` copied the pointer `storedValue`. Thus `a.storedValue`, `b.storedValue`, and `c.storedValue` all point at the same `int` value. These copies are shallow: The pointers, rather than the pointees, are copied. A second less obvious problem is a memory leak. The `int` initially allocated by a's constructor remains allocated and needs to be reclaimed. The `int` allocated by c's constructor is no longer referenced by any pointer variable, so it also needs to be reclaimed, but we no longer have a pointer to it. These problems are illustrated in Figures 4-15 and 4-16.

To fix these problems, we implement the Big Three. The result is shown in Figure 4-17. Generally speaking, if a destructor is necessary to reclaim memory, then the defaults for copy assignment and copy construction are not acceptable.

4.6.6   Linked Data Structures

Linked data structures, such as linked lists and binary search trees, provide classic examples in which the Big Three need to be written. Although the Standard Library provides implementations

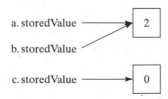

Figure 4-15   After line 5 in Figure 4-14, the default copy constructor generates shallow copies

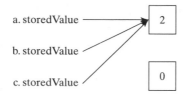

Figure 4-16 After line 7 in Figure 4-14, the default `operator=` generates a shallow copy and leaks memory

of stacks, queues, lists, sets, and maps, you may on occasion find that you need to implement your own. For instance, the linked list (and thus queue) implementations in the Standard Library use doubly linked lists, although a singly linked list can be implemented faster and with less space. In this section we illustrate a singly linked list implementation of a queue; minor syntactical improvements are given in sections that follow. Our interest in this implementation is concerned mostly with memory management and the Big Three.

```
1   class IntCell
2   {
3     public:
4       explicit IntCell( int initialValue = 0 )
5         { storedValue = new int( initialValue ); }
6       IntCell( const IntCell & rhs )
7         { storedValue = new int( *rhs.storedValue ); }
8
9       ~IntCell( )
10        { delete storedValue; }
11
12      const IntCell & operator=( const IntCell & rhs )
13      {
14          if( this != &rhs )
15              *storedValue = *rhs.storedValue;
16          return *this;
17      }
18
19      int getValue( ) const
20        { return *storedValue; }
21
22      void setValue( int val )
23        { *storedValue = val; }
24
25    private:
26      int *storedValue;
27  };
```

Figure 4-17 Data member is a pointer; Big Three needs to be written

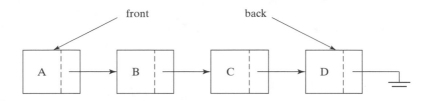

Figure 4-18 Linked list implementation of the queue

Recall that a queue supports insertion at one end (the back) and deletion at the other end (the front). These operations are `enqueue` and `dequeue`, respectively. As Figure 4-18 shows, a singly linked list in which we store a pointer to both the front and the back of the list can be used to represent a queue. In an empty queue, the data member `front` is NULL. In this case, the linked list contains list nodes that each store the data and a pointer to the next node in the list, and this is implemented in a `ListNode` class as shown in Figure 4-19. The class uses public data because the data members need to be accessed from the queue class. There are several alternate solutions, including the use of nested classes, that we will discuss in Sections 4.7 – 4.9.

Figure 4-20 shows that to enqueue a new integer x, we create a new `ListNode` and attach it after the last node in the list, in the process updating `back`. Figure 4-21 shows that to dequeue the front item, we simply advance `front` after saving the data in the front node so it can be returned. In Java, when we advance `front`, the node that was formerly referenced by `front` becomes unreferenced and eligible for garbage collection. In C++, we must clean up the memory ourselves.

In fact, we can now see that several other routines require that we clean up memory: two obvious candidates are `makeEmpty` and the destructor, both of which must clean up all the nodes in the list. Furthermore, if we write a destructor, we must write `operator=`, and if we copy a large queue into a small queue, it is evident that nodes will have to be reclaimed.

```
1   class ListNode
2   {
3     public:
4        int    element;
5        ListNode *next;
6
7        ListNode( int theElement, ListNode * n = NULL )
8          : element( theElement ), next( n ) { }
9   };
```

Figure 4-19 `ListNode` class

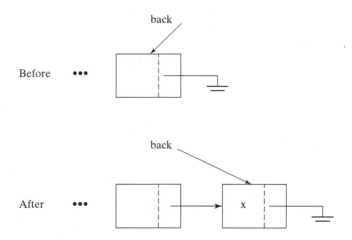

Figure 4-20 enqueue operation for linked-list-based implementation

The implementation of the queue is provided in the `IntQueue` class that begins in Figure 4-22. `UnderflowException` is simply a class that is used if `getFront` or `dequeue` is attempted on an empty queue. We will discuss exceptions in more detail in Chapter 8, but for now we remark that `UnderflowException` behaves exactly like a Java runtime exception that is uncaught. We show the two data members at the top of the `IntQueue` class declaration instead of at the bottom simply so we can see them in this discussion. Normally, the private section is placed at the end of a C++ class declaration.

The zero-parameter constructor, shown at lines 10 and 11, does no more than initialize `front` and `back` to NULL; this is NOT done by default. The copy constructor at lines 13 to 15

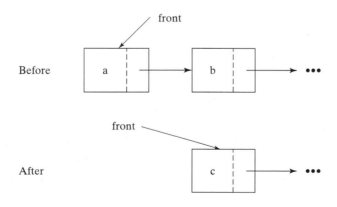

Figure 4-21 dequeue operation for linked-list-based implementation

```
 1   class UnderflowException { };
 2
 3   class IntQueue
 4   {
 5     private:
 6       ListNode *front;
 7       ListNode *back;
 8
 9     public:
10       IntQueue( ) : front( NULL ), back( NULL )
11         { }
12
13       IntQueue( const IntQueue & rhs )
14           : front( NULL ), back( NULL )
15         { *this = rhs; }
16
17       ~IntQueue( )
18         { makeEmpty( ); }
19
20       const IntQueue & operator= ( const IntQueue & rhs )
21       {
22           if( this != &rhs )
23           {
24               makeEmpty( );
25               ListNode *rptr = rhs.front;
26               for( ; rptr != NULL; rptr = rptr->next )
27                   enqueue( rptr->element );
28           }
29           return *this;
30       }
31
32       void makeEmpty( )
33       {
34           while( !isEmpty( ) )
35               dequeue( );
36       }
```

Figure 4-22   Linked-list-based queue class (part 1 of 2)

first makes the queue empty and then copies rhs into it using operator=. Since operator= might try to reclaim nodes in this queue prior to the copy, it is important that this queue be placed into a respectable state prior to invoking the copy assignment operator. The destructor is shown at lines 17 and 18. Instead of reclaiming the memory itself, it delegates the dirty work to makeEmpty, which presumably cleans up the memory. The copy assignment operator, operator=, is shown at lines 20 to 30. After the alias test, it empties out this queue and then steps through rhs, enqueueing each item it sees. The alias test is crucial here, since otherwise, a self-assignment makes the queue empty!

makeEmpty is shown at lines 32 to 36. Recall that the destructor was relying on makeEmpty to reclaim all the list nodes. makeEmpty is implemented simply by calling dequeue until the queue is empty, thus delegating the dirty work of memory management yet again.

isEmpty, getFront, and enqueue are all shown in Figure 4-23. They are relatively straightforward (in some cases trivial) given that they are only a few lines of code each and do not involve reclaiming memory. Reclaiming memory however, can only be deferred for so long, and finally in dequeue, shown in lines 55 to 62, we have to bite the bullet. As the code shows, a call at line 57 to getFront gives us the frontItem that can be returned at line 61 (or throws an UnderflowException that is unhandled). Prior to advancing front at line 59, we save a pointer to it (line 58) so we can reclaim the node (line 60) by invoking the delete operator. Thus we have managed to funnel all memory management to three lines of code, which is generally your best strategy, since memory management is so bug-prone.

```
37        bool isEmpty( ) const
38          { return front == NULL; }
39
40        int getFront( ) const
41        {
42            if( isEmpty( ) )
43                throw UnderflowException( );
44            return front->element;
45        }
46
47        void enqueue( int x )
48        {
49            if( isEmpty( ) )
50                back = front = new ListNode( x );
51            else
52                back = back->next = new ListNode( x );
53        }
54
55        int dequeue( )
56        {
57            int frontItem = getFront( );
58            ListNode *old = front;
59            front = front->next;
60            delete old;
61            return frontItem;
62        }
63    };
```

Figure 4-23 Linked-list-based queue class (part 2 of 2)

4.6.7 Default Constructor

If no constructors (not including the special copy constructor) are provided for a class, then a default constructor is automatically generated. The default takes no parameters. Each data member that is a class type is initialized by its zero-parameter constructor. However, the primitive members of objects allocated on the runtime stack or from the memory heap are not guaranteed to be initialized.

4.6.8 Disabling Copying

Both `operator=` and the copy constructor can be disabled (independently) by placing their declarations in the private section of the class. It is still worthwhile to provide an implementation of these methods. Similarly as in Java, constructors can be private; as in Java, this is common in the case of factory classes (such as `InetAddress`) that provide static methods to create object instances. C++ supports the same idiom. Destructors should generally not be private.

If the class contains data members that do not have the ability to copy themselves, then the default `operator=` will not work.

 ## 4.7 Friends

Typically we would like to make data members (and occasionally member functions) private, but as we saw in Section 4.6.6, it often is inconvenient to do so, because there may be one other class (or possibly a few select classes) that needs access to implementation details. However, making the members public grants access to everyone.

Java has an intermediate visibility modifier, package visibility, in which specific members are marked as being accessible to other classes. However, while this allows access only to classes that happen to be in the same package (typically not a severe limitation), the access is granted to all such classes.

In C++, there is no such visibility modifier. Instead, the class can grant waivers of the normal privacy restrictions to others. Such a waiver would apply to the access of all of the class' private members. This waiver can be granted only by the class that is willing to allow access to its private members. The recipient of the waiver can be either an entire class or a specific function. There is no limit to the number of waivers that a class can grant. A waiver is known as a *friend declaration*.

4.7.1 Classes as Friends

Figure 4-24 offers an alternative to the `ListNode` class that was previously declared in Figure 4-19. Notice that here the class contains private members only and, thus, with no friend declarations, is unusable (even instances cannot be created). The friend declaration at line 10 allows any of the `IntQueue` member functions to access the private members.

4.7.2 Methods as Friends

A class can also grant access to a specific function. For instance, although it makes little sense,

```
    friend int main( );
```

grants `main` access to private data.

```
1   class ListNode
2   {
3     private:
4       int    element;
5       ListNode *next;
6
7       ListNode( int theElement, ListNode * n = NULL )
8         : element( theElement ), next( n ) { }
9
10      friend class IntQueue;
11  };
```
Figure 4-24 `ListNode` class with friend declaration

A member function can be granted access by using the `::` operator (we discuss the `::` operator in Section 4.11) to specify the class that it is part of. For instance,

    friend void IntQueue::enqueue(int x);

grants access to `IntQueue`'s `enqueue` member function that takes an `int`. The friend declaration is very specific:

    friend int IntQueue::getFront( );

does not grant access to the `getFront` member function implemented in Figure 4-23, because the `getFront` method is an accessor and the declaration that was provided signals that the waiver was granted to a mutator. The friend declaration

    friend int IntQueue::getFront( ) const;

fixes the problem.

As a matter of style, just as package visibility is often an inferior design decision, friend declarations are generally best avoided, because they weaken the encapsulation and information hiding benefits that the private section offers. An alternative approach to our original problem of granting `IntCell` access to `ListNode` internals is to use nested classes; this is discussed in the next section.

4.8 Nested Classes

Like Java, C++ supports *nested classes*. Specifically, the nested class in C++ behaves in a manner that is similar to the static nested class in Java. Figure 4-25 shows that we can hide the `ListNode` class inside of the `IntCell` class.

If the `ListNode` class were public, outside of `IntCell` it would be known as `IntCell::ListNode`, but the point of the idiom is to hide the class, so it is placed in the private section.

Unlike Java, private members of the nested classes are not visible from instances of the enclosing class, so the members in `ListNode` need to be public. However, this is of little consequence, since the `ListNode` type itself is hidden. Alternatively, the `IntCell` class could declare `ListNode` as a friend and then `ListNode` could have private members.

```
1   class IntQueue
2   {
3     public:
4       ...
5
6     private:
7       class ListNode
8       {
9         public:
10          int   element;
11          ListNode *next;
12
13          ListNode( int theElement, ListNode * n = NULL )
14            : element( theElement ), next( n ) { }
15      };
16
17      ListNode *front;
18      ListNode *back;
19  };
```

Figure 4-25   Nested `ListNode` class

Similarly, unlike Java, private members of the enclosing class are not visible from instances of the nested class. Here the most sensible way to remedy this limitation is for the enclosing class to use a friend declaration to grant access to instances of the nested class.

C++ does not support Java-style inner classes in which instances of the inner class are constructed with the hidden reference to an outer object that caused its creation. Thus the C++ nested class is simply used as a convenience to hide one type inside another type.

C++ allows local classes in which a class is declared inside a function. However, their utility is dubious, because, unlike Java, automatic local variables in the enclosing function cannot be accessed (static local variables can be accessed, but this hardly seems like sufficient justification to introduce the added complexity of using a local class).

C++ does not allow anonymous classes.

 ## 4.9   The `struct` Type

In C++, the `struct` type is a relic from the C programming language. A `struct` in C++ is essentially a class in which the members default to public. Recall that in a class, the members default to private. Thus in Figure 4-25 we can use `struct` instead of `class` at line 7 and then omit line 9. Clearly the `struct` type is not needed, but you will often see it and it is commonly used by programmers to signify a type that contains mostly data that are accessed directly, rather than through member functions.

4.10 Return-by-Constant Reference Revisited

Let us return to an issue raised earlier about how objects are returned. Recall that the default return mechanism is return-by-value. In return-by-value, the value of the expression is copied back to the caller. If the return type is an object that is expensive to copy, then this can be undesirable. There are occasions when it is worth returning by constant reference, in an attempt to avoid copying the return value, but this is tricky and there are two important issues.

First, as Figure 4-26 shows, if you are returning a constant reference, then the expression that is being returned must have a lifetime that extends past the end of the function. Thus findMaxWrong is incorrect because it returns a reference to maxValue, and maxValue does not exist once this function returns. The first implementation is correct, since it is guaranteed that the array item exists when the function returns. Notice that a return expression such as

```
return arr[ maxIndex ] + "";
```

does not work. The result of the string concatenation is an unnamed temporary string whose destructor will be called as soon as the function terminates.

```
1    const string & findMax( const vector<string> & arr )
2    {
3        int maxIndex = 0;
4
5        for( int i = 1; i < arr.size( ); i++ )
6            if( arr[ maxIndex ] < arr[ i ] )
7                maxIndex = i;
8
9        return arr[ maxIndex ];
10   }
11
12   const string & findMaxWrong( const vector<string> & arr )
13   {
14       string maxValue = arr[ 0 ];
15
16       for( int i = 1; i < arr.size( ); i++ )
17           if( maxValue < arr[ i ] )
18               maxValue = arr[ i ];
19
20       return maxValue;
21   }
```

Figure 4-26 Two versions to find the maximum string (alphabetically); only the first version is correct

Ensuring that the return expression has a long lifetime is only half of the task. Consider the following three calls to findMax.

```
string s1 = findMax( arr );              // copies
const string & s2 = findMax( arr );  // no copy
string & s3 = findMax( arr );            // illegal
```

The first call is legal, but defeats the entire purpose of returning by constant reference. Specifically, the object s1 is a string, it is being created, and its initial value is another string, so this statement causes execution of a string copy constructor. The similar code

```
string s1;
s1 = findMax( arr );
```

is no better; it creates a default string and then the second line causes execution of the string copy assignment operator.

The second call, in which we initialize s2 is the correct way to avoid the copy. The declaration says that s2 is a reference variable. Thus, it is not a new string. The initialization states that s2 references the same string object as the return value of findMax. Since findMax returns by (constant) reference, its return value references the maximum string that is actually contained in arr. Thus s2 references the maximum string that is actually contained in arr.

If findMax returned by value, then this would appear to be dubious code, because s2 would be referencing an unnamed temporary, whose destructor could be called as soon as the statement terminated. Using s2 at the next line could result in an attempt to access an already destructed string. However, the language specification has specifically contemplated this scenario and it is guaranteed that the temporary variable will not be destroyed while the reference variable is active. Even so, in this situation, the return-by-value causes a copy to create the temporary variable. Thus, to avoid the copy, both of the following steps must be taken:

• Return by (const, if appropriate) reference.
• Have the caller use a (const, if appropriate) reference variable to access the return value.

The third call should not compile, because it attempts to throw away the const-ness of the reference variable returned by findMax. Specifically, findMax was returning a reference that could now be used to modify the referenced object, and if this declaration were to be allowed by the compiler, then s3 could be used to modify the referenced object, in violation of the expectation of findMax.

However, the const-ness can be cast away using the special const_cast:

```
string & s3 = const_cast<string &> ( findMax( arr ) );
```

Now an attempt to change the object that was being referenced compiles (although if the object was actually stored in read-only memory, the code may fail at runtime). Needless to say, using a const_cast to circumvent const-ness is almost always inadvisable and is best avoided.

4.11 Separation of Interface and Implementation

If a program consists of many separate source files that use a class type, each source file must be able to see the class declaration. The easiest way to do this is to put the entire class definition in a header file (.h) and then have each .cpp file that uses a class type provide include directives. Because the include directive causes the contents of an entire file to logically replace the include directive, two serious downsides emerge:

First, normally, in a separate compilation model, only the files that have changed are recompiled, but this clearly is not the case here, since header files themselves are never directly compiled. As a result, any change to the implementation of any of the member functions in a class requires the recompilation of every file that uses the class.

Second, the recompilation is expensive, because if the class is used in numerous .cpp source files, the compiler must repeatedly parse the entire contents of the header file.

To solve these problems, C++ allows separation of the class specification from its implementation. The specification lists the class and its members (data and functions). The implementation provides implementations of the member functions. Often the specification by itself is called a *class declaration*, while the complete class, with member functions implemented, is the *class implementation*. The class declaration is also known as the *class specification* and is sometimes known as the *class interface*.

Figure 4-27 shows the class declaration for `IntCell`, which we last saw in Figure 4-6. The class implementation is shown in Figure 4-28. Observe that we use the `::` scoping operator to signify that we are implementing member functions, rather than plain (nonmember) functions. The main program is shown in Figure 4-29.

The same syntax is used whether these member functions are public or private. The signature of the member functions in the implementation file must exactly match the signature in the class specification, including parameter-passing mechanism, return mechanism, and all uses of `const`. The names of the formal parameters do not have to match and, in fact, may be omitted in the class declaration.

```
1   class IntCell
2   {
3     public:
4       explicit IntCell( int initialValue = 0 );
5
6       int getValue( ) const;
7       void setValue( int val );
8
9     private:
10      int storedValue;
11  };
```

Figure 4-27 Third version of C++ class that stores an `int` value, now with class declaration separate from implementation (still needs more work)

```
1   #include "IntCell.h"
2
3   IntCell::IntCell( int initialValue )
4     : storedValue( initialValue )
5   {
6   }
7
8   int IntCell::getValue( ) const
9   {
10      return storedValue;
11  }
12
13  void IntCell::setValue( int val )
14  {
15      storedValue = val;
16  }
```

Figure 4-28   Third version of C++ class that stores an `int` value; class implementation (final version)

It is illegal to provide an implementation of a member function that was not listed in the class declaration. If a member function is listed in the class declaration, but is not implemented, the program will still compile. It will link and run if the missing member function is never actually invoked. This allows the programmer to implement and debug the class in stages.

```
1   #include "IntCell.h"
2   #include <iostream>
3   using namespace std;
4
5   int main( )
6   {
7       IntCell m1;
8       IntCell m2 = 37;
9       IntCell m3( 55 );
10
11      cout << m1.getValue( ) << " " << m2.getValue( )
12                          << " " << m3.getValue( ) << endl;
13      m1 = m2;
14      m2.setValue( 40 );
15
16      cout << m1.getValue( ) << " " << m2.getValue( ) << endl;
17
18      return 0;
19  }
```

Figure 4-29   Example showing the use of `IntCell` when class is separated (no changes)

The compilation mechanism is the same as described in Section 2.1.7. The `.cpp` files (`main.cpp` and `IntCell.cpp`) would be compiled as part of the project and the `.h` files would automatically be handled by the include directives.

If the implementation of a member function in `IntCell.cpp` changes, then only `IntCell.cpp` needs to be recompiled. If the class declaration in `IntCell.h` changes, then all `.cpp` files that have referenced the class declaration must be recompiled.

We do remark that implementing a member function inside the class declaration does have the advantage that an aggressive compiler can perform inline optimization. Thus, often trivial one-liners that are not likely to undergo changes in future versions are implemented in the class declaration. Most notably, this often includes constructors and destructors.

 ## 4.12 #ifndef and #endif

Suppose the code in Figure 4-29 is changed to contain a duplicate of the include directive at line 1. In other words, the altered code begins with

```
#include "IntCell.h"
#include "IntCell.h"
```

Whereas function declarations can be repeated and the declarations subsequent to the first are simply ignored, a class declaration cannot be repeated within a single `.cpp` file. Thus this revision does not compile.

Of course, nobody would deliberately write this kind of code. Unfortunately, in a complicated project, we often require that some of the `.h` files have include directives that reference other `.h` files. In that case, it is possible that the effect of a series of include directives is to include the same `.h` file more than once, and it may be impossible to avoid this scenario.

Figure 4-30 shows the C++ idiom that is used to avoid this problem. This idiom is placed inside the header file and the idea is that the compiler should be directed to read the `.h` file only

```
1   #ifndef INTCELL_H
2   #define INTCELL_H
3
4   class IntCell
5   {
6     public:
7       explicit IntCell( int initialValue = 0 );
8
9       int getValue( ) const;
10      void setValue( int val );
11
12    private:
13      int storedValue;
14  };
15  #endif
```

Figure 4-30   Final version of C++ class that stores an `int` value, with class declaration separate from implementation, includes ifndef/endif idiom

once per compilation of a `.cpp` file. At line 2, prior to reading the class declaration for `IntCell`, the preprocessor defines the symbol `INTCELL_H`. Presumably, this is a unique symbol, based on the name of the header file, for which no other attempts have ever been made to define. Thus, at line 1, if the `INTCELL_H` symbol is NOT defined, it is safe to read the class declaration. So `#ifndef` is a preprocessor directive and stands for "not defined." The `#endif` at line 15 closes the body of the `#ifndef`. As a matter of safe programming, this idiom, which we refer to as the *ifndef/endif idiom*, should be used in all header files. Even if there is no class declaration in the header file, using this idiom allows the compiler to avoid some parsing effort if the file appears a second time in a chain of include directives.

 ## 4.13 Static Members

Like Java, C++ allows static members. A static data member of a class is not part of any instance, but instead is part of the class. Whether there are 0, 1, or 20 instances of the class, there is exactly one shared instance of the static data member. In this regard, static data members in C++ are identical to their Java counterparts.

Member functions can access static data. If such a function accesses only static data and no instance data, then the member function should be declared static, since even in the case where there are 0 instances of the class, it still makes sense to call the member function. Additionally, if there are 0 instances of the class, it clearly would be impossible to invoke a nonstatic member function. Again, this is exactly the same as in Java.

The main difference between C++ and Java with regard to static members concerns their initialization. Java has precise rules on when the initialization occurs and the initialization can be done both inline or in a static initializer block. Generally speaking, C++ allows neither.

An example that illustrates both static data members and static member functions is the `Ticket` class shown in Figure 4-31. For brevity, we do not separate interface and implementation. Each ticket stores its `id`, and we would like `id`s to be unique. One way to do this is to assign the `id`s sequentially, keeping track of the number of tickets. When a new ticket is constructed, we increment the number of tickets and use the new number as the ticket `id`.

In this scenario, the ticket `id` is a data member that is part of each unique ticket instance, but the ticket count is shared data and is thus static. `ticketCount` is declared at line 15 as being a static variable. Unfortunately, this does not cause the creation of the shared `ticketCount` object; this must be provided separately as shown on line 30. Note that this definition cannot be placed in the header file, because if the header file is included in separate `.cpp` files, `ticketCount` will be multiply defined. (The ifndef/endif idiom only avoids multiple reading of the file for each `.cpp` file, not for separate `.cpp` files.) `ticketCount` is initialized when it is defined.

The constructor, shown at lines 4 and 5, increments `ticketCount` and uses it to initialize `id`. `getTicketCount` is a static method, since it could theoretically return 0 if invoked prior to the first creation of a ticket. Also, observe the idiom of disabling the copy constructor and copy assignment operator at lines 17 to 27 by placing them in the private section. Allowing a real copy would create duplicate tickets with identical `id`s, but using the implementation that is provided is not really a copy, so in this case it seems reasonable to disable both forms of copying.

```
1   class Ticket
2   {
3     public:
4       Ticket( ) : id( ++ticketCount )
5         { }
6
7       int getID( ) const
8         { return id; }
9
10      static int getTicketCount( )
11        { return ticketCount; }
12
13    private:
14      int id;
15      static int ticketCount;
16
17      Ticket( const Ticket & rhs )
18      {
19          id = ++ticketCount;
20      }
21
22      const Ticket & operator= ( const Ticket & rhs )
23      {
24          if( this != &rhs )
25              id = ++ticketCount;
26          return *this;
27      }
28  };
29
30  int Ticket::ticketCount = 0;   // place this line in Ticket.cpp
```

Figure 4-31   Static data member defined in implementation file

Disabling the copy constructor means, among other things, that a Ticket object may not be passed using call-by-value nor returned using return-by-value.

To invoke the getTicketCount member function, we once again use the :: scoping operator, as shown in both lines 3 and 6 in Figure 4-32.

When a static data member involves a complex initialization, Java processes the initialization in a *static initializer block*. C++ does not have a static initializer block, but the effect can be achieved as follows: Define a private static member function staticInit and use a call to this static member function to initialize the static data member. If the static data member does not have appropriate copy semantics that would easily allow this, fabricate a second private static data member of type bool and have it invoke staticInit. Inside staticInit, you can

```
1   int main( )
2   {
3       cout << Ticket::getTicketCount( ) << " tickets" << endl;
4
5       Ticket t1, t2, t3;
6       cout << Ticket::getTicketCount( ) << " tickets" << endl;
7       cout << "t2 is " << t2.getID( ) << endl;
8
9       return 0;
10  }
```

Figure 4-32   Invoking static member functions

then explicitly initialize all the static data members of the class. An example of this strategy is shown in Figure 4-33.

Because a static member function does not affect any particular instance of a class, static member functions are never marked as accessors. Normally, static member functions will be implemented in the .cpp file along with the nonstatic member functions.

```
1   class MathUtils
2   {
3       ...
4     private:
5       static vector<int> primes;
6       static bool forceStaticInit;
7
8       static bool staticInit( int n )
9       {
10          // Use Sieve of Erastothenis to eliminate non-primes
11          vector<bool> nums( n + 1, true );
12          for( int i = 2; i * i <= n; i++ )
13              for( int j = i * 2; j <= n; j += i )
14                  nums[ j ] = false;
15
16          for( int k = 2; k <= n; k++ )
17              if( nums[ k ] )
18                  primes.push_back( k );
19
20          return true;
21      }
22  };
23
24      // In implementation file
25  vector<int> MathUtils::primes;
26  bool        MathUtils::forceStaticInit = staticInit( 1000 );
```

Figure 4-33   Simulating the static initializer in C++: initialize array with prime numbers less than or equal to 1,000

```
1   class Utilities
2   {
3     public:
4       static const int BITS_PER_BYTES = 8;
5       ...
6   };
7
8     // In Utilities.cpp
9   const int Utilities::BITS_PER_BYTES;
```

Figure 4-34   Constant static integral members initialized in class declaration

If a static data member is a constant integer type (`int`, `short`, `long`, `char`, etc.), its initialization can be performed in the class declaration. However, it must still be defined in the `.cpp` file and the definition must not have any initialization. This hardly seems worth the effort except that initializing this way makes the static data member a constant integral expression, and qualifies it to be used as a case in a switch statement and a few other places where constant integral expressions are specifically required. Figure 4-34 illustrates the syntax.

 ## 4.14 Anonymous Objects

Occasionally, we need to construct anonymous objects (often temporaries). In that case, the name of the class, with parameters appropriate for its constructors, can be used. For instance, suppose we want to generalize the `Student` constructor at line 5 in Figure 4-11. Recall that the constructor is implemented as

```
Student( const string & n, const Date & b, double g )
  : name( n ), birthDate( b ), gpa( g )
{ }
```

Suppose we want to add defaults. The default `string` is "" and the default `double` is 0.0, but we need a default `Date`. Presumably there is an appropriate constructor, so assuming the existence of a zero-parameter constructor, `Date()` represents a default date. Thus the constructor is

```
Student( const string & n = "", const Date & b = Date( ),
        double g = 0.0 )
  : name( n ), birthDate( b ), gpa( g )
{ }
```

 ## 4.15 Namespaces

The C++ equivalent of packages is the *namespace*. To declare a namespace, we simply write

```
namespace namespaceName
{
...
}
```

where `namespaceName` is the name of the namespace. Inside the braces can be functions, objects, and class declarations. A class `ClassName` declared in namespace `namespaceName` is formally known as `namespaceName::ClassName`.

As with Java packages, entities inside a namespace can be accessed without specifying the namespace. Like packages, namespaces are open-ended, so one can have several separate namespace declarations.

As in Java, it can be inconvenient to write the complete class name, which includes the namespace name. A *using directive* is the equivalent of an import directive. The first form,

```
using namespaceName::ClassName;
```

allows `ClassName` to be used as a shorthand for `namespaceName::ClassName`. The second form,

```
using namespace namespaceName;
```

is the equivalent of the Java wild-card import directive (that ends `.*`) and allows all entities in the namespace `namespaceName` to be known by their shorthands. (Older compilers handle this wild-card form better than the more specific using directive above, so C++ code tends to use the wild-card using directive).

In Java, classes can be declared as public or package visible. No such syntax exists in C++; all (top-level) classes in the namespace are visible outside of the namespace. Namespaces can be nested, with the `::` operator used to access the nested namespace. Namespace names are normal C++ identifiers and do not include the dot (`.`) that is typical in Java namespaces.

Classes, functions, and objects that are declared outside of any namespace are considered to be in the global namespace. These can always be accessed with a leading `::`, as in `::IntCell`. This may be necessary from code that is inside another namespace that also contains a class called `IntCell`.

Classes, functions, and objects can be declared in an anonymous namespace. Such entities are not visible outside of the compilation unit (i.e., `.cpp` file) in which they are declared. This allows us to declare classes without fear of conflict.

 ## 4.16 Incomplete Class Declaration

Consider the following situation:

```
class A
{
    ...
    B *data;
};

class B
{
    ...
    A *data;
};
```

Here, both class A and class B contain a data member that is a pointer to an object of the other class type. The declaration of class A will generate an error, because the compiler does not know that B is a class type. Clearly, switching the order of declaration for classes A and B won't work. The solution is an *incomplete class declaration* that serves solely to allow the compiler to know the existence of the class type. In our example,

```
class B;      // incomplete class declaration
class A
{
    ...
    B *data;
};

class B
{
    ...
    A *data;
};
```

Note that if a class makes more active use of another class, an incomplete class declaration may not be sufficient. For instance, if class A contained a data member of type B, rather than simply a pointer, the compiler would still complain. In this case, the complete class declaration of B (the implementation is not needed, but the memory layout is) would have to precede A. Then class B could not have a data member of type A (since this would imply A and B are infinitely large), but could have a data member that is a pointer to A.

4.17 Technical Differences

Although many of the differences are simply syntactic and, of course, the entire object model is different, there are some differences that are subtle and worth mentioning, because they can cause confusion for Java programmers.

4.17.1 Member Functions and Data Members Cannot Have the Same Name

In Java, a class can use a name for both methods and data at the same time. This is not allowed in C++. In Java, the name of class can be used as a method in that class (although usually this just means that the programmer, intending to write a constructor, mistakenly provided a `void` return type, which becomes legal). In C++, the compiler will not allow a member function to have the same name as the class in which it is declared.

4.17.2 Inline Data Member Initialization

In Java, by default data members can be initialized inline. In C++ this is illegal and a compiler error will result. Data members in C++ can only be initialized in a constructor.

4.17.3 Default Data Member Initialization

In Java, data members will by default be initialized to zero for primitive types and to `null` for reference variables. No such guarantee is provided in C++. Primitive types and pointer variables are not guaranteed default initialization unless they are global or static. Nonprimitive data members are guaranteed initialization by a zero-parameter constructor by default. If no such constructor is present for the data member, then the lack of a constructor for the class will generate a compiler error.

4.17.4 Default Visibility

In Java, the default visibility is package visibility. In C++, the default visibility is private for classes and public for structs.

Key Points

- C++ classes consist of the declaration and the definition. Sometimes they are combined, but for large applications, it is common to place the declaration in a `.h` header file and the definition in a `.cpp` implementation file.
- The header files should use the ifndef/endif idiom to avoid being processed more than once per implementation file.
- Like Java, constructors are used to create objects. However, primitive data members are not initialized by default.
- A copy constructor is always called whenever a brand new object is created that is initialized to be a copy of an existing object. This includes formal parameters that are passed using call-by-value.
- A copy assignment (`operator=`) is always called whenever an already existing object's state is changed to be a copy of another already existing object.
- When an object goes out of scope, its destructor is invoked. A destructor is needed for any class that allocates resources (heap memory, file handles, etc.).
- If a destructor is written, then typically a copy constructor and a copy assignment operator also need to be written to provide deep copy semantics.
- C++ requires that the class designer differentiate accessor member functions (`const` member functions) from mutator member functions (non-`const` member functions). The const-ness of a member function is part of its signature.
- A one-parameter constructor implies the existence of a typecast operator. The typecast operator may be used by the system implicitly unless the constructor is declared `explicit`.

- Initializer lists are used by the constructor to initialize data members by invoking their constructors. A constant data member or a data member without a zero-parameter constructor must be initialized in the initializer list.
- A friend of a class is able to access private members of the class. Typically a class grants friendship to an entire other class, but it can also grant friendship on a function-by-function basis.
- C++ supports nested classes but not inner classes or anonymous classes. Although local classes are allowed, because automatic variables in the function are not accessible, they have less utility than their Java counterparts.
- C++ allows static members. Although there is no static initializer, one can relatively easily write a function that simulates the behavior of the static initializer. Static data members must be declared in the class declaration and defined in the implementation file.
- Member functions can return parameters by constant reference to avoid copying, but it is fairly tricky to do so.
- C++ namespaces are the rough equivalent of packages. The using directive is the equivalent of the import directive.
- Incomplete class declarations are used to inform the compiler of the existence of a class and is used if two or more classes refer to each other circularly.

Exercises

1. How are public and private class members listed in C++?
2. What is the difference between the class interface and implementation in C++?
3. In Java, it is legal to declare a method with the same name as the class; the result is not a constructor. Is this also legal in C++?
4. What is the C++ alternative to using `this` to invoke another constructor?
5. How are accessors and mutators differentiated in C++?
6. What is an implicit type conversion?
7. What does the `explicit` reserved word do?
8. What is an initializer list and when must it be used?
9. What is the Big Three, what does it default to, and when is the default unacceptable?
10. How can copying be disabled for a class type?
11. What is a friend declaration?
12. What are the semantics of nested classes in C++?
13. How does the C++ programmer achieve separate compilation?
14. What is the ifndef/endif idiom and why is it used?
15. How are static members declared and defined in C++?

16. What is an anonymous object?

17. What Java construct most closely mirrors the C++ namespace?

18. What is an incomplete class declaration and why is it used?

19. Implement a `Stack` class that stores `ints` and supports `size`, `isEmpty`, `clear`, `push`, `pop`, and `peek` (as in Java). Provide two different implementations: an array and a singly linked list. Implement the Big Three if appropriate.

20. Implement a `Set` class that stores `strings` and supports `size`, `isEmpty`, `clear`, `add`, `remove`, and `contains` (as in Java). Provide five different implementations: a sorted array, an unsorted array, a sorted singly linked list, an unsorted singly linked list, and an unbalanced binary search tree. Implement the Big Three if appropriate.

Operator Overloading 5

Chapter Outline

In contrast with Java, C++ is designed around making objects appear to be as similar as possible to primitives. In Chapter 4, we saw that this decision introduces significant complications that Java does not have.

In this chapter, we describe *operator overloading*, which is the ability to define a meaning for the existing operators when applied to new class types. In doing so, we can write classes such as `Rational`, `ComplexNumber`, and `BigDecimal` without resorting to named methods such as `add`. This makes these types look as if they were primitive types built in to the language from day 1. Operator overloading is a feature of C++ that is not part of Java at all and has a few subtleties, but for the most part, with reasonable care, it is a useful feature that is not at all that complex. Indeed, more than a few programmers list operator overloading as a feature they would like added to Java.

 ## 5.1   Basics of Operator Overloading

We begin our discussion with the Person class sketched in Figure 5-1. Once again, we will not separate the class declaration and implementation except when needed later to illustrate syntax. Our minimal Person class provides a constructor that initializes a name and a social security number (a presumably unique identifier of the person), as well as accessors for those data members and a print routine. Obviously we would expect more data members, accessors, and perhaps some mutators, but this class by itself is sufficient to illustrate some basic principles.

In Java, a class such as this would normally be expected to provide an equals method (and also a hashCode method). So we have provided an equals method that compares two Person objects (we will declare two Persons equal if they have the same ssn). Given two Person objects p1 and p2, the result of p1.equals(p2) is the same in this method as it would be in Java.

```
1    class Person
2    {
3      public:
4        Person( int s, const string & n = "" )
5          : ssn( s ), name( n )
6        { }
7
8        const string & getName( ) const
9          { return name; }
10
11       int getSsn( ) const
12         { return ssn; }
13
14       void print( ostream & out = cout ) const
15         { out << "[ " << ssn << ", " << name << " ]"; }
16
17       bool equals( const Person & rhs ) const
18         { return ssn == rhs.ssn; }
19
20     private:
21         const int ssn;
22         string name;
23   };
```

Figure 5-1   Person class with print and equals

However, primitive types are compared with ==. It would be nice if we could write p1==p2. This is what operator overloading allows us to do. The syntax in this case is easy: We replace the member function name `equals` with the name `operator==` and, voila, it works. There is no reason to remove `equals` and we could, in fact, keep both names as shown in Figure 5-2.

It is clear from this syntax that if `lhs` and `rhs` are of type `Person`, then `lhs==rhs` is simply a shorthand for `lhs.operator==(rhs)` that the compiler winds up calling behind the scenes. In fact, this is true. Both `lhs==rhs` and `lhs.operator==(rhs)` will compile, although obviously using the latter form defeats the whole purpose of defining `operator==` in the first place.

In the declaration for both `equals` and `operator==`, observe that `rhs`, which is the second operand, is passed using constant reference to signify that it is for input only. The member functions are declared as accessors, signifying that `lhs`, which is the first parameter, is to not be altered.

```
1   class Person
2   {
3     public:
4       Person( int s, const string & n = "" )
5         : ssn( s ), name( n )
6       { }
7
8       const string & getName( ) const
9         { return name; }
10
11      int getSsn( ) const
12        { return ssn; }
13
14      void print( ostream & out = cout ) const
15        { out << "[ " << ssn << ", " << name << " ]"; }
16
17      bool equals( const Person & rhs ) const
18        { return ssn == rhs.ssn; }
19
20      bool operator==( const Person & rhs ) const
21        { return equals( rhs ); }
22
23    private:
24      const int ssn;
25      string name;
26  };
```

Figure 5-2   Person class with overloaded operator==

Not only can we overload `operator==`, we can overload all six of the relational and equality operators. Note that we have already overloaded `operator=`, the copy assignment operator. If it made sense, we could overload operators such as +, +=, <<, >>, etc. Of most interest is `operator<<`, which we discuss in the next section.

 ## 5.2   Overloading I/O

Given the `Person` class as defined in Figure 5-2, we can send an instance to any output stream by invoking the `print` method. If the `print` method has no parameters, the output is sent to the standard output stream `cout`. With parameters, we could send it elsewhere, such as `cerr` or a file stream. Although we do not discuss I/O until Chapter 9, it is not too much to admit that `istream` and `ostream`, like the Java `InputStream` and `OutputStream`, are base classes in an inheritance hierarchy that covers all input streams and output streams.

Again, examining the parameters to `print`, we see that the `ostream` is passed by reference, signalling that after the `Person` is processed, the state of the `ostream` can (and must) be changed. The `print` routine is an accessor, signifying that the `Person` itself does not change.

So given a `Person p`, `p.print(cout)` or simply `p.print()` outputs `Person p` to `cout`. However, for primitive types, we are used to invoking the `<<` operator, as shown in the implementation of `print` at line 15, and since we have operator overloading, shouldn't we be able to overload `operator<<`?

The answer to the question is yes. However, if we attempt to place `operator<<` in the `Person` class, we see a problem. If the operator signature takes one parameter, as in

```
operator<< ( ostream & out ) const
```

then it must be invoked as `p<<cout`, so that the compiler rewrites it as `p.operator<<(cout)`. Of course, we write the expression as `cout<<p`, suggesting that we need to go into the `ostream` class and add

```
operator<< ( const Person & p ) const
```

Needless to say, changing the `ostream` class is not going to be a viable solution. Instead, C++ provides an alternative: We can define `operator<<` as a nonclass function. In that case, a respectable implementation is as shown in Figure 5-3. Here we see that `operator<<` takes two parameters: first, the `ostream`, passed by reference, as expected, and second, a `Person`, passed by constant reference, since it is not to be changed and can be a large object that is expensive to copy. Since calls to `<<` are typically chained, we want `operator<<` to return a reference to `out`, so that

```
cout << p1 << " " << p2;
```

evaluates to

```
( cout << p1 ) << " " << p2;
```

Then the left-hand operand of the second `<<` is still an `ostream`.

```
1    ostream & operator<< ( ostream & out, const Person & p )
2    {
3        p.print( out );
4        return out;
5    }
```

Figure 5-3 Implementation of `operator<<` as a non-member function

The implementation of `operator<<` simply invokes the `print` member function of `Person` p. (Note that if this member function was not declared as an accessor in Figure 5-2, then this invocation would not compile.) We then return the `ostream`.

This code is boilerplate: Any class can provide an implementation of a `print` member function and an overloaded `operator<<` that invokes it. If all classes do so, then we can always print objects using `operator<<`. This convention, in effect, replaces Java's convention of every class providing a `toString` method.

5.3   Global vs. Class Operators

The discussion thus far suggests that an operator can be overloaded either as a member function or as a nonmember function. It also suggests that if it is overloaded as a member function, then the first operand of the operator must be of the class type, since it becomes `*this`. In other words, in `lhs==rhs`, when `operator==` is a member function, `*this` is `lhs`. So if the first operand cannot be of the class type in which the overloaded operator would be a member, as in the case of `operator<<` where the first operand is `ostream`, then we must use a nonmember function.

Overloading an operator as a nonmember function has a significant disadvantage: Since it is not a member of the class, the implementation cannot access any private data unless it is made a friend of the class. Thus, the following code does not compile unless `Person` has declared that `operator<<` is a friend:

```
ostream & operator<< ( ostream & out, const Person & p )
{
    out << "[ " << p.ssn << ", " << p.name << " ]";
    return out;
}
```

On the other hand, the implementation of member function `operator==` can access private data, since it is a member function of class `Person`:

```
bool operator==( const Person & rhs ) const
    { return ssn == rhs.ssn; }
```

In reality, the fact that nonmember functions cannot access private data is rarely a significant liability because the class designer often can implement nonmember functions by invoking public member functions of the class. Furthermore, the member function implementation of `operator==` has its own subtle problem. Recall that in Java, we expect `equals` to be symmetric: `a.equals(b)` and `b.equals(a)` should give the same result if both are not `null`.

The implementation of `operator==` given above fails this requirement. Specifically, because the `Person` constructor is not declared `explicit` and because a one-parameter constructor is available (a default parameter can be used for the `name`), the following code compiles and returns true:

```
Person p1( 123, "Joe" );
cout << ( p1 == 123 ) << endl;
```

In trying to invoke `p1==Person`, the compiler finds an inexact match, but can use the one-parameter constructor to generate a temporary `Person` object from the `int` 123. However,

```
cout << ( 123 == p1 ) << endl;
```

does not compile: When using operator overloading, if the implementation is a class member function, the first parameter MUST be exact. Implicit type conversions are not allowed.

If instead of implementing `operator==` as a member function, it was implemented as a nonmember function,

```
bool operator== ( const Person & lhs, const Person & rhs )
{
    return lhs.equals( rhs );
}
```

both calls to `==` above would compile and yield `true`. In the nonmember definition, we now have two parameters. Both parameters are input parameters only, and being potentially large, are thus passed using call-by-constant reference. Since the function is not a member function, it cannot be an accessor function. Observe that the fact that this member function cannot access private data does not limit us.

It is illegal to provide both versions of `operator==`, since invoking `p1==p2` would be ambiguous. In our particular situation, the most sensible approach would be to make the constructor `explicit`, in which case we would not need to worry about this.

However, there are many cases where implicit type conversions make sense. For instance, if we have a `BigInteger` class, it would be nice to be able to write the following code:

```
int log2( const BigInteger & x )
{
  int result = 0;
  for( BigInteger b = x; b != 1; b /= 2 )
    result++;
  return result;
}
```

Certainly, we would expect that using `1!=b` in the for loop would also work. [We'll presume that `int`s are 32 bits and that a `BigInteger` has less than 2,000,000,000 (2^{31}) bits. Given that this would require 250 Megabytes to represent, that's probably not too unreasonable a limit.] Looking at `BigInteger`, to support `b!=1` and `1!=b` we have several choices.

Choice 1 is to provide a single nonmember function:

```
bool operator!= ( const BigInteger & lhs, const BigInteger & rhs )
```

Both b!=1 and 1!=b will generate a temporary BigInteger and in either case, the original BigInteger and the temporary BigInteger will be compared.

An alternative is to provide a member function and a nonmember function. While they cannot clash, we can still overload, yielding both:

```
bool operator!= ( int lhs, const BigInteger & rhs )
bool BigInteger::operator!= ( const BigInteger & rhs ) const
```

Of course, the second function would also be declared in the BigInteger class declaration.

With this approach, two BigIntegers are compared with operator!=: b!=1 generates a temporary, then the member version of operator!= is used, and finally 1!=b is an exact match for the nonmember function. Although for the nonmember function we can always provide the implementation

```
bool operator!= ( int lhs, const BigInteger & rhs )
{
    return rhs != lhs;
}
```

we might be able to do better with sufficient effort, based on the fact that lhs must be small. If this is not the case, we are probably better off with the first choice above. If it is the case, then it stands to reason that it is worth defining three overloaded functions

```
bool operator!= ( int lhs, const BigInteger & rhs )
bool BigInteger::operator!= ( const BigInteger & rhs ) const
bool BigInteger::operator!= ( int rhs ) const
```

since any slick algorithm for the nonmember version could also be used to implement the member function that takes int rhs as a parameter.

Which of these design decisions is best depends on the particular application. The string class, for instance, provides a host of overloaded operators that handle primitive strings, characters, and other string objects, rather than relying on the temporaries that are created in an implicit conversion. The cost of the temporaries is not only the cost to construct them, but also the cost to invoke their destructors, and in the case of string (and BigInteger) this is certain to involve calls to new and delete.

5.4 What Can Be Overloaded?

In C++, all but four operators can be overloaded. The four nonoverloadable operators are the dot operator ., the rarely used .*, the ternary operator ?:, and sizeof. Additionally, although it is legal to overload && and ||, doing so is of dubious utility, since these operations guarantee left-to-right short circuit evaluation and when overloaded, that guarantee is impossible to replicate. Also the comma operator, which is dubious in the first place, is best not overloaded.

When overloading operators, the operator precedence and associativity cannot be changed. That is, a+b/c/d is always a+((b/c)/d). Thus overloading ^ in an attempt to implement exponentiation is dubious because exponentiation associates right to left and should have higher precedence than multiplication, neither of which is true for operator^.

Arity (whether an operator is unary or binary) cannot be changed, so, for example, we cannot write a unary / operator or a binary ~. Finally, only existing operators can be overloaded; new operators cannot be created. This disallows, for instance, overloading ** to achieve exponentiation. Foiled again!

The rules above tell us that almost all of the sensible operators are overloadable. For classes such as BigDecimal or Rational, this would include basic arithmetic operators +, -, *, etc.; assignment operators =, +=, -=, etc.; the bit operators &, ∧, and |; the equality and relational operators; the shifting operators (both for bit shifting and I/O); the unary + and - operators; ++ and --;. We will see all of these operators overloaded when we discuss the Rational class in Section 5.5.

There are other operators that surprisingly can be overloaded. The most obvious is the array indexing operator [], since we know it is overloaded in vector. We will discuss the issues involved in overloading operator[] in Section 5.6.

Other operators that can be overloaded include the unary pointer dereferencing operator*, operator->, operator(), and the typecast operator. We will eventually see uses for all of these, but not in this chapter.

 ## 5.5   A Rational Number Class

The classic use of operator overloading is to implement a numeric type such as BigInteger, BigDecimal, ComplexNumber, or Rational. The code in Figure 5-4 illustrates a program that

```
1    #include "Rational.h"
2    #include <iostream>
3    using namespace std;
4
5    // Rational number test program
6    int main( )
7    {
8        Rational x;
9        Rational sum = 0;
10       int n = 0;
11
12       cout << "Type as many rational numbers as you want" << endl;
13
14       for( sum = 0, n = 0; cin >> x; sum += x, n++ )
15           cout << "Read " << x << endl;
16
17       cout << "Read " << n << " rationals" << endl;
18       cout << "Average is " << ( sum / n ) << endl;
19
20       return 0;
21   }
```

Figure 5-4   Using the Rational class

uses a rational number class, `Rational`. To run the program, simply type in rational numbers separated by white space. Terminate the input with either the end-of-file marker (control-Z on Windows[®]; control-D on Unix) or simply type something that is not a `Rational`.

The program computes the average of its input numbers. If the input numbers are typed as

    3 8/6 -2/5

the program replies with 59/45. If no numbers are typed (prior to the end-of-file marker), the program replies with indeterminate. If we examine the program, we see that the `Rational` type behaves exactly as any other primitive numeric type.

Figure 5-5 shows the first half of the `Rational` class declaration, which contains all of the public members. Figure 5-6 shows the second half and also includes operators that are non-members. The contents of these figures reside entirely in `Rational.h`.

Many of the operations are similar (e.g., < and >), so only a representative set of operators is implemented in the code that follows. The implementation of the class follows in a host of separate code fragments that are all placed in `Rational.cpp`.

A rational number consists of a numerator and a denominator. The constructors allow, among other things, a single `int` as the initializer, and this constructor is not marked `explicit`, so we can take advantage of mixing `Rational` and `int` types.

We maintain the invariant that the denominator is never negative and that the rational number is expressed in lowest form. Thus the `Rational` 9/-6 would be represented with numerator −3 and denominator 2. We allow the denominator to be zero, thus representing infinity, negative infinity, or (if the numerator is also zero) indeterminate. These invariants are maintained internally by applying `fixSigns` and `reduce` as appropriate. Thus, not only is the data representation private, but so are `fixSigns` and `reduce`, as shown in Figure 5-7. `reduce` uses a greatest-common-divisor algorithm, which illustrates the most interesting facet of Figure 5-7. Although we could make this routine a private static member function, we have chosen to simply make it a nonmember function, but to avoid conflict with other functions that have the same name, we limit its scope to the `.cpp` file by placing it in the anonymous namespace (Section 4.15). Also, since the behavior of the % operator is undefined if the operands are negative, we insure that they are not by having `gcd` switch the sign of a negative numerator prior to calling `gcdRec`.

Our class defines several named member functions that are all trivial. `toDouble` and `toInt` are used to create a `double` or `int` from the `Rational`. An implicit type conversion is not supported. We could have tried to allow it by using operator overloading to implement type conversion operators:

```
operator double ( ) const        // Allows type cast to double
    { return toDouble( ); }
operator int ( ) const           // Allows type cast to int
    { return toInt( ); }
```

```
1    #ifndef RATIONAL_H
2    #define RATIONAL_H
3    #include <iostream>
4    using namespace std;
5
6    class Rational
7    {
8      public:
9          // Constructors
10         Rational( int numerator = 0 )
11           : numer( numerator ), denom( 1 ) { }
12         Rational( int numerator, int denominator )
13           : numer( numerator ), denom( denominator )
14           { fixSigns( ); reduce( ); }
15
16         // Assignment Ops
17         const Rational & operator+=( const Rational & rhs );
18         const Rational & operator-=( const Rational & rhs );
19         const Rational & operator/=( const Rational & rhs );
20         const Rational & operator*=( const Rational & rhs );
21
22         // Unary Operators
23         const Rational & operator++( );        // Prefix
24         Rational operator++( int );            // Postfix
25         const Rational & operator--( );        // Prefix
26         Rational operator--( int );            // Postfix
27         const Rational & operator+( ) const;
28         Rational operator-( ) const;
29         bool operator!( ) const;
30
31         // Named Member Functions
32         double toDouble( ) const              // Do the division
33           { return static_cast<double>( numer ) / denom; }
34         int toInt( ) const                    // Do the division
35           { return numer >= 0 ? numer / denom :
36                           - ( -numer / denom ); }
37         bool isPositive( ) const
38           { return numer > 0; }
39         bool isNegative( ) const
40           { return numer < 0; }
41         bool isZero( ) const
42           { return numer == 0; }
43         void print( ostream & out = cout ) const;
```

Figure 5-5   Rational declaration (public section)

```
44      private:
45          // A rational number is represented by a numerator and
46          // denominator in reduced form
47        int numer;                          // The numerator
48        int denom;                          // The denominator
49
50          void fixSigns( );                  // Ensures denom >= 0
51          void reduce( );                    // Ensures lowest form
52    };
53
54      // Math Binary Ops
55    Rational operator+( const Rational & lhs, const Rational & rhs );
56    Rational operator-( const Rational & lhs, const Rational & rhs );
57    Rational operator/( const Rational & lhs, const Rational & rhs );
58    Rational operator*( const Rational & lhs, const Rational & rhs );
59
60      // Relational & Equality Ops
61    bool operator< ( const Rational & lhs, const Rational & rhs );
62    bool operator<=( const Rational & lhs, const Rational & rhs );
63    bool operator> ( const Rational & lhs, const Rational & rhs );
64    bool operator>=( const Rational & lhs, const Rational & rhs );
65    bool operator==( const Rational & lhs, const Rational & rhs );
66    bool operator!=( const Rational & lhs, const Rational & rhs );
67
68      // I/O
69    ostream & operator<< ( ostream & out, const Rational & value );
70    istream & operator>> ( istream & in, Rational & value );
71    #endif
```

Figure 5-6   `Rational` declaration (private section and nonmembers)

However, this is a bad idea because it can result in ambiguities. Specifically, if r is a `Rational`, then r==0 becomes ambiguous given the set of operators that we have defined. This is because the `Rational` constructor allows 0 to be typecast up to a `Rational` (invoking the constructor would create a `Rational`), while at the same time `operator int` allows r to be typecast down to an `int`. The compiler has no way to decide which cast is better, so in the absence of an exact match, it declares an ambiguity. This is known as a *dual-direction implicit conversion*. We recommend against allowing dual direction implicit conversions because it can eventually result in an ambiguity and, even worse, the ambiguity is not detected unless it actually occurs, meaning that you might not realize that your class has potential problems.

The remainder of this section examines operator overloading issues. We will not be overly concerned with efficiency issues, and instead focus on keeping the code simple.

```
1   namespace
2   {
3           // n is guaranteed non-negative
4       int gcdRec( int n, int m )
5       {
6           if( n % m == 0 )
7               return m;
8           else
9               return gcdRec( m, n % m );
10      }
11
12      int gcd( int m, int n )
13      {
14          if( m > 0 )
15              return gcdRec( n, m )
16          else
17              return gcdRec( n, -m );
18      }
19  }
20
21  void Rational::fixSigns( )
22  {
23      if( denom < 0 )
24      {
25          denom = -denom;
26          numer = -numer;
27      }
28  }
29
30  void Rational::reduce( )
31  {
32      int d = 1;
33
34      if( denom != 0 && numer != 0 )
35          d = gcd( numer, denom );
36      if( d > 1 )
37      {
38          numer /= d;
39          denom /= d;
40      }
41  }
```

Figure 5-7   Private member routines and local gcd to keep Rationals in normalized
                   form

5.5.1 Assignment Operators

The various assignment operators use concepts that are identical to the copy assignment operator
(operator=) discussed in Section 4.6. operator+= is representative and is shown in Figure 5-8.

```
1    const Rational & Rational::operator+=( const Rational & rhs )
2    {
3        numer = numer * rhs.denom + rhs.numer * denom;
4        denom = denom * rhs.denom;
5        reduce( );
6
7        return *this;
8    }
```

Figure 5-8   Assignment operator

Although it is not an issue here, it is always important to consider the possible effects of aliasing prior to making changes to data members.

As an example, the implementation of operator/=,

```
const Rational & Rational::operator/=( const Rational & rhs )
{
    numer *= rhs.denom;
    denom *= rhs.numer;
    fixSigns( );
    reduce( );
    return *this;
}
```

fails to work correctly when it is invoked using r/r. To fix the problem, either a special aliasing test can be used or temporaries can be used. Both ideas are implemented in Figure 5-9.

It is important to note that the existence of operator+= does not imply anything about operator+.

5.5.2   Arithmetic Operators

Arithmetic operators such as addition and subtraction can be implemented either as member functions or outside of the class. Recall that as member functions they have access to private implementation details. However, when implemented as a nonmember function, the first operand does not have to be an exact match if an implicit type conversion is available. Thus we choose to use a nonmember function for maximum flexibility.

The existence of operator+ does not imply anything about operator+=. However, it is customary to ensure that these two operations have consistent semantics. The implementation in Figure 5-10 shows the typical idiom that works whether or not we implement operator+ as a member function, does not require access to any private details, and guarantees that operator+ is implemented consistently with respect to operator+=. Because neither operand is mutable, there are no aliasing issues. Also, observe that the return type is by value, because we are returning an object (the sum) that did not exist prior to the call and that is created as a stack-allocated local variable.

```
1   const Rational & Rational::operator/=( const Rational & rhs )
2   {
3       if( this == & rhs )
4           numer = denom = 1;
5       else
6       {
7           numer *= rhs.denom;
8           denom *= rhs.numer;
9           fixSigns( );
10          reduce( );
11      }
12      return *this;
13  }
```

```
1   const Rational & Rational::operator/=( const Rational & rhs )
2   {
3       int newNumer = numer *= rhs.denom;
4       int newDenom = denom *= rhs.numer;
5
6       numer = newNumer;
7       denom = newDenom;
8       fixSigns( );
9       reduce( );
10      return *this;
11  }
```

Figure 5-9   Two possible implementations of `operator/=`

5.5.3   Relational and Equality Operators

As was the case for the binary arithmetic operators, we choose to implement the relational and equality operators as nonmembers. Importantly, the existence of == does not imply anything about != and, similarly, each of the relational operators must be implemented. We implement the most complicated of the group in Figure 5-11.

```
1   Rational operator+( const Rational & lhs, const Rational & rhs )
2   {
3       Rational answer( lhs );    // Initialize answer with lhs
4       answer += rhs;             // Add the second operand
5       return answer;             // Return answer by copy
6   }
```

Figure 5-10   Addition operator

```
1   bool operator<=( const Rational & lhs, const Rational & rhs )
2   {
3       return !(lhs - rhs).isPositive( );
4   }
```

Figure 5-11   Relational operator

5.5.4   Input and Output Operators

Figure 5-12 shows the output routines using the idiom we discussed in Section 5.2. For input, we use `istream` instead of `ostream`, `>>` instead of `<<`, and the second parameter is passed by reference, since the point of the operator is to change the state of the `Rational` parameter.

The implementation is shown in Figure 5-13. Since I/O is not discussed until Chapter 9, we will simply remark that the basic algorithm attempts to read an integer; then it tries to read a /. If it reads a character and it is a /, then it reads the denominator, otherwise, it puts the character back on the input stream and assumes the denominator is 1. A anonymous temporary `Rational` object is created and then assigned to value at line 17, and the stream is returned at line 18.

```
1   void Rational::print( ostream & out ) const
2   {
3       if( denom != 0 )
4       {
5           out << numer;
6           if( denom != 1 )
7               out << '/' << denom;
8       }
9         // Messy code for denom == 0
10      else if( numer == 0 )
11          out << "indeterminate";
12      else
13      {
14          if( numer < 0 )
15              out << '-';
16          out << "infinity";
17      }
18  }
19
20  ostream & operator<<( ostream & out, const Rational & value )
21  {
22      value.print( out );
23      return out;
24  }
```

Figure 5-12   Output operator

```
1   istream & operator>>( istream & in, Rational & value )
2   {
3       int num;
4       int den = 1;
5
6       in >> num;
7
8       char ch;
9       in.get( ch );        // try to read the /
10
11      if( !in.eof( ) )    // if read has hit EOF, eof is true
12          if( ch == '/' )
13              in >> den;
14          else
15              in.putback( ch );
16
17      value = Rational( num, den );
18      return in;
19  }
```

Figure 5-13   Input operator

Observe that this implementation accesses no private information from the `Rational` class. The creation of the temporary `Rational` at line 17 could have been avoided if this function was made a friend of the `Rational` class or if a `setValue` member function had been provided. In that case, the value's numerator and denominator could have been set once `num` and `den` were known.

5.5.5   Unary Operators

We continue with the ++ and -- operators. We will examine the auto-increment operator. As in Java, there are two flavors: prefix (before the operand) and postfix (after the operand). Both add 1 to an object, but the result of the expression (which is meaningful when used in a larger expression) is the new value in prefix form and the original value in postfix form. These forms are completely different in semantics and precedence. Consequently, we need to write separate routines for each form. Since they have the same name, they must have different signatures to be distinguished. This is done in C++ by specifying an empty parameter list for the prefix form and a single (anonymous and unused) `int` parameter for the postfix form. ++x calls the zero-parameter `operator++`; x++ calls the one-parameter `operator++`. This `int` parameter is never used; it is present only to give a different signature.

The prefix and postfix forms shown in Figure 5-14 add 1 by increasing `numer` by the value of `denom`. In the prefix form we can then return *`this` by constant reference, as done

```
1    const Rational & Rational::operator++( )  // Prefix form
2    {
3        numer += denom;
4        return *this;
5    }
6
7    Rational Rational::operator++( int )        // Postfix form
8    {
9        Rational tmp = *this;
10       numer += denom;
11       return tmp;
12   }
13
14   bool Rational::operator!( ) const
15   {
16       return !numer;
17   }
18
19   const Rational & Rational::operator+( ) const
20   {
21       return *this;
22   }
23
24   Rational Rational::operator-( ) const
25   {
26       return Rational( -numer, denom );
27   }
```

Figure 5-14   Unary operators

for the assignment operators. The postfix form requires that we return the initial value of
*this; thus we use a temporary. Because of the temporary, we have to use return-by-value
instead of return-by-reference. Even if the copy constructor for the return is optimized away,
the use of the temporary suggests that, in many cases, the prefix form will be faster than the
postfix form.

The three remaining unary operators have straightforward implementations, as shown in
Figure 5-14. operator! returns true if the object is zero; this is done by applying ! to the
numerator. Unary operator+ evaluates to the current object; a constant reference return can be
used here. operator- returns the negative of the current object by creating a new object whose
numerator is the negative of the current object. The return must be by copy because the new
object is a local variable. However, there is a trap lurking in operator-. If the word Rational

is omitted on line 26, then the comma operator evaluates (-numer,denom) as denom and an implicit conversion gives the Rational denom/1, which is returned. Have we had enough of the comma operator yet?

 ## 5.6   Matrix Class (for **double**s)

C++ does not provide a library type for two-dimensional arrays. However, it is easy to create a class that supports two-dimensional arrays in the same style as Java. We will call this class MatrixOfDouble. In Chapter 7, we discuss how to generalize this to support two-dimensional arrays of any type.

Recall that in Java, in the declaration

```
double [ ][ ] mat = { { 3, 2 }, { 4, 1, 3 }, { 5, 2 } };
```

mat.length is 3 (because there are three rows), and each row is itself a one-dimensional array. Thus, mat[0] is of type double[] and mat[0].length is 2. Similarly mat[1].length is 3 and mat[2].length is 2.

As shown in Figure 5-15, our class will store the two-dimensional array using a vector of vectors (at line 33). Note that in the declaration of array, white space must separate the two > characters; otherwise, the compiler will interpret the >> token as a shift operator. In other words, we must write

```
vector<vector< double> > array;   // white space needed
```

and not

```
vector<vector<double>> array;     // oops!
```

The constructor first constructs array as having rows entries each of type vector<double>. Since each entry of array is constructed with the zero-parameter constructor, it follows that each entry of array is a vector<double> object of size 0. Thus we have rows zero-length vectors of double. The body of the constructor is then entered and each row is resized to have cols columns. Thus the constructor terminates with what appears to be a two-dimensional array. (Note that the doubles themselves are not guaranteed any initialization.)

Because vectors know how to clean up their own memory, we do not need to worry about a destructor, copy constructor, or copy assignment operator.

The numrows and numcols accessors are easily implemented as shown. As we will see, it is possible for the user to make the two-dimensional array nonrectangular, in which case the result from numcols is meaningless.

We also provide member functions to change the number of rows and columns. Note that when the number of rows is changed by resizing the array, any additional rows have length 0 (i.e., no columns).

```cpp
1   #ifndef MATRIX_OF_DOUBLE_H
2   #define MATRIX_OF_DOUBLE_H
3
4   #include <vector>
5   using namespace std;
6
7   class MatrixOfDouble
8   {
9     public:
10      MatrixOfDouble( int rows, int cols ) : array( rows )
11        { setNumCols( cols ); }
12
13      int numrows( ) const
14        { return array.size( ); }
15      int numcols( ) const
16        { return numrows( ) > 0 ? array[ 0 ].size( ) : 0; }
17
18      void setNumRows( int rows )
19        { array.resize( rows ); }
20      void setNumCols( int cols )
21        { for( int i = 0; i < rows; i++ )
22            array[ i ].resize( cols );
23        }
24      void setDimensions( int rows, int cols )
25        { setNumRows( rows ); setNumCols( cols ); }
26
27      const vector<double> & operator[]( int row ) const
28        { return array[ row ]; }
29      vector<double> & operator[]( int row )
30        { return array[ row ]; }
31
32    private:
33        vector< vector<double> > array;
34  };
35
36  #endif
```

Figure 5-15   Java class to represent two-dimensional array of double

As our Java example illustrated, the key operation is [], which in C++ can be overloaded as operator[]. The result of mat[r] is invocation of mat.operator[](r), which returns a vector corresponding to row r of matrix mat. Thus we have a skeleton:

```cpp
vector<double> operator [] ( int row )
    { return array[ row ]; }
```

The main question is whether this is an accessor or a mutator, and what the return mechanism should be. If we consider the routine

```
void copy( MatrixOfDouble & to, const MatrixOfDouble & from )
{
    for( int r = 0; r < to.numrows( ); r++ )
        to[ r ] = from[ r ];
}
```

in which we copy each row of from into the corresponding row of to, we see contradictions.

If operator[] returns a vector<double> by value, then to[r] cannot appear on the left-hand side of the assignment. The only way to affect a change of the elements stored in to is if operator[] returns a reference to a vector. Unfortunately, doing so would allow

```
from[ r ] = to[ r ];
```

to compile, in violation of from's const-ness. That cannot be allowed in a good design.

Thus we see that we need operator[] to return a constant reference for from, but a plain reference for to. In other words, we need two versions of operator[], which differ only in return types. That is not allowed for two members that otherwise have the same signature, and therein lies the trick: Whether a member function is an accessor or a mutator is part of the signature. Thus the version that returns a constant reference will be marked as an accessor and the version that returns a reference will be marked as a mutator. This is shown at lines 27 to 30.

It is worth emphasizing two points. First, to resolve the call, the compiler will always choose the mutator unless it is not a candidate (because the object it is acting upon is a constant). Second, any member function that returns a reference to private data implicitly allows the private data to be changed later on by anyone who retains that reference. As such, the technique should generally be avoided except in cases such as this one where this is a desired outcome, and member functions that return by reference should not be marked as accessors, even though the call itself does not change the state of the object.

To see how this works, the expression mat[0][1]=3.14 consists of

```
vector<double> & row0 = mat.operator[] ( 0 );   // matrix [] mutator
double         & item01 = row0.operator[] ( 1 ); // vector [] mutator
item01 = 3.14;
```

Here row0 is a reference to (i.e., another name for) mat.array[0] that is stored internally in mat, representing row 0. item01 is a reference to mat.array[0][1], stored internally. So changing item01 to 3.14 changes the entry in mat.array[0][1].

Notice that although we are invoking operator[] twice, we are invoking two different versions of operator[]. Notice that both versions are mutators, but do not make any changes on their own to the objects they are acting upon. However, by returning references to the object, they open the door for later changes.

5.7   Liabilities of Operator Overloading

When used properly, operator overloading can provide spectacular results, as can be seen by the `Rational` class. So why is it not part of Java? The main reason is that programmers tend to abuse a good thing.

For instance, suppose we have a `Company` class and a `Person` class. Occasionally we want to add or remove a `Person` from a `Company`. The sensible thing to do is to define `add` and `remove` member functions in the `Company` class. However, the overly aggressive operator overloader will instead overload `operator+=` and `operator-=` in place of `add` and `remove`, and then we get code such as

```
Company c;
Person p;
...
c += p;
```

which is not intuitive and can be hard to read. Pretty soon operators are used everywhere and nobody can understand the code. Operator overloading should never be used in place of named member functions when the operators do not provide intuitive semantics.

Key Points

- Operator overloading allows us to define meanings for the existing operators when applied to nonprimitive types.
- When an operator is overloaded as a member function, the first operand is accessible as `*this` and subsequent operands are parameters. The first operand must be an exact match of the class type; implicit type conversions are not acceptable.
- When an operator is overloaded as a nonmember function, all operands are parameters, but the implementation does not, by default, have access to private members of any class.
- All but a few operators can be overloaded. The most common operators to overload include the assignment operator(s), equality and relational operators, and the input and output stream operators. Later we will see that the function call operator can also be overloaded.
- `operator<<` should be overloaded for all class types. Typically this is done by providing a companion `print` member function.
- `operator+=` and `operator+` must be overloaded separately, and consistently. Typically `operator+` simply invokes `operator+=`.

- When `operator++` is overloaded, typically both a prefix and a postfix version are provided.
- When `operator[]` is overloaded, typically both an accessor and a mutator version are provided.

Exercises

1. Which operators cannot be overloaded?
2. Under what circumstances can the precedence, associativity, or arity of an operator be changed?
3. Explain the difference between overloading `operator=` as a member function versus a nonmember function.
4. When must an operator be overloaded as a nonmember function?
5. Under what circumstances is it a dangerous idea to overload the type conversion operator?
6. Explain how `this` is used in the implementation of assignment operators.
7. How are `operator+=` and `operator+` implemented to ensure compatible semantics?
8. Implement a `Complex` class that supports complex numbers. Provide as many operations as you can.
9. Implement a `BigInteger` class that supports arbitrary precision integers, providing as many operations as you can with reasonable efficiency. Provide two implementations: one to maintain the digits in an array and a second to maintain the digits in a linked list.
10. Implement a `Polynomial` class that supports single-variable polynomials. Support `operator+`, `operator-`, and `operator*`, as well as the corresponding assignment operators, `operator==` and `operator!=`, as well as an overloaded input and output operator. Add a public method, `eval`, that evaluates the polynomial at a particular point. You should use a good separation of interface and implementation. The polynomial is implemented as a sorted `vector` of pairs, in which each pair represents a coefficient and an exponent. For instance, the polynomial x^2+4 is represented by a vector of size 2, with index 0 containing (4, 0) and index 1 containing (1, 2). If this polynomial is represented by p, then `p.eval(2)` returns 8. You may assume that all coefficients are of type `double` and exponents are nonnegative integers. A polynomial can be constructed by passing a `string`. For simplicity, you may assume that there are no spaces in the `string`. This makes it easy to implement the required `operator<<`. An example of a call to the constructor is

```
Polynomial p( "x^2+8x+15" );
```

11. Implement a Map class that stores keys and values that are both strings. Like the Java Map, your map will support isEmpty, size, clear, get, put, and remove. Additionally, support operator[], which takes a key as a parameter and returns a reference to the corresponding value in the map. If the key is not present, operator[] will insert it with a default value and return a reference to the newly inserted value. This implies that operator[] is a mutator. Add an accessor version with similar semantics, but have it throw an exception if the key is not found. Provide two separate implementations: one to maintain the items in an array and a second to maintain the items in a linked list. In both cases, each key and value is stored together in a Pair, which is a nested class that you should define.

Object-Oriented Programming: Inheritance

6

Chapter Outline

Like Java, C++ supports inheritance. Most of the features associated with inheritance that are found in Java have equivalent implementations in C++. In some cases, these features are not the default behavior, and thus the C++ programmer must be more careful than a Java programmer.

In other cases, the behavior of similar constructs is slightly different. Additionally, C++ supports some techniques, such as multiple inheritance, that Java does not allow.

In this chapter, we describe the basics of Java inheritance, see some of the extra code that the C++ programmer must write to avoid subtle errors, discuss multiple inheritance in C++, and examine the differences between similar C++ and Java constructs.

 ## 6.1   Basic Syntax

To illustrate the basics of inheritance, we begin with a simple `Person` class in Figure 6-1 and then a simple `Student` class in Figure 6-2 that extends `Person`. The `Person` class duplicates Figure 5-1, but has some subtle errors that eventually must be fixed. First, let's examine the basic syntax in the `Student` class.

Instead of the extends clause that is found in Java, an *IS-A* relationship is signalled in C++ by using the syntax seen at line 1 in Figure 6-2:

```
class Student : public Person
```

The reserved word `public` is required; otherwise, we get private inheritance, which does not model an *IS-A* relationship (see Section 6.10.2) and is typically not what we want.

```
1   class Person
2   {
3     public:
4       Person( int s, const string & n = "" )
5         : ssn( s ), name( n )
6       { }
7
8       const string & getName( ) const
9         { return name; }
10      int getSsn( ) const
11        { return ssn; }
12
13      void print( ostream & out = cout ) const
14        { out << ssn << ", " << name; }
15
16    private:
17      int ssn;
18      string name;
19  };
20
21  ostream & operator<< ( ostream & out, const Person & p )
22  {
23      p.print( out );
24      return out;
25  }
```

Figure 6-1   `Person` as a base class (version 1, slightly flawed)

```
1   class Student : public Person
2   {
3     public:
4       Student( int s, const string & n = "", double g = 0.0 )
5         : Person( s, n ), gpa( g )
6       { }
7
8       double getGpa( ) const
9         { return gpa; }
10
11      void print( ostream & out = cout ) const
12        { Person::print( out ); out << ", " << gpa; }
13
14    private:
15      double gpa;
16  };
```

Figure 6-2   Student as a derived class (not flawed)

Initialization of the subclass requires a call to the superclass constructor. As in Java, by default, this initialization is a call to the zero-parameter superclass constructor. By using an initializer list, we can specify a call to any superclass constructor, and as in Java, this is required if the superclass does not have a zero-parameter constructor. In our example, the initializer list at line 5 in Figure 6-2 illustrates the syntax.

At line 12, we see the equivalent to Java's super.print: We simply use the :: scoping operator to specify the call to the Person's implementation of print.

Otherwise, the rest of the class is similar to what would be seen in Java. The memory layout of Student includes the data members specified in Person, but these data members cannot be accessed from member functions implemented in class Student. The print routine in Student intends to override the print routine in Person. The getName and getSsn member functions from Person are inherited by Student. Thus,

```
Person p( 987654321, "Bob" );
Student s( 123456789, "Jane", 4.0 );
p.print( );
s.print( );
cout << s.getName( ) << " " << s.getGpa( ) << endl;
```

produces the expected output.

Additionally, we implement operator<< for Person, and expect that a Student can be passed as a parameter because a Student *IS-A* Person. Indeed this is true. However, there is a subtle bug in Person's print member function that causes the call to operator<< to print the wrong information when a Student is passed as a parameter. We can easily fix this problem in the next section.

6.2 Dynamic Dispatch

As we mentioned, the `print` routine in `Person` has a serious, yet easily fixable, error that is illustrated by the code

```
Student s( 123456789, "Jane", 4.0 );
const Person & p = s;                    // p and s are same object
s.print( );                              // calls Student::print
p.print( );                              // calls wrong print!!
```

Clearly p and s are the same object. So if we invoke the `print` member function on either p or s, we expect the same answer; certainly this basic polymorphic behavior is what happens in Java. However, in our code, `s.print` invokes `Student::print` on our student, while `p.print` invokes `Person::print` on our student.

The problem is that in the call to `p.print`, the compile-time type of p is `Person`, while the runtime type (the type of object p actually references when the program is run) is `Student`. In C++, by default, the decision on which member function to invoke is made on the basis of the compile-time type of p. This is known as *static dispatch*. Java always uses the runtime type for instance methods, which is known as *dynamic dispatch*.

Dynamic dispatch is almost always the preferred course of action. However, dynamic dispatch incurs some runtime overhead because it requires that the program maintain extra information and that the compiler generate code to determine which member function to invoke. This overhead was once thought to be significant and would be incurred even if no inheritance was actually used, so C++ did not make it the default. This is unfortunate, because we now know that the overhead of dynamic dispatch is relatively minor.

To achieve dynamic dispatch, the C++ programmer must mark the base class method with the reserved word `virtual`. A *virtual function* uses dynamic dispatch. A *nonvirtual function* uses static dispatch. Thus if we rewrite the `print` member function in class `Person` as

```
virtual void print( ostream & out = cout ) const
  { out << ssn << ", " << name; }
```

the code at the start of this section behaves as expected. This also is the minor change that fixes `operator<<`.

As a general rule, if a method is overridden in a derived class, it should be declared virtual in the base class to ensure that the correct method is always selected. In fact, a stronger statement applies: If a method might reasonably be expected to be overridden in a derived class, it should be declared virtual in the base class. Once a method is marked virtual, it is virtual from that point down in the inheritance hierarchy.

Only if a member function is intended to be invariant in an inheritance hierarchy (or if an entire class is not intended to be extended) does it make sense to not mark it as virtual. Thus `getName` and `getSsn` are not marked as virtual. In Java, these would be marked `final` to signify that it is illegal to attempt to override. C++ does not have final methods or final classes, so the lack of `virtual` in a method declaration is a signal to the reader that the method is intended to be final, and those semantics are guaranteed if invoked through a base class reference (or pointer).

When the class declaration and implementation are separate, the virtual declaration must be in the member function declaration and should not be in the separate member function definition.

 ## 6.3   Constructors, the Big Three, and Inheritance

In the subclass, like all classes, we need to consider whether we can accept defaults for the destructor, copy constructor, and copy assignment operator or whether we need to write our own.

6.3.1   Defaults

First, we need to decide what the defaults are. For all three, the inherited component is considered to be a data member. Thus, by default:

- The copy constructor is implemented by invoking a copy constructor on the base class(es), followed by invoking copy constructors on each of the newly added data members. If any of the required copy constructors cannot be called (because they are private), then an attempt to invoke a default copy assignment operator will generate a compiler error.
- The copy assignment operator is implemented by invoking a copy assignment operator on the base class(es), followed by invoking copy assignment operators on each of the newly added data members. If any of the required copy assignment operators cannot be called (because they are private, or the data member is constant or otherwise not assignable), then an attempt to invoke a default copy assignment operator will generate a compiler error.
- The destructor is implemented by invoking destructors on each of the newly added data members, followed by invoking the destructor on the base class(es).

6.3.2   Implementing the Big Three Explicitly

If any default is unacceptable, then it can be implemented explicitly. Generally, if one of the defaults is unacceptable, all three are. The typical scenario is that the base class operations are fine, because if the base class does not support copying, it generally makes little sense to allow the subclasses to do so. In this scenario, the newly added data members allocate memory from the heap without cleaning it up automatically,

Figure 6-3 shows an explicit implementation of the defaults for the Student class. To implement the copy constructor, we need to make sure to include a call to the base class copy constructor in the initializer list. To implement the destructor, we simply list the additional actions that must be taken in addition to the default. To implement the copy assignment operator, we need to make sure that we chain up to the base class.

In short, to implement copy semantics, we must chain up to the base class, while in the destructor, the chaining up is automatic.

```
1   class Student
2   {
3       . . .
4       Student( const Student & rhs )
5         : Person( rhs ), gpa( rhs.gpa )
6       { }
7
8       ~Student( )
9       {
10          // automatically chains up
11      }
12
13      const Student & operator= ( const Student & rhs )
14      {
15          if( this != & rhs )
16          {
17              Person::operator= ( rhs );
18              gpa = rhs.gpa;
19          }
20          return *this;
21      }
22          . . .
23  };
```

Figure 6-3   Explicit implementation of the Big Three defaults for `Student`

6.3.3   Virtual Destructor

A much trickier aspect of the Big Three concerns polymorphism. Consider the code

```
Student *s1 = new Student( "123456789", "Jane", 4.0 );
Person *p1 = s1;
delete p1;
```

Here, s1 points at a `Student` object and certainly the second assignment is legal, since `Student` *IS-A* `Person`. So when `delete` is invoked, whose destructor is used?

Since the destructor is a member function, the answer depends on whether or not the destructor is declared virtual. In our original code in Figure 6-1, it is not, so we invoke the `Person` destructor instead of the `Student` destructor. This means that any memory in the `Student` data fields that was allocated from the memory heap either directly (via calling `new`), or indirectly (e.g., if there is a `string` or `vector` as a data member) is never reclaimed and we have a subtle memory leak.

Thus we see an important rule: In a base class, a destructor should always be declared virtual to ensure polymorphic destruction. As with all virtual methods, this costs some space and time, so classes that are intended to be final can avoid declaring their destructors virtual. The reason it is easy to do this incorrectly is that the base class destructor should be virtual even if defaults are used

```
1    class Person
2    {
3      public:
4        Person( int s, const string & n = "" )
5          : ssn( s ), name( n )
6          { }
7
8        virtual ~Person( )
9          { }
10
11       const string & getName( ) const
12         { return name; }
13
14       int getSsn( ) const
15         { return ssn; }
16
17       virtual void print( ostream & out = cout ) const
18         { out << ssn << ", " << name; }
19
20     private:
21       int ssn;
22       string name;
23   };
24
25   ostream & operator<< ( ostream & out, const Person & p )
26   {
27       p.print( out );
28       return out;
29   }
```

Figure 6-4   `Person` as a base class (correct version)

in the entire hierarchy. Otherwise, as we just mentioned, memory that was allocated indirectly and that otherwise would have been released will leak.

Figure 6-4 shows the `Person` class with correct virtual declarations. The `Student` class in Figure 6-1 needs no changes from the original.

6.4   Abstract Methods and Classes

In Java, abstract methods are methods that serve as placeholders, with implementations deferred to concrete subclasses. Such methods are declared with the reserved word `abstract`. A class with at least one abstract method must also be marked as abstract, and an abstract class cannot be instantiated; instead it serves as a common superclass.

In C++, a method is abstract if:

1. It is declared virtual.
2. The declaration is followed by =0.

For instance, the member function `area` is declared abstract as follows:

```
virtual double area( ) const = 0;
```

In C++, a class is abstract if it has at least one abstract method, and, like Java, abstract classes cannot be instantiated. A C++ class with no abstract methods is not abstract. This rule is different than Java: Abstract classes in Java do not have to have an abstract method (e.g., `java.awt.event.WindowAdapter`). C++ escapes this rule by allowing a virtual method that has an implementation to be declared abstract. The sole purpose of doing so seems to be to allow the class to be abstract.

A common place where this trick is used is the destructor, because an abstract class must be extended and thus must have a virtual destructor. The destructor must have an implementation (since the derived classes chain up to it), but if we mark it as abstract, then the class is now automatically abstract, even if no other abstract methods are present. Abstract methods in C++ are often denoted as *pure virtual methods*.

Figure 6-5 shows an abstract `Shape` class and a `Circle` class that implements all the abstract methods. A `Square` class would be similar and is not shown (we use all three classes later). A `Shape` stores its type information as private data, so this data must be initialized in the constructor (since the subclasses do not have access to private data). Thus like Java, abstract classes do provide constructors that are used by the subclasses. The destructor at line 5 is marked virtual (we do not make it abstract, since we have other abstract methods).

`getType`, shown at lines 7 and 8, is not marked virtual, which signifies that it is intended as a final method. Although subclasses can provide different implementations, if `getType` is invoked through a `Shape` reference or pointer, we will always invoke the `Shape`'s `getType` method, which is similar to the behavior we would get in Java.

Abstract method `getArea` is declared at line 10 and is overridden in the `Circle` class. The `print` method is virtual, signalling that we expect that the default implementation we have provided may need to be overridden. The fact that `Circle` and `Square` do not override `print` in our implementation does not justify removing the virtual declaration. The declaration is there to express that the `print` method is not invariant and may need to be overridden.

In the `Circle` class, we see that the `Circle` constructor invokes the `Shape` constructor at line 27 to initialize its inherited components.

 ## 6.5   Slicing

In our discussion of virtual member functions, we have talked about accessing derived classes by pointers and reference variables. So why not by direct base class objects? The reason is relatively simple: It doesn't work!

Consider the following example:

```
Student s( 123456789, "Jane", 4.0 );
Person p( 987654321, "Bob" );
p = s;
p.print( );
```

```
1   class Shape
2   {
3     public:
4       Shape( const string & s ) : shapeType( s ) { }
5       virtual ~Shape( ) { }
6
7       const string & getType( ) const
8         { return shapeType; }
9
10      virtual double getArea( ) const = 0;
11      virtual void print( ostream & out ) const
12        { out << getType( ) << " of area " << getArea( ); }
13
14    private:
15      string shapeType;
16   };
17
18   ostream & operator<< ( ostream & out, const Shape & s )
19   {
20       s.print( out );
21       return out;
22   }
23
24   class Circle : public Shape
25   {
26     public:
27       Circle( double r ) : Shape( "Circle" ), radius( r )
28         { }
29
30       double getArea( ) const
31         { return 3.14 * radius * radius; }
32
33     private:
34       double radius;
35   };
36
37   class Square : public Shape
38   {
39       // similar implementation as Circle not shown
40   };
```

Figure 6-5   Shape hierarchy with an abstract base class

Clearly the first two lines create two objects. The first object is of type Student and the second is of type Person, as shown in Figure 6-6. Equally clearly, the third statement copies s into the already existing object p. As Figure 6-6 shows, p only has room for the name and ssn data members, so those are the only members that can be copied. As shown in Figure 6-7, s's gpa cannot be copied into p because the Person p has no room for it.

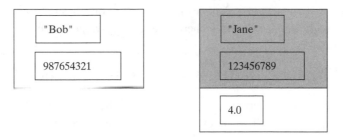

Figure 6-6   Memory layout of base class and derived class object; shaded portions are
inherited data and might not be visible

As this example shows, if a derived class object is copied into a base class object, only the
base class portion is actually copied. The derived class object has been *sliced,* and this effect is
known in C++ as *slicing*.

Slicing occurs in all forms of object copying. Thus, if s is a Student,

```
Person p = s;
```

constructs a new Person object, but only using a slice of s.

Slicing also occurs when objects are passed using call-by-value. For instance, even if
print is declared virtual in class Person, if we mistakenly write operator<< passing Person
using call-by-value,

```
ostream & operator<< ( ostream & out, Person p )
{
    p.print( out );
    return out;
}
```

then the call

```
cout << s << endl;
```

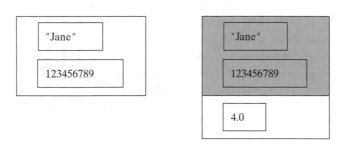

Figure 6-7   Result of copying Person into Student

does not work, because s is passed using call-by-value and only a slice of s is copied into p. Inside operator<<, the print method is thus invoked on a Person object. As a result, call-by-value should never be used in conjunction with inheritance: Call-by-value and inheritance don't mix.

6.6   Why Inheritance Is Harder in C++ Than Java

It is common to hear that inheritance is harder in C++ because methods are not virtual by default. This is simply not true. The reason that inheritance is harder in C++ than Java is because of the slicing problem.

In Java, if we want to store a collection of shapes, we can simply throw them in an array of Shape, and then safely invoke the print and area methods with automatic dynamic dispatch. What we actually have is not an array of Shape objects, but rather, an array of reference variables that all reference objects that are (subtypes of) Shapes.

In C++, we cannot store an array of Shape, because of slicing. As soon as we try to place a derived class object into the array, it will be sliced. All calls would be on Shape objects. Of course Shape is abstract, so that is another problem, but the abstractness of Shape is not really the critical issue. It is the slicing problem.

We can use an array of pointers to Shapes and then the code will look exactly like Java. In fact, if

1. we declare every method as virtual
2. only allocate objects using new
3. access all objects by pointers
4. use collections of pointers

we can, for the most part, do everything that we do in Java, with one important exception: Java does garbage collection, while in C++ we must eventually call delete, and that's the hard part.

Using inheritance in C++ implies that we must make significant use of pointers and allocate objects on the memory heap. This means we are stuck with the thorny issue of cleaning up memory, which is quite a nuisance in C++ and notoriously error-prone.

As an example of how we use pointers with inheritance to achieve polymorphic behavior, the code in Figure 6-8 shows how we store Circles and Squares (and, in general, any kind of Shape) in a single collection.

The main routine, shown at lines 36 to 40 simply invokes testShapes, mostly so we can clarify that any allocated memory in testShapes must be cleaned up. In testShapes, line 25 is the C++ equivalent of creating an empty ArrayList; then lines 27 to 29 are the equivalent of calling add. We do not have any slicing problems since the vector is storing pointers, so we are never copying Shape objects themselves. We can then pass the vector to methods such as printArray and totalArea, which will scan through the vector and invoke the appropriate print and area methods on the Shapes being pointed at.

```
1    void printShapes( const vector<Shape*> & a )
2    {
3        for( int i = 0; i < a.size( ); i++ )
4            cout << *a[ i ] << endl;
5    }
6
7    double totalArea( const vector<Shape*> & a )
8    {
9        double sum = 0.0;
10
11        for( int i = 0; i < a.size( ); i++ )
12            sum += a[ i ]->getArea( );
13
14        return sum;
15    }
16
17   void cleanup( vector<Shape *> & a )
18   {
19       for( int i = 0; i < a.size( ); i++ )
20           delete a[ i ];
21   }
22
23   void testShapes( )
24   {
25       vector<Shape *> arr;
26
27       arr.push_back( new Circle( 2.0 ) );
28       arr.push_back( new Square( 2.0 ) );
29       arr.push_back( new Square( 4.0 ) );
30
31       printShapes( arr );
32       cout << "Total area is " << totalArea( arr ) << endl;
33       cleanup( arr );
34   }
35
36   int main( )
37   {
38       testShapes( );
39       return 0;
40   }
```

Figure 6-8   Heterogeneous collection of shapes

In testShapes, arr is a local variable allocated on the runtime stack. This means that when testShapes returns, arr's destructor will be called. This will free the vector, but not the Shapes that were being pointed at. Since testShapes created objects from the memory heap, it must reclaim them, and this is the job of cleanup.

`cleanup` simply steps through the array invoking `delete`. Observe that this would not work if the `Shape` class did not correctly declare a virtual destructor. `printShapes` and `totalArea` are similar and simply illustrate different syntax. Since `operator<<` accepts any `Shape` and `*a[i]` is an object that is a (subtype of) `Shape`, we can pass it to `operator<<` at line 4. The `getArea` method can be invoked using the normal `->` operator, as shown at line 12. The code here is not much different than the equivalent Java code, except that we must write `cleanup`.

 ## 6.7   Type Conversions

In Java, the typecast operator is used in conjunction with inheritance to cast down the inheritance hierarchy (i.e., from a superclass or interface reference down to a subclass reference). This is used to invoke methods on the actual object that were not defined by the compile-time reference type. For instance, in C++, if we have the line of code

```
Person *p = new Student( "123456789", "Jane", 4.0 );
```

then invoking `p->gpa()` is not legal.

In C++, one can use a typecast to cast down the inheritance hierarchy. This makes most sense when casting a pointer type or a reference type, since, as we've already seen, accessing objects directly in C++ doesn't work well with inheritance because of slicing. So in the code above, after

```
Student *s = (Student *) p;
```

`s->gpa()` is legal, as would be `((Student *) p)->gpa()`.

Although this code works, it is not the preferred way to do a downcast. This is because it would run even if `p` was actually pointing at a `Person` at runtime. In other words, unlike Java, this typecast is not checked at runtime. In Java, this code would generate a `ClassCastException`, but in C++, the code may well run, producing garbage.

To alleviate this problem, C++ introduced the *dynamic cast*. If we use

```
Student *s = dynamic_cast<Student *>( p );
```

then `dynamic_cast` returns NULL if the runtime type of `p` is not compatible with `s`. `dynamic_cast` can also be used to cast references:

```
Student jane( "123456789", "Jane", 4.0 );
Person & pref = jane;
Student & sref = dynamic_cast<Student &>( pref );
```

If the cast fails because the object is of the wrong type or if the cast is not applied to a pointer or a reference, then a `bad_cast` exception is thrown. The `dynamic_cast` works only with types that are polymorphic, meaning that the class type must have at least one virtual method.

Casting in C++ is much less common than in Java, because most uses of Java casting involve casting down from `Object` in generic collections (e.g., the `java.util` classes). As we will see in Chapter 7, C++ uses a different mechanism, known as *templates*, to support generic algorithms, removing almost all uses of casting.

C++ does not provide an `instanceof` operator. With pointer variables and the dynamic cast, the `instanceof` operator can be simulating by invoking a dynamic cast and verifying that the return value is not NULL. However, using `instanceof` in Java is relatively rare in well-designed object-oriented programs, and the idiom in C++ is even more rare.

 ## 6.8   Multiple Inheritance and Interfaces

C++ does not provide a special interface type. Instead, one simply implements *pure abstract base classes,* which are classes that contain only abstract member functions. For instance, Figure 6-9 shows two interfaces, `Printable` and `Serializable`. We can now have a class that implements both of these interfaces, as shown in Figure 6-10. As in Java, `Person` is now type-compatible with `Printable` and `Serializable`, and of course, `Person` could also easily extend a class that was not a Java-style interface.

Since C++ does not distinguish between interfaces and noninterfaces, `Person` could extend several classes that had implementations. When properly done, this can be very useful. For instance, C++ defines an `istream` class, an `ostream` class, and then an `iostream` class, which supports both input and output at the same time.

However, multiple implementation inheritance, in which two or more base classes are not done in the interface style, creates significant complications because the implementations that are inherited could be conflicting.

For instance, consider the scenario in Figure 6-11. The `Person` class has subclasses `Student` and `Employee`, and then `StudentEmployee` extends both `Student` and `Employee`, thus having the functionality of both.

```
1   class Printable
2   {
3     public:
4        virtual ~Printable( ) { }
5        virtual void print( ostream & out = cout ) const = 0;
6   };
7
8   class Serializable
9   {
10     public:
11        virtual ~Serializable( ) { }
12        virtual void readMe( istream & in = cin ) = 0;
13        virtual void writeMe( ostream & out = cout ) const = 0;
14   };
```

Figure 6-9   Example of declaring interfaces

```
1   class Person : public Printable, public Serializable
2   {
3     public:
4       ...
5         // Complicated, so probably implement in .cpp
6         void print( ostream & out = cout ) const;
7         void readMe( istream & in = cin );
8         void writeMe( ostream & out = cout ) const;
9       ...
10  };
```

Figure 6-10   Example of implementing multiple interfaces

Now consider the problems that have to be resolved in StudentEmployee. Since getHours is defined in both classes, which is inherited? Since there is an ambiguity, either both are inherited (then the invoker must make it plain which of the methods is to be used) or both are overridden in the StudentEmployee class. The first possibility leads to ugly code. In the second option, StudentEmployee will not be computing the same information as both Student and Employee, violating at least one *IS-A* relationship. Most likely, we would want to change just the method name to avoid this conflict.

More tricky is the memory layout. Since Student and Employee both define an hours data member, it seems that StudentEmployee needs two copies of hours. This is certainly true, as seen if we change the name of one of the getHours, but leave the data member intact. A basic tenet of inheritance is that the subclasses inherit the superclass' data.

Now what about name? Both Student and Employee have a name data member, so according to our logic, there should be two copies. However, that's no good, since Student and Employee inherited name from Person. By default, however, we get two copies. To get only one copy, we must use *virtual inheritance*. When Person is extended, the subclasses use virtual to signal that any inherited data from Person are stored in a different manner. When multiple such subclasses are themselves extended, the compiler will be able to distinguish between data members like hours that were created in the subclasses and data members like name that are really all part of a single ancestor class.

If the ancestor class supplies some of the data, it makes sense that its constructor should be invocable. Thus with virtual inheritance, not only can a superclass constructor be invoked, but also the constructor of an ancestor class that is virtually extended can be invoked in the initializer list. All other initializations of the ancestor's data by other initializers in the initializer list are ignored.

The result of all these changes, with an illustration of the syntax, is shown in Figure 6-12. Observe the deficiency of this approach: Although the conflict is at StudentEmployee, it is the Student and Employee classes that are responsible for using virtual inheritance. Thus if the base classes have not already declared their use of virtual inheritance, it is difficult to inherit from both of them without having to disturb existing code.

```
1    class Person
2    {
3      public:
4        Person( const string & n, const string & t )
5          : name( n ), ptype( t ) { }
6        virtual ~Person( )
7          { }
8      private:
9        string name;
10       string ptype;
11   };
12
13   class Student : public Person
14   {
15     public:
16       Student( const string & n )
17         : Person( "Student", n ) { ... }
18       int getHours( ) const;    // number of credit hours taken
19
20     private:
21       int hours;
22   };
23
24   class Employee : public Person
25   {
26     public:
27       Employee( const string & n )
28         : Person( "Employee", n ) { ... }
29       int getHours( ) const;    // number of vacation hours left
30
31     private:
32       int hours;
33   };
34
35   class StudentEmployee : public Student, public Employee
36   {
37     public:
38       // Constructor sets type to StudentEmployee???
39       // ??? getHours ???
40
41     private:
42       // ??? name ???
43       // ??? hours ???
44   };
```

Figure 6-11   Example of conflicting implementations (needs fixing)

```
1   class Person
2   {
3      public:
4         Person( const string & t, const string & n )
5            : ptype( t ), name( n ) { }
6         virtual ~Person( )
7            { }
8      private:
9         string ptype;
10        string name;
11  };
12
13  class Student : virtual public Person
14  {
15     public:
16        Student( const string & n, int h )
17           : Person( "Student", n ), hours( h ) { ... }
18        int getCreditHours( ) const;    // credit hours taken
19
20     private:
21        int hours;
22  };
23
24  class Employee : virtual public Person
25  {
26     public:
27        Employee( const string & n, int h )
28           : Person( "Employee", n ), hours( h ) { ... }
29        int getVacationHours( ) const;   // vacation hours left
30
31     private:
32        int hours;
33  };
34
35  class StudentEmployee : public Student, public Employee
36  {
37     public:
38        StudentEmployee( const string & n, int ch, int vh )
39           : Person( "StudentEmployee", n ),
40             Student( "ignored", ch ), Employee( "ignored", vh )
41           { }
42     private:
43        // one name, two hours are inherited in memory layout
44  };
```

Figure 6-12   Example of implementing multiple interfaces

6.9   Protected and Friends

Under normal public inheritance, *protected members* in C++ are visible only in the class in which they are declared and any subclasses. The visibility rules do not use the arcane rules from Java that depend on the invocation being through a subtype reference. As with Java, use of protected data members is often poor design, because it encourages subclasses to access these data members directly and results in more changes being required should there be changes to the data members. Protected member functions are used to provide an implementation of a helper function that is logically private, but can be used by subclasses.

Friendship in C++ is not inherited. If a class or method is a friend of class `Base`, and class `Derived` extends `Base`, then the class or method can only access the portions of `Derived` that were inherited from `Base`. It cannot access the private details of `Derived`.

 6.10   Technical Differences

Our discussion mentioned several differences between inheritance in Java and C++. In addition to those differences, we mention several technical points that sometimes are of interest to C++ programmers. (There are also a host of complex and subtle points that we avoid discussing; after all, these are two different languages.)

6.10.1 No Root Class

C++ does not have a root base class that is similar to `Object`. As we discuss in Chapter 7, C++ uses templates in many of the places where `Object` is used in Java.

6.10.2 Nonpublic Inheritance

C++ allows not only public inheritance, but also private (and protected) inheritance. The default is private inheritance, which you will certainly run into when you forget to type the reserved word `public`.

In private inheritance, all of the inherited base components become private in the derived class. An *IS-A* relationship no longer holds (except inside the implementation of the derived class), so a derived class pointer or reference can no longer be passed as an argument that requires a base class pointer or reference.

Private inheritance sometimes models a HAS-A relationship and is typically used to change the visible interface of an existing object. For instance, in the `IntCell` class in Chapter 4, if we decided that we did not like the names `getValue` and `setValue`, but instead liked `get` and `put`, we could use private inheritance instead of the Java style of delegation. This is shown in Figure 6-13. If we used public inheritance, then `NewCell` would be type-compatible with `IntCell` and would still have `getValue` and `setValue`. With private inheritance, `getValue` and `setValue` are only visible inside of `NewCell`, although they can be used in the implementation of `get` and `put`, but not outside of the `NewCell` class, and `NewCell` is not type compatiable with `IntCell`.

```
1    class NewCell : private IntCell
2    {
3      public:
4        explicit NewCell( int initialValue = 0 )
5          : IntCell( initialValue ) { }
6
7        int get( ) const
8          { return getValue( ); }
9
10       void put( int value )
11         { setValue( value ); }
12   };
```

Figure 6-13   Private inheritance to change an interface; avoids delegation

6.10.3 Reducing Visibility When Overriding

C++ allows you to reduce the visibility of a method. If a method is public in a base class and private in a derived class, then it is visible when invoked through a base class reference and invisible otherwise. This is not a pretty picture because it violates the contract of an *IS-A* relationship. Specifically, what would happen if a public virtual function in a base class were overridden by a private function and then the function was invoked through a base class pointer that is actually pointing at a derived class object? In C++, the method is invoked using dynamic dispatch and so the private method would be used. This seems like bad semantics.

6.10.4 New Methods Hide Originals in Base Classes

The overloading algorithms in C++ and Java are different. Consider the code in Figure 6-14. In the code, we have a base class and a derived class. The base class declares member function `foo` with no parameters and the derived class declares member function `foo` with an `int` parameter.

In Java, only the zero-parameter `foo` is available when `foo` is invoked by a `Base` reference. The same is true in C++. However, in Java, both versions of `foo` are available when `foo` is invoked by a derived class reference; in C+ this is not true. Instead, when a method is declared in a derived class, it *hides* all methods of the same name in the base class. Thus `foo` with no parameters is no longer accessible through a derived class reference, even though it would be accessible through a base class reference.

There are two ways around this problem. The first is to override all of the hidden methods and redefine them in the derived class with an implementation that chains to the base class. Thus in class `Derived`, we add

```
        void foo( ) { Base::foo( ); }    // place in class Derived
```

The other alternative is to provide a *using declaration* in the derived class. In class `Derived`, we add

```
        using Base::bar;                 // place in class Derived
```

```
1    class Base
2    {
3      public:
4        virtual void foo( );
5    };
6
7    class Derived : public Base
8    {
9      public:
10       void foo( int x );
11   };
12
13   void test( Base & arg1, Derived & arg2 )
14   {
15       arg1.foo( );         // OK
16       arg1.foo( 4 );       // Illegal, as expected
17       arg2.foo( 4 );       // Legal, as expected
18       arg2.foo( );         // Illegal; not like Java
19   }
```

Figure 6-14   Derived class methods hide base class methods with the same name

One reason why this rule is important is that an accessor hides a mutator. Most likely this was unintentional, but many compilers will warn you, and what they are saying, in effect, is that you made a slight change to the signature when you overrode the original member function. Pay attention to these warnings.

6.10.5 Overriding with Different Return Type

C++ allows the return type of an overriding method to be slightly changed. Specifically, if the original return type is a pointer (or reference) to a class type B, the new return type may be a pointer (or reference) to class D, provided D is a publicly derived class of B. This condition simply states that you can change the return type to be a subclass of the original return type, as long as an *IS-A* relationship holds. This is useful for overriding methods such as

```
virtual const Base & Base::operator++( );
```
with
```
virtual const Derived & Derived::operator++( );
```

6.10.6 Type Compatibility

In Java, a variable that is an array of subclass types is type-compatible with an array of super-class types. For instance,

```
Object [ ] arr = new Employee[ 10 ];    // Legal Java
```
This type compatibility doesn't make much sense, when one sees that

```
arr[ 0 ] = new Basketball( );                // Compiles in Java
```

must be allowed to compile, since at compile time `arr[0]` is of type `Object` and `BasketBall` is an `Object`. Of course at runtime this throws an exception, but the whole point of the typing system is to try to avoid runtime problems.

In C++, the equivalent scenario would be an array of pointers, and C++ does not allow an array of subclass pointers to be type-compatible with an array of superclass pointers.

6.10.7 Reflection

C++ has little support for reflection. About all you can do is invoke the `typeid` method by passing an expression. It returns an object of type `type_info` that represents the runtime type of the expression. Standard C++ guarantees that this object contains a public data member called `name` and that you can compare `type_info` objects with `==` and `!=`. Thus,

```
Person *p = new Student( 123456789, "Jane", 4.0 );
cout << typeid( *p ).name << endl;                    // prints Student
cout << ( typeid( *p ) == typeid( Person ) ) << endl; // false (0)
```

6.10.8 Dynamic Dispatch in Constructors

In Java, when an instance method is invoked (via `this`) in a constructor, dynamic dispatch is always used. In C++, dynamic dispatch is not used. This is really of minimal consequence, since invoking nonfinal instance methods in Java is known to be a dangerous practice.

6.10.9 Default Parameters

Java does not allow default parameters. The most likely reason is that, in C++, default parameters are bound at compile time. Changing the default value in a derived class is unsafe, because doing so can create an inconsistency with virtual functions, which are bound at runtime. Thus if you provide default parameters in a base class method, keep them unchanged in the overridden derived class method.

Key Points

- The *IS-A* relationship is modelled in C++ with public inheritance.
- Private inheritance is the (probably wrong) default and can be used to model a *HAS-A* relationship.
- Because of slicing, polymorphism requires that objects be accessed with either base class pointers or references.
- Dynamic dispatch is performed only if a member function is declared virtual.
- Constructors are never declared virtual.

- Destructors are always declared virtual in a base class.
- Abstract methods are implemented as virtual member functions with =0 at the end of their declarations. A class with at least one abstract method is an abstract class.
- An initializer list call to a base class constructor replaces the Java call to `super`.
- Chaining to a base class method is achieved using the `::` scope operator.
- If `operator=` is overridden for the derived class, the base class `operator=` should be invoked as part of the implementation.
- The dynamic cast is the preferred form of downcasting in C++. It can be used to implement `instanceof`, although it is rarely needed in C++.
- C++ does not have interfaces, but the effect can be achieved with an abstract base class that contains only abstract methods and a virtual destructor.
- C++ allows multiple inheritance. If two implementations conflict, both of those implementations should have been declared using virtual inheritance to avoid replication of data members.
- Protected members are visible in derived class implementations, regardless of how they are accessed.
- Friendship is not inherited.
- There is no root class that is equivalent to `Object`. Instead templates are used to implement generic algorithms.
- Although it is bad style, C++ allows the reduction of visibility of a method in a derived class.
- Methods declared in the derived class hide base class methods with the same name.
- The return type of a derived class method can be changed from the base class method if it is replaced with a subclass of the original return type.
- An array of a derived type is not type-compatible with an array of the base type.
- C++ does not support reflection.

Exercises

1. What is the C++ equivalent of the `extends` clause?
2. What does `virtual` do?
3. What is slicing?
4. Why is it bad to declare a base class parameter using call-by-value?
5. How is the superclass constructor invoked in C++?
6. What are the defaults for the Big Three in a derived class?
7. Why is the default base class destructor unacceptable?
8. How are abstract classes declared in C++?

9. What is a pure virtual function?

10. Why is inheritance harder to do in C++ than in Java?

11. How are heterogeneous collections stored in C++?

12. What are the semantics of `dynamic_cast`?

13. How is the Java interface programmed in C++?

14. What are the rules for protected and friends with respect to inheritance?

15. What is virtual inheritance?

16. What is private inheritance?

17. What does it mean for a derived class method to hide a base class method?

18. Add a `Rectangle` class to the hierarchy in Figure 6-5 and modify Figure 6-8 appropriately to include objects of type `Rectangle`.

19. Define an abstract base class called `Employee` that contains a name (`string`), a social security number (`string`), and the respective accessor functions, and contains an abstract method that gets and sets a salary. It also contains a method called `print` whose task is to output the name and social security number. You should not use protected members. Include a two-parameter constructor, using initializer lists, and give all parameters default values. Carefully decide which members should be virtual. Next, derive a class called `Hourly` that adds a new data member to store an hourly wage (`double`). Its `print` method must print name, social security number, and salary (with the phrase `"per hour"`). It will certainly want to call the base class `print`. Provide an accessor and mutator for the salary, and make sure that its constructor initializes a salary. Next, derive another class called `Salaried` that adds a new data member to store a yearly salary (`double`). Its `print` method must print name, social security number, and salary (with the phrase `"annual"`). Provide an accessor and mutator for the salary, and make sure that its constructor initializes a salary. Exercise the classes by declaring objects of type `Salaried` and `Hourly` via constructors and calling their `print` methods. Provide a single `operator<<` that prints an `Employee` (by calling `print`). This method will automatically work for anything in the `Employee` hierarchy. To hold all employees, create a class called `Roster` that is able to hold a variable number of `Employee` * objects. `Roster` should have a `vector` of `Employee` *. Provide the capability to add an employee and print the entire roster of employees. To add an employee, `Roster::add` is passed a pointer to an `Employee` object and calls `vector::push_back`. Don't worry about error checks. To summarize, `Roster` has public methods named `add` and `print`. Write a short test program in which you create a `Roster` object, call `new` for both kinds of `Employee`, sending the result to `Roster::add`, and output the `Roster` via a call to `print`.

20. Define a hierarchy that includes `Person`, `Student`, `Athlete`, `StudentAthlete`, `FootballPlayer`, `BasketballPlayer`, `StudentFootballPlayer`, `StudentBasketballPlayer`, and `StudentFootballAndBasketballPlayer`. Give a `Person` a name, a `Student` a GPA, an `Athlete` a uniform number, a `FootballPlayer` a boolean representing true for offense, and false for defense, and a

BasketballPlayer a scoring average (as a double). Define appropriate data representations, constructors, destructors, and methods, and make use of virtual inheritance. Observe that StudentFootballAndBasketballPlayer will have two uniform numbers. Write a test program that obtains both numbers.

Templates

7

Chapter Outline

In Java, inheritance is used to write type-independent code. In C++, however, a different alternative is used: the *template*.

In this chapter, we begin by reviewing how generic algorithms are implemented in Java, and then see the basics of how templates are written for functions and classes. We will also see how templates are used to implement function objects, which in Java are implemented via inheritance and interfaces. We discuss how templates affect separate compilation and, finally, we will briefly mention some of the advanced uses of templates.

136

7.1   Review of Generic Programming in Java

Java uses inheritance to implement generic programming. For instance, all of the Collections API classes are written in terms of the `Object` class, and since all objects in Java are instances of this class, these collections are usable by all class types. In other parts of the language, a generic algorithm is implemented in terms of an interface type and thus works for any class that implements the interface.

However, this approach has some limitations. For instance, since primitive types are not objects, they cannot be directly added into a standard Java collection. Instead, wrapper classes such as `Integer` must be used. Java 1.5 will fix this deficiency by automatically wrapping primitives when they are passed as arguments to parameters of type `Object` (a process known as *boxing*). A second problem is that using inheritance leads to excessive downcasting, because the return type of the generic methods tends to be `Object` or an interface type. The downcasting is not only time consuming, it tends to delay typing errors from compile time until runtime, which is less desirable. Java 1.5 adds *generics* to the language, which will detect many typing errors at compile time.

 ## 7.2   Function Templates

C++ provides function templates. A *function template* is not an actual function, but instead is a pattern for what could become a function. Figure 7-1 illustrates a function template `findMax` that is virtually identical to the (correct) routine for `string` shown in Figure 4-26. Line 4 indicates that `Comparable` is the template argument: It can be replaced by any type to generate a function (both `class` and `typename` can be used interchangeably here). For instance, if a call to `findMax` is made with a `vector<string>` as a parameter, then a function will be generated by replacing `Comparable` with `string`. A general rule of thumb is that a function template is not a function; rather, it is simply a function wannabe. When it is expanded, the result is a function. Figures 7-2 and 7-3 illustrate that function templates are expanded automatically as needed.

```
1   // Return the maximum item in array a.
2   // Assume a.size( ) > 0.
3   // Comparable objects must provide operator<
4   template <typename Comparable>
5   const Comparable & findMax( const vector<Comparable> & a )
6   {
7       int maxIndex = 0;
8
9       for( int i = 1; i < a.size( ); i++ )
10          if( a[ maxIndex ] < a[ i ] )
11              maxIndex = i;
12
13      return a[ maxIndex ];
14  }
```

Figure 7-1   `findMax` function template

```
1   #include "IntCell.h"
2   #include <string>
3   using namespace std;
4
5   int main( )
6   {
7       vector<int>       v1( 37 );
8       vector<double>    v2( 40 );
9       vector<string>    v3( 80 );
10      vector<IntCell>   v4( 75 );
11      vector<int>       v5( 75 );
12
13        // Additional code to fill in the vectors not shown
14
15      cout << findMax( v1 ) << endl; // OK: Comparable = int
16      cout << findMax( v2 ) << endl; // OK: Comparable = double
17      cout << findMax( v3 ) << endl; // OK: Comparable = string
18      cout << findMax( v4 ) << endl; // Illegal: no operator<
19      cout << findMax( v5 ) << endl; // OK: uses findMax, line 15
20
21      return 0;
22  }
```

Figure 7-2   Using the findMax function template

Specifically, Figure 7-2 shows the code that the programmer would write, and then Figure 7-3 shows the code that the compiler generates internally to expand the function template into real functions. An expansion for each new type generates additional code; this is one example of *code bloat* when it occurs in large projects. However, once the template is expanded for a particular type, it is not expanded a second time for the same type. Thus internally, in Figure 7-3, only one function is shown for the expansion with int.

Note also, that in Figure 7-2, the call at line 18 will result in a compile-time error. This is because when Comparable is replaced by IntCell, line 39 in Figure 7-3 becomes illegal: There is no operator< defined for IntCell. Since this line (line 39 in Figure 7-3) is internally generated, the compiler will most likely flag the calling code (line 18 in Figure 7-2) and the corresponding line in the template declaration (line 10 in Figure 7-1) in the error message that it outputs. To help the users of a template avoid these kinds of errors, it is customary to include, prior to any template, comments that explain what assumptions are made about the template argument(s). This includes assumptions about what kinds of constructors are required. In findMax, a zero-parameter constructor and copy constructor are both required by vector, but it is reasonable to assume that the user has satisfied the requirements of the parameters, and thus we have not included those requirements in the comments.

When line 18 in Figure 7-2 is commented out, the result is that there are three separate overloaded versions of findMax that have been expanded from the template.

```
1   const int & findMax( const vector<int> & a )
2   {
3       int maxIndex = 0;
4
5       for( int i = 1; i < a.size( ); i++ )
6           if( a[ maxIndex ] < a[ i ] )
7               maxIndex = 1;
8
9       return a[ maxIndex ];
10  }
11
12  const double & findMax( const vector<double> & a )
13  {
14      int maxIndex = 0;
15
16      for( int i = 1; i < a.size( ); i++ )
17          if( a[ maxIndex ] < a[ i ] )
18              maxIndex = i;
19
20      return a[ maxIndex ];
21  }
22
23  const string & findMax( const vector<string> & a )
24  {
25      int maxIndex = 0;
26
27      for( int i = 1; i < a.size( ); i++ )
28          if( a[ maxIndex ] < a[ i ] )
29              maxIndex = i;
30
31      return a[ maxIndex ];
32  }
33
34  const IntCell & findMax( const vector<IntCell> & a )
35  {
36      int maxIndex = 0;
37
38      for( int i = 1; i < a.size( ); i++ )
39          if( a[ maxIndex ] < a[ i ] )
40              maxIndex = i;
41
42      return a[ maxIndex ];
43  }
```

Figure 7-3   findMax function template expanded (including a bad expansion for IntCell)

Because template arguments can assume any class type, when deciding on parameter passing and return passing conventions, it should be assumed that template arguments are not primitive types. That is why we have returned by constant reference.

Error messages relating to function templates are generally of two types. Type-independent errors, such as missing semicolons, are detected when the template is compiled. Type sensitive errors, such as undefined operators and methods are detected when a particular expansion causes a problem.

Because a function template is not a function (it is just a wannabee), function templates can be placed in header files without causing multiple definitions. In fact, this is probably the simplest way to compile function templates.

Not surprisingly, there are many arcane rules that deal with function templates. Most of the problems occur when the template cannot provide an exact match for the parameters, but can come close. There must be ways to either declare or resolve the ambiguity. For instance, consider the code in Figure 7-4, which illustrates a max2 function template and also a specific max2

```
1   #include "IntCell.h"
2   #include <string>
3   using namespace std;
4
5   template <typename Comparable>
6   const Comparable & max2( const Comparable & lhs,
7                            const Comparable & rhs )
8   {
9       return lhs > rhs ? lhs : rhs;
10  }
11
12  const string & max2( const string & lhs, const string & rhs )
13  {
14      return lhs > rhs ? lhs : rhs;
15  }
16
17  int main( )
18  {
19      string s = "hello";
20      int    a = 37;
21      double b = 3.14;
22
23      cout << max2( a, a ) << endl;    // OK: expand with int
24      cout << max2( b, b ) << endl;    // OK: expand with double
25      cout << max2( s, s ) << endl;    // OK: not a template
26      cout << max2( a, b ) << endl;    // Ambiguous
27
28      return 0;
29  }
```

Figure 7-4   max2 function might be ambiguous

function that is not a template. Four calls to max2 are made in main. The first two are expanded with int and double as Comparable, respectively. The third call, at line 25, uses the nontemplate function that is defined at lines 12 to 15. Thus if there is an expandable template and a nontemplate, and both are equivalent matches, then the nontemplate wins. The fourth call, at line 26, is ambiguous because when we expand with either an int or a double, in both cases, one parameter is an exact match and one is an approximate match.

 ## 7.3   Class Templates

In the simplest version, a *class template* works much like a function template. Figure 7-5 shows an ObjectCell class template that is virtually identical to the IntCell class seen earlier in Figure 4-6, but works for any type Object that has a zero-parameter constructor, a copy constructor, and an assignment operator. Since we presume that objects have these requirements normally, we have omitted the comments, letting the typename Object speak for itself. Note that Object is passed by constant reference, since it could be large. Also, notice that the default parameter for the constructor is not 0, because 0 might not be a valid Object. Instead, the default parameter is an Object created with its zero-parameter constructor.

Figure 7-6 shows how ObjectCell can be used to store objects of several types. Notice that ObjectCell is not a class; it is only a class template. Like function templates, class templates are wannabee classes. In Figure 7-6, the actual classes are ObjectCell<int> and ObjectCell<double>.

```
1   #ifndef OBJECTCELL_H
2   #define OBJECTCELL_H
3
4   template <typename Object>
5   class ObjectCell
6   {
7     public:
8       explicit ObjectCell( const Object & initValue = Object( ) )
9         : storedValue( initValue )
10        { }
11
12      const Object & getValue( ) const
13        { return storedValue; }
14      void setValue( const Object & val )
15        { storedValue = val; }
16
17    private:
18      Object storedValue;
19  };
20  #endif
```

Figure 7-5   Class template that stores any Object value

```
1   #include "ObjectCell.h"
2   #include <iostream>
3   using namespace std;
4
5   int main( )
6   {
7       ObjectCell<int>    m1;
8       ObjectCell<double> m2( 3.14 );
9
10      m1.setValue( 37 );
11      m2.setValue( m2.getValue( ) * 2 );
12
13      cout << m1.getValue( ) << endl;
14      cout << m2.getValue( ) << endl;
15
16      return 0;
17  }
```

Figure 7-6   Using the `ObjectCell` class template

It should be clear that the `vector` class is in reality a class template. It turns out that the `string` class is an instantiated class template (the class template is `basic_string`). A third class template is `complex`, which is most often instantiated as `complex<double>` and is found in the standard header file `complex`. Finally, `ostream` and `istream` are actually instantiations of class template `basic_ostream` and `basic_istream`.

Many of the classes that we have seen earlier are excellent candidates to be class templates. Two obvious examples are the matrix class from Section 5.6 and the queue class in Section 4.6.6. Figure 7-7 shows a `Matrix` class template that is virtually identical to the `MatrixOfDouble` class seen earlier in Figure 5-15, but works for any type `Object` that has the requisites of a `vector`. The `Matrix` class template is easily used, as shown in Figure 7-8.

7.4   Separate Compilation

If we implement a class template entirely in its declaration, then, as we have seen, there is very little syntax. Many class templates are, in fact, implemented this way because compiler support for separate compilation of templates historically has been weak and platform specific. Thus, in many cases, the entire class with its implementation is placed in a single header file. Popular implementations of the Standard Library follow this strategy to implement class templates.

The recent Standard has attempted to rectify this situation, so separation of the class template's declaration from its implementation, which has long been part of the language, is becoming more appealing. The ideas are the same for templates as for nontemplates.

```
1    #ifndef MATRIX_H
2    #define MATRIX_H
3    #include <vector>
4    using namespace std;
5
6    template <typename Object>
7    class Matrix
8    {
9      public:
10        Matrix( int rows, int cols ) : array( rows )
11          { setNumCols( cols ); }
12
13        int numrows( ) const
14          { return array.size( ); }
15        int numcols( ) const
16          { return numrows( ) > 0 ? array[ 0 ].size( ) : 0; }
17
18        void setNumRows( int rows )
19          { array.resize( rows ); }
20        void setNumCols( int cols )
21          { for( int i = 0; i < numrows( ); i++ )
22              array[ i ].resize( cols );
23          }
24        void setDimensions( int rows, int cols )
25          { setNumRows( rows ); setNumCols( cols ); }
26
27        const vector<Object> & operator[]( int row ) const
28          { return array[ row ]; }
29        vector<Object> & operator[]( int row )
30          { return array[ row ]; }
31
32      private:
33        vector< vector<Object> > array;
34    };
35
36    #endif
```

Figure 7-7   Java class to represent a two-dimensional array of `double`

Figure 7-9 shows the declaration for the `ObjectCell` class template. This part is, of course, simple enough, since it is just a subset of the entire class template that we have already seen.

For the implementation, we have a collection of function templates. This means that each function must include the template declaration and, when using the scope operator, the name of the class must be instantiated with the template argument. Thus in Figure 7-10, the name of the class is `ObjectCell<Object>`. Although the syntax seems innocuous enough, it can get quite

```
1   #include <iostream>
2   #include "Matrix.h"
3   using namespace std;
4
5   int main( )
6   {
7       Matrix<int> m( 2, 2 );
8       m[ 0 ][ 0 ] = 1; m[ 0 ][ 1 ] = 2;
9       m[ 1 ][ 0 ] = 3; m[ 1 ][ 1 ] = 4;
10
11      cout << "m has " << m.numrows( ) << " rows and "
12                        << m.numcols( ) << " cols." << endl;
13
14      cout << m[ 0 ][ 0 ] << " " << m[ 0 ][ 1 ] << endl <<
15              m[ 1 ][ 0 ] << " " << m[ 1 ][ 1 ] << endl;
16
17      return 0;
18  }
```

Figure 7-8   Using the `Matrix` class

cumbersome. For instance, to define `operator=` in the specification requires no extra baggage. In the implementation, we would have the brutal code[1]

```
1   #ifndef OBJECTCELL_H
2   #define OBJECTCELL_H
3
4   template <typename Object>
5   class ObjectCell
6   {
7     public:
8       explicit ObjectCell( const Object & initValue = Object( ) );
9
10      const Object & getValue( ) const;
11      void setValue( const Object & val );
12
13    private:
14      Object storedValue;
15  };
16  #endif
```

Figure 7-9   Class template that stores any `Object` value

---

1. Note that some occurences of `ObjectCell<Object>` (those after `::`) can be omitted, with the compiler interpreting `ObjectCell` as `ObjectCell<Object>`.

```
1    #include "ObjectCell.h"
2
3    template <typename Object>
4    ObjectCell<Object>::ObjectCell( const Object & initValue )
5      : storedValue( initValue )
6    {
7    }
8
9    template <typename Object>
10   const Object & ObjectCell<Object>::getValue( ) const
11   {
12       return storedValue;
13   }
14
15   template <typename Object>
16   void ObjectCell<Object>::setValue( const Object & val )
17   {
18       storedValue = val;
19   }
```

Figure 7-10 Implementation of the ObjectCell class template

```
template <typename Object>
const ObjectCell<Object> &
ObjectCell<Object>::operator= ( const ObjectCell<Object> & rhs )
{
    if( this != &rhs )
        storedValue = rhs.storedValue;
    return *this;
}
```

Even with this, the issue now becomes how to organize the class template declaration and the member function template definitions. The main problem is that the implementations in Figure 7-10 are not actually functions; they are still wannabees. They are not even expanded when the ObjectCell template is instantiated. Each member function template is expanded only when it is invoked.

7.4.1   Everything in the Header

The first option is to put both the declaration and implementation in the header file. This would not work for classes, since we could get multiply defined functions if several different source files had include directives that processed this header, but since everything here is a wannabee, there is no problem.

With this strategy, it might be a little easier for reading purposes to simply have the header file issue an include directive (prior to the #endif) to automatically read in the implementation file. With this strategy, the .cpp files that store the templates are not compiled directly.

```
1  #include "ObjectCell.cpp"
2
3  template class ObjectCell<int>;
4  template class ObjectCell<double>;
```

Figure 7-11   Instantiation file `ObjectCellExpand.cpp`

7.4.2   Explicit Instantiation

On some compilers we can achieve many of the benefits of separate compilation if we use explicit instantiation. In this scenario, we set up the `.h` and `.cpp` files as would normally be done for classes. Thus both Figure 7-9 and Figure 7-10 would be exactly as currently shown. The header file would NOT have an include directive to read the implementation. The `main` routine would only have an include directive for the header file. So Figure 7-6 would be unchanged also. If we compile both `.cpp` files, we find that the instantiated member functions are not found. We fix the problem by creating a separate file that contains explicit instantiations of the `ObjectCell` for all the types we use. An example of these explicit instantiations is shown in Figure 7-11. This file is compiled as part of the project. We have had success using this technique with several older compilers. The downside is that all of the template expansions have to be listed by the programmer, and when the class template uses other class templates, sometimes those have to be listed too. The advantage is that if the implementation of the member functions in `ObjectCell` changes, only `ObjectCellExpand.cpp` needs to be recompiled.

7.4.3   The export Directive

Newer compilers support the *export directive*, which is a recent language addition. If we issue an export directive prior to the class template declaration, as shown in Figure 7-12, then the extra file that we added in Section 7.4.2 becomes unnecessary and the program links as we would have expected. Don't expect to see this correctly implemented on all compilers. The export directive also works for function templates.

```
1  #ifndef OBJECTCELL_H
2  #define OBJECTCELL_H
3
4  template <typename Object>
5  export class ObjectCell
6  {
7      ...
```

Figure 7-12   The export directive

7.5   Specialized Templates

There are numerous other features of templates that can be used to produce fairly bizarre code. Rather than list all of them, we concentrate on a few features that are commonly used.

7.5.1   Multiple Template Parameters

The template parameter list can have more than one parameter. For instance, a map, in which we store keys and values can be declared as

```
template <typename KeyType, typename ValueType>
class Map
{
    ...
};
```

An instantiation of the `Map` to store names and birthdates, in which a name is a `string` and a birthdate is of type `Date`, would be

```
Map<string,Date> birthdays;
```

In fact, `map` (the class template name is all lowercase) is part of the Standard Library and mimics the `TreeMap` found in `java.util`.

7.5.2   Template Nontype Parameters

Template parameter lists can include nontype parameters. For instance,

```
template <typename Object, int size>
class Buffer
{
    ...
};
```

A nontype parameter must be a compile-time constant. Legal instantiations of the `Buffer` template would then include

```
Buffer<string,1024> buf1;
Buffer<string,2048> buf2;
```

The advantage of using a nontype parameter is that `size` can be used in places that require constant expressions (such as primitive arrays), so a data member such as

```
Object buf[ size ];    // Primitive array instead of vector
```

would be legal in this class template, but would not be legal if `size` was simply a parameter to a `Buffer` constructor, in which only `Object` was in the template parameter list. The disadvantage, of course, is the potential for code bloat.

Additionally, note that `buf1` and `buf2` above have different types. This may be an advantage or a disadvantage.

7.5.3   Default Template Parameters

Template parameter lists can have default values for both type and nontype parameters. For instance,

```
template <typename Object=char, int size=4096>
class Buffer
{
    ...
};
```

A nontype parameter must be a compile-time constant. Legal instantiations of the Buffer template would then include

```
Buffer<int>    buf1;           // Buffer<int,4096>
Buffer<>       buf2;           // Buffer<char,4096>
```

Default template parameters are relatively new and not implemented on many compilers.

7.5.4   Member Templates

Member templates are member functions that are themselves templates; this is basically a template inside of a template. As an example of its use, consider the code in Figure 7-13. Even though a float can be used in place of a double and an int can be used in place of a long, if we have

```
Pair<int,float>   p1( 3, 4.0 );
Pair<long,double> p2 = p1;
```

the code does not compile because p1 and p2 are not type compatible and so the default copy constructor is not applicable. Member templates allow us to solve this problem by providing a constructor that accepts any Pair, instead of the specific Pair.

This strategy is illustrated in Figure 7-14. Lines 9 to 12 contain the member template. Observe that the constructor for Pair accepts a Pair with arbitrary types and as long as the types are compatible, the constructor template will expand. If the types are not compatible, we get a compile-time error due to line 11, which is behavior that we want.

```
1    template <typename Type1, typename Type2>
2    class Pair
3    {
4      public:
5        Pair( const Type1 & f, const Type2 & s )
6          : first( f ), second( s )
7        { }
8
9          ...
10
11        Type1 first;
12        Type2 second;
13   };
```

Figure 7-13 Pair class template that is very picky about types

```
1    template <typename Type1, typename Type2>
2    class Pair
3    {
4      public:
5        Pair( const Type1 & f, const Type2 & s )
6          : first( f ), second( s )
7        [ ]
8
9        template <typename Type3, typename Type4>
10       Pair( const Pair<Type3,Type4> & rhs )
11         : first( rhs.first ), second( rhs.second )
12       { }
13
14          ...
15
16       Type1 first;
17       Type2 second;
18   };
```

Figure 7-14   Pair class template that allows construction from any type-compatible Pair using a member template

Member templates are also a relatively new addition to C++, so many compilers do not support them. The use shown here, extending type compatibility among different template instantiations, is probably its most common.

7.6   Templates for Function Objects

In Java, inheritance can be used to implement function objects. In fact, we can use inheritance in C++ in almost the same way. Our example begins with a basic rectangle class as shown in Figure 7-15.

If we want to find the maximum rectangle using the findMax function template in Figure 7-1, then we need to have operator< defined for rectangles. This might not be easy to do. For instance, it might already be defined to return the maximum area, but we are interested in the maximum perimeter, or maximum length, or, worse, we want to find the maximum based on several different criteria.

7.6.1   The Java Solution

In Java, we typically solve this problem by passing a second parameter to findMax, which is a function object. The function object is an instance of a class that implements some interface. In this case, the interface is Comparator (in java.util), which specifies a method that can compare any two objects. Since we do not have a root class of Object in C++, we can simulate the Java idea by declaring that Comparator is a class template, and have the findMax template

```
1   class Rectangle
2   {
3     public:
4       explicit Rectangle( int len = 0, int wid = 0 )
5         : length( len ), width( wid ) { }
6
7       int getLength( ) const
8         { return length; }
9
10      int getWidth( ) const
11        { return width; }
12
13      void print( ostream & out = cout ) const
14        { out << "Rectangle " << getLength( ) << " by "
15                                << getWidth( ); }
16
17    private:
18      int length;
19      int width;
20  };
21
22  ostream & operator<< ( ostream & out, const Rectangle & rhs )
23  {
24      rhs.print( out );
25      return out;
26  }
```

Figure 7-15   Simple rectangle class used in function object examples

accept a Comparator<Object> as a second parameter. A better plan is to make the Comparator a template parameter, so that a Comparator that compares base class objects can be used on a vector of derived class objects. This resulting Comparator class template and findMax function template is shown in Figure 7-16. Since we expect the Comparator to be a base class, it probably should have a virtual destructor and be passed using call-by-constant reference, instead of call-by-value, but as we will see, this turns out not to be necessary.

Now main can invoke findMax if it passes a vector of Rectangles and an appropriate function object. main is shown in Figure 7-17. The comparator is an anonymous instance of class LessThanByLength, which implements the Comparator interface and is shown in Figure 7-18. Specifically, it extends an instantiated Comparator template by implementing isLessThan.

Except for the template baggage that replaces the use of Object as a superclass, this implementation is exactly equivalent to the Java idiom for function objects.

```
1    template <typename Object>
2    class Comparator
3    {
4      public:
5        virtual bool isLessThan( const Object & lhs,
6                                 const Object & rhs ) const = 0;
7    };
8
9    // Generic findMax, with a Java-style function object.
10   template <typename Object, typename Comparator>
11   const Object &
12   findMax( const vector<Object> & a, Comparator cmp )
13   {
14       int maxIndex = 0;
15
16       for( int i = 1; i < a.size( ); i++ )
17           if( cmp.isLessThan( a[ maxIndex ], a[ i ] ) )
18               maxIndex = i;
19
20       return a[ maxIndex ];
21   }
```

Figure 7-16   Java-style comparator and findMax routine

7.6.2   Avoiding Inheritance

If we examine the code carefully, we see that the Comparator class template is not used at all! Thus we can simplify Figure 7-18 and remove the Comparator class template completely. The revised version is shown in Figure 7-19. Otherwise findMax and main are unchanged.

7.6.3   Function Objects with operator()

We can use operator overloading to make the implementation of the function object look slicker. To do this, we replace isLessThan with operator(), as shown in Figure 7-20.

```
1    int main( )
2    {
3        vector<Rectangle> a;
4
5        a.push_back( Rectangle( 1, 10 ) );
6        a.push_back( Rectangle( 10, 1 ) );
7        a.push_back( Rectangle( 5, 5 ) );
8
9        cout << findMax( a, LessThanByLength( ) ) << endl;
10
11       return 0;
12   }
```

Figure 7-17   main that invokes findMax with a comparator

```
1  class LessThanByLength : public Comparator<Rectangle>
2  {
3    public:
4      bool isLessThan( const Rectangle & lhs,
5                       const Rectangle & rhs ) const
6        { return lhs.getLength( ) < rhs.getLength( ); }
7  };
```

Figure 7-18 Class that implements the comparator interface for rectangles (preliminary)

```
1  class LessThanByLength
2  {
3    public:
4      bool isLessThan( const Rectangle & lhs,
5                       const Rectangle & rhs ) const
6        { return lhs.getLength( ) < rhs.getLength( ); }
7  };
```

Figure 7-19 Class that implements the comparator for rectangles without `Comparator`

In the implementation of `findMax`, the call at line 17 becomes

```
        if( cmp.operator() ( a[ maxIndex ], a[ i ] ) )
```

Since `operator()` is the function call operator, this can be rewritten as

```
        if( cmp( a[ maxIndex ], a[ i ] ) )
```

At this point it makes sense to change the name of the parameter to `findMax` from `cmp` to `isLessThan`. Thus we get the code in Figure 7-21.

To summarize, the function object is declared in Figure 7-20 and provides an implementation of the function call operator. The routine that uses the function object is a template, and the type of the function object is a template parameter. Syntactically, when the function object is used, it looks like a normal global function call. The template routine can itself be invoked as in Java by passing an instance of the function object. The compiler will do all the type resolution.

Function objects are used extensively in the STL, which is the C++ equivalent of the Collections API. The STL is discussed in Chapter 10.

```
1  class LessThanByLength
2  {
3    public:
4      bool operator( ) ( const Rectangle & lhs,
5                         const Rectangle & rhs ) const
6        { return lhs.getLength( ) < rhs.getLength( ); }
7  };
```

Figure 7-20 Overloading the function call operator for a function object

```
1    template <typename Object, typename Comparator>
2    const Object & findMax( const vector<Object> & a,
3                            Comparator isLessThan )
4    {
5        int maxIndex = 0;
6
7        for( int i = 1; i < a.size( ); i++ )
8            if( isLessThan( a[ maxIndex ], a[ i ] ) )
9                maxIndex = i;
10
11       return a[ maxIndex ];
12   }
```

Figure 7-21   Implementation of findMax with operator() (final version)

Key Points

- Templates in C++ replace the use of inheritance in Java to implement type-independent algorithms. Templates allow many mismatched types to be detected at compile time.
- Function templates are not functions; they are function wannabees.
- When a function template is expanded, the result is a function.
- Class templates are wannabee classes.
- Separate compilation of templates is complicated by the fact that the templates are not real functions or member functions. Various mechanisms can be used, depending on the compiler.
- Parameters to a function that are template parameters should rarely be passed using call-by-value. An exception is function objects.
- Templates can be instantiated with multiple parameters.
- Templates can be instantiated with nontype parameters, such as an int.
- Template parameters can have defaults.
- Member templates are member function templates inside of templates.
- Function objects are implemented in C++ by overloading the function call operator.

Exercises

1. When using templates, what kinds of errors are detected at compile time that are not detected until runtime in Java?
2. When are errors in a template definition detected by the compiler?

3. What is code bloat?
4. What strategies are used for separate compilation of templates?
5. What is a member template?
6. How are templates used for function objects?
7. Implement a function template that takes a single vector as a parameter and sorts the vector (using any simple sorting algorithm).
8. Implement a function template that takes a single vector as a parameter and a function object that represents the comparator as a second parameter, and sorts the vector using the comparator as the basis for ordering (using any simple sorting algorithm).
9. Reimplement Exercise 4.19 using templates to generalize the types of the objects in the stack.
10. Reimplement Exercise 4.20 using templates to generalize the types of the objects in the set.
11. Reimplement Exercise 5.11 using templates to generalize the types of the keys and values in the map.

Abnormal Control Flow $\qquad$ 8

Chapter Outline

Java is notoriously concerned with not allowing unsafe programs to execute. The compiler will catch many programming errors and the runtime system will throw exceptions when invalid operations occur. C++ was designed with a different mentality.

In this chapter, we discuss how C++ programs typically handle errors and then we examine exceptions in C++. Although the syntax has similarities (`try` and `catch`), C++ exception handling is a shell of what Java provides.

8.1   The Design of C++

From day 1, Java was defined with code safety in mind. C++ was designed with code efficiency in mind, which was certainly justifiable given the speed of computers in the 1980s. Although error handling in C++ is important, the language specification does not go out of its way to detect programming errors at either compile time or runtime; often a program will terminate due to an error only if the underlying hardware complains.

As an example, we know that in Java, all variables have a definite value prior to use, so the Java equivalent of the code in Figure 8-1 would be illegal and would not compile. Older C++ compilers say nothing about this code, while newer compilers issue warnings about the two uninitialized variables. However, most C++ compilers will still compile the code and let the user run it.

A second example is shown in Figure 8-2. Here we see the old-style cast used to convert between two completely unrelated pointer types. This code compiles, probably with a warning, and runs, producing some bizarre output. Of course the dynamic_cast can be used to solve this problem, but Java does not allow type confusion of the sort shown here at all. Similar nonsense can be seen in Figure 8-3: Here we allow assigning to a constant object. Although C++ puts in a good-faith effort to disallow the assignment, if we use the const_cast, we can change an object that we promised not to change.

```
1   class Account
2   {
3     public:
4       Account( int b = 0 )
5         : balance( b ) { }
6
7       int getBalance( ) const
8         { return balance; }
9       void deposit( int d )
10        { balance += d; }
11
12    private:
13      int balance;
14  };
15
16  int main( )
17  {
18      Account *acc1 = new Account( );
19      Account *acc2;
20
21      acc1->deposit( 50 );
22      cout << acc1->getBalance( ) << endl;
23      cout << acc2->getBalance( ) << endl;
24
25      return 0;
26  }
```

Figure 8-1   C++ code that compiles (probably with a warning)

```
1   class Barbell
2   {
3     public:
4       Barbell( double b ) : weight( b ) { }
5
6       double getWeight( ) const
7          { return weight; }
8     private:
9       double weight;
10  };
11
12  int main( )
13  {
14      Barbell *bb  = new Barbell( 15.6 );
15      cout << bb->getWeight( ) << endl;
16
17      Account *acc = (Account *) bb;
18      cout << acc->getBalance( ) << endl;
19      acc->deposit( 40 );
20      cout << bb->getWeight( ) << endl;
21
22      return 0;
23  }
```

Figure 8-2   C++ code that might generate a warning but compiles, allowing type confusion

Certainly the most evil of C++ issues is shown in Figure 8-4. Here we have an obvious array index that is out of bounds. Almost any language would detect this at runtime, but not C++. Instead, it uses the four bytes that follow arr[9] as its guess for arr[10]. If arr[10] were on the left-hand side of the assignment operator, we could even change the value of those four bytes. Almost certainly this would be some other variable in the program, leading to hard-to-find bugs.

In C, on which primitive C++ arrays are based, the lack of bounds checking was justified on the grounds that the implementation simply stored a pointer variable. Additionally, being a language of the 1970s, which was used instead of assembly language to implement operating systems, certainly speed was an important criterion.

The vector class was added in the mid 1990s, and not including bounds checking as an automatic part of the indexing operator seems inexcusable. Yet it accurately reflects the C++ philosophy of not forcing the user to pay at runtime for anything more than the bare necessities and certainly not paying for a feature that was free in C.

In C++, error handling in general seems to follow this trend. The compiler and runtime systems are less likely to signal errors than in Java. Even when such errors are signalled, in many

```
1   int main( )
2   {
3       const string h = "hello";
4
5         // two failed attempts to change h
6       h[ 0 ] = 'j';        // does not compile, thankfully
7       string & href = h;   // does not compile, thankfully
8
9         // third time is a charm
10      string & ref = const_cast<string &> ( h );
11      ref[ 0 ] = 'j';
12      cout << h << endl;   // prints jello
13
14      return 0;
15  }
```

Figure 8-3   C++ code that allows changes to constants

cases the programmer can avoid acknowledging that the error has occurred and can thus continue executing code while the program is no longer in a good state.

This contrasts with Java, where if the Virtual Machine signals an exception, the Virtual Machine will shut down (the erroneous thread) if the exception is not handled, and where the programmer is explicitly required to write some code that acknowledges that a checked exception might occur (even if that code simply declares a throws list that allows the exception to propagate).

 ## 8.2   Nonexception Error Handling

In this section, we discuss two widely used error handling techniques that predate exception handling.

8.2.1   abort and exit

If the programmer has detected an unrecoverable error, there are plausible solutions. The best is to throw an exception and not handle it (or possibly handle the exception in main, and let main

```
1   int main( )
2   {
3       int i;
4       vector<int> arr( 10, 37 );   // 10 items, all with val 37
5
6       for( i = 0; i <= 10; i++)
7           cout << i << " " << arr[ i ] << endl;
8
9       return 0;
10  }
```

Figure 8-4   Array bounds are not checked in C++

return with a nonzero return value). In a pre-exception world, there are two common ways to abnormally terminate a program from inside any function.

The functions `abort` and `exit`, both declared in the standard header file `cstdlib`, cause the program to terminate. `exit` can provide a parameter that will be used in place of a return value for `main`. The signatures of `abort` and `exit` are

```
void abort( );
void exit( int status );
```

`abort` causes the program to terminate abruptly. No destructors are invoked in the process. `exit` causes the destructors of static objects to be called, but not any local objects that are in pending function calls. Do not call `exit` inside the destructor of a static object. (Why?)

Because few destructors are invoked, both `abort` and `exit` are inferior to throwing an uncaught exception. Furthermore, `exit` should never be used outside of `main` to handle a normal termination, since a normal termination should guarantee that all appropriate destructors are invoked.

As part of the termination process, `exit` invokes functions that are registered with `atexit` in reverse order of their registrations (the functions are also invoked if termination is normal). Such functions accept no parameters and return `void`, and the number of registered functions is implementation dependent. The signature for `atexit` is

```
int atexit( void f( void ) );
```

with `atexit` returning 0 if the limit of registered functions has already been reached. Figure 8-5 illustrates the use of `atexit`. If `foo` returns normally, without calling `abort` (or throwing an unhandled exception), `printExit` will be invoked as the program terminates. `printExit` will also be invoked if `foo` calls `exit`.

8.2.2   Assertions

The `assert` preprocessor macro (see Section 12.1 for a discussion of preprocessor macros) is made available by including the standard header file `cassert`.

If NDEBUG is defined, calls to `assert` are ignored. Otherwise, if the parameter to `assert` is zero, an error message is printed and the program is aborted by calling `abort`. Recall that no

```
1    void printExit( )
2    {
3        cout << "Invoking the printExit method..." << endl;
4    }
5
6    int main( )
7    {
8        atexit( printExit );
9        foo( );
10   }
```

Figure 8-5   Example of calling `atexit`

```
1   #include <iostream>
2   #include <string>
3   #include <cassert>
4   using namespace std;
5
6   void foo( string *s )
7   {
8       assert( s != NULL );
9           ...
10  }
```

Figure 8-6   Example of calling `assert`

destructors are invoked, so this is rather drastic. The error message includes the actual expression as well as the source code filename and line number.

For instance, in Figure 8-6, if a call to `foo` is made with a NULL pointer, an error message similar to

    Assertion failed: s != NULL, file Fig8-6.cpp, line 8

will appear (on the standard error) and the program will terminate abnormally. If NDEBUG is defined prior to line 8 via

    #define NDEBUG

`assert` will be ignored.

8.2.3   Error States

Many older C++ libraries, including the I/O library use the notion of an error state. If an error occurs, it is returned in an error code, or a global error code is set, or the object records that it is in an error state (in an internal data member). In all cases, the error state can be tested and possibly cleared if the user invokes appropriate functions. We will discuss how this works with I/O in Chapter 9. In general, this solution is inferior to exceptions.

8.3   Exception Handling

Exception handling in C++ is based on a similar model popularized in a language called Ada. In the 1980s and 1990s, Ada was the language of choice for U.S. Government applications because, unlike C and C++, but like Java that followed, it attempted to catch many errors at compile time and to do extensive runtime checking in an attempt to avoid programming errors in mission-critical systems. Java exception handling is a refinement of C++'s model.

8.3.1   Basic Syntax

The basic C++ syntax is similar to Java, in that a member function can throw an exception, and a caller can either ignore the exception and let it propagate to its caller or attempt to handle the exception with a try/catch block.

8.3.2   No finally Clause

C++ does not have a finally clause. However, it is guaranteed that if a function returns either normally with no active exception or abnormally with an active exception, all its destructors will be invoked. Thus local objects that allocate heap memory indirectly will free the heap memory back to the system automatically, assuming their destructors are correctly written. This leaves only heap memory that was directly allocated and is accessed by local pointer variables. In such a case, the `auto_ptr`, which we discuss in Section 8.4, can be used. The basic idea of the `auto_ptr` is that it wraps a pointer variable and has a destructor that calls `delete`, so if we create an `auto_ptr`, the heap memory can be freed by its destructor.

8.3.3   The Throw List and Unexpected Exceptions

In C++, we can specify a *throw list* cosmetically like Java. Notice that the reserved word is `throw`, rather than `throws`, to avoid an additional reserved word in the language. We say that this is cosmetic because unlike Java, the throw list in C++ is not examined at compile time. So if the method throws an exception that is not in the throw list, the program will still compile. However, at runtime, if an exception is thrown that was not in the throw list, then a call to `std::unexpected` will occur, which normally calls `abort`. It is possible to change the behavior of `std::unexpected` by invoking `set_unexpected`.

The throw list syntax in C++ is slightly different from Java:

```
void foo( ) throw( UnderflowException, OverflowException );
```

An empty (as opposed to missing) throw list signals that no exceptions are expected to be thrown. If an expected exception is thrown but not caught, the function `std:terminate` will be invoked. This function is also called if the exception handling mechanism determines that the runtime stack has been corrupted or if a destructor that is executed as part of the handling of an exception itself throws an exception (to avoid infinite recursion). Calling `set_terminate` allows the programmer to supply a function that contains different behavior for the `terminate` function.

8.3.4   Missing Throw List

A missing (as opposed to empty) throw list signals that any exception might be thrown. Thus, nothing is unexpected. Missing throw lists are part of C++ so as to preserve backward compatibility when exceptions were added. Of course, this is why compile-time checking of throw lists is not feasible. Most C++ code omits the throw list.

8.3.5   What Can Be Thrown

In Java, only objects that are subclasses of `Throwable` (or `Throwable` itself) can be thrown as exceptions. In C++, any object can be thrown as an exception, but clearly, it is better to create a class type that can store information about why the exception was thrown.

In Java, `Throwable` objects contain a stack trace as part of their data. Since there is no root exception class in C++, you cannot count on much information from the exception object besides its type.

8.3.6   Standard Exception Classes

Although there is no root exception class, C++ attempts to provide an inheritance hierarchy for its exceptions. These exceptions are shown in Figure 8-7. In Java, most of these exceptions would be considered runtime exceptions and would not be caught by the programmer. The only method in class `exception`, besides the Big Three and a zero-parameter constructor is the `what` method, which returns a primitive string that gives you some information. `exception` and its subclasses promise not to throw any exception (specifically `bad_alloc`) when their methods are invoked.

8.3.7   Rethrowing Exceptions

An exception can be rethrown simply by providing a throw statement in a catch block:

```
catch( domain_error e )
{
    // do some cleanup (not shown)
    throw;   // rethrow e
}
```

8.3.8   Catching All Exceptions

Because there is no root hierarchy, special syntax is needed to catch all exceptions. If ... is used in a catch handler, it matches any exception. However, the exception object will not be available (since there is no way to provide its type). As in Java, if there are multiple catch clauses, the first match wins. Thus ... has to be the last catch block in a series.

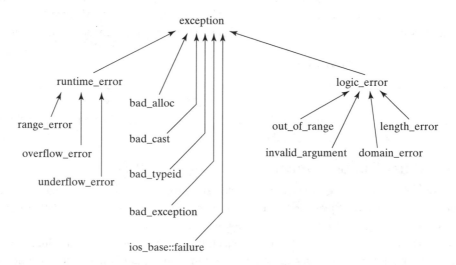

Figure 8-7   Standard exceptions

8.3.9 Inheritance and Exceptions

When inheritance is used, an exception object of a type `DerivedException` can be caught by a handler for `BaseException`. To achieve polymorphism, call-by-reference (or constant reference) should be used, since call-by-value slices the exception object.

Figure 8-8 illustrates truly nonsensical code, including a throw list for each method. Since the call at line 22 could cause either of two kinds of exceptions, but both are subtypes of `logic_error`, we can simply catch `logic_error` in the same way we would in Java. Most of the rules that concern inheritance are similar in C++ and Java.

The throw list in an overriding method cannot add exceptions. The catch clauses are tried in sequence, so a derived exception class must be listed before a base exception class, and all must be listed before `...` (the compiler will check this). If the exceptions form inheritance hierarchies and the methods are marked `virtual`, dynamic dispatch will occur when the exception's methods are invoked, as long as the exception is not passed by value.

```
1    double mysqrt( double x ) throw( domain_error )
2    {
3        if( x < 0 )
4            throw domain_error( "sqrt of neg number" );
5        else
6            return sqrt( x );
7    }
8
9    double myexp( double x ) throw( out_of_range )
10   {
11       double result = exp( x );   // call routine in cmath
12       if( result == HUGE_VAL )
13           throw out_of_range( "exp too large" );
14       else
15           return result;
16   }
17
18   double f( double x )
19   {
20       try
21       {
22           return mysqrt( x ) + myexp( x );
23       }
24       catch( logic_error & e )
25       {
26           cout << e.what( ) << endl; // invoke correct what
27           return -1.0;       // can't be answer for any other x
28       }
29   }
```

Figure 8-8   Nonsense example to illustrate inheritance

The alert reader may be wondering why the reference to the exception, e, at line 26 is not stale. After all, in both cases, a local temporary was storing the exception object and the function in which that temporary was created has terminated. Clearly if this was true, exceptions would have to be passed using call-by-value, which would be impossible with inheritance (since call-by-value and inheritance do not mix). Thus, as a special case, the exception handling mechanism guarantees that the exception object will not have its destructor called until it is no longer an active exception. This means the object is valid until it is caught and the catch block that it is caught in terminates, unless the catch block rethrows the exception, in which case the object retains its validity as if the catch block was never executed.

8.3.10 Templates and Exceptions

Templates and exceptions don't mix. Specifically, do not put a throw list on any function template. The reason is that you have to worry not only about the logic in your function, but whether the various operations on the instantiated types might themselves throw an exception. This becomes an impossible task and is typical of what happens when two separate features are added to a language at a late stage. The features often are not 100% compatible.

8.4   The auto_ptr Class

When a pointer variable is allocated locally, it can be hard to reclaim its memory. For instance,

```
void foo( )
{
    Person *p = new Student( 123456789, "Jane", 4.0 );
    p->print( );
        ...
    delete p;
}
```

Even if we have done all the correct things, such as declaring a virtual destructor for Person, this code could leak memory if foo abruptly terminates with an unhandled exception. Because C++ does not have a finally block, it is difficult to guarantee that the delete statement is executed. However, it is guaranteed that all local variables will have their destructors called.

Thus, C++ provides a wrapper class template, the auto_ptr, declared in the standard header file memory. The idea of auto_ptr is that it wraps a pointer variable, provides sufficient operator overloading so that the wrapped variable can be accessed without any additional baggage, and, since its instances are objects, we can expect a destructor to be invoked. The destructor can call delete on the pointer variable that it is wrapping. The auto_ptr also provides a get routine in case access to the wrapped pointer is needed and reliance on an implicit type conversion is not appropriate. In a simple example,

```
void foo( )
{
    auto_ptr<Person> p( new Student( 123456789, "Jane", 4.0 ) );
    p->print( );
        ...
}
```

Now, even if `print` or some other routine throws an exception that is not handled, the Student's destructor is invoked. The call to `print` works because `auto_ptr` overloads `operator->`. Also overloaded are `operator*`, the type conversion operator (a cast to `Person *`, in our example), copying, and copy construction.

If an `auto_ptr` is constructed to point at an object that was not heap-allocated, disaster can ensue, so don't do that. If two `auto_ptrs` are constructed to point at the same heap-allocated object, disaster can ensue, because of double-deletion, so don't do that either.

If an `auto_ptr` is copied into another `auto_ptr`, either by copy construction or by copy assignment, then we have double-deletion potential. To avoid double-deletion, the `auto_ptr`'s destructor calls `delete` only if it is the owner of the pointer. When the `auto_ptr` is initialized with a pointer, it becomes the owner. If it is copied to another `auto_ptr`, ownership transfers. The first `auto_ptr` will no longer attempt to call `delete`. This ownership transfer allows two other uses of the `auto_ptr`.

In the first additional use, a function allocates an object from the heap memory and returns a pointer to the object back to the caller. Now the caller is responsible for reclaiming the memory. With an `auto_ptr`, the function wraps the pointer in an `auto_ptr` and returns it using return-by-value. The caller saves a copy of the return value in a local `auto_ptr`, which transfers ownership and thus the memory will be automatically reclaimed.

In the second additional use, we pass an `auto_ptr` to a function that we invoke and let that function clean up the memory, because we have no use for it after the return. Although this works, it also implies that we need to be very careful when we pass `auto_ptrs` to other routines, since on the return, the allocated memory is likely to have been reclaimed.

An important consequence is that placing `auto_ptrs` into standard containers, such as `vectors`, is a terrible idea (and is, in fact, illegal in Standard C++). Once it is in a `vector`, it will tend to get copied over and over again, possibly into a temporary variable. If the temporary variable winds up with ownership, then when it is destroyed, it will dynamically reclaim the memory.

Key Points

- For robust code, avoid calling `exit` outside of `main`. Try to use exceptions instead.
- `assert` can be used to debug code, but might be inappropriate for production code. However, a simple replacement for `assert` that substitutes a call to `abort` with throwing of an exception can easily be written (Section 12.1).

- Exceptions in Java are based on exceptions in C++, but the C++ implementation doesn't work well, mainly because of the need for backward compatibility with earlier versions of C++.
- Few C++ library routines signal errors by throwing an exception. Instead, many incorporate error states into either return codes, global variables, or object state.
- C++ does not have a finally block. Instead, attempt to ensure that all of your heap-allocated objects are wrapped inside a stack-allocated object, so that they can be freed by calls to destructors. One way to do this is to use the `auto_ptr`.
- A throw list specifies exceptions that can be expected to occur. If an exception is thrown from a method that is not in the method's throw list, function `std::unexpected` is invoked.
- A missing throw list indicates that any exception can occur.
- Any object can be thrown in C++.
- The Standard Library defines a small hierarchy of what would be Java errors and runtime exceptions that can be extended by the programmer. This hierarchy is rooted at class `exception`.
- Inside a catch block, we can rethrow an exception simply by issuing `throw`. The exception is not required in the throw statement.
- To catch all exceptions use `....`.
- Many of the Java rules that relate to exceptions are, in effect, implemented in C++.
- Exceptions should always be caught using call-by-reference or call-by-constant reference. Catching by reference allows the state of the exception object to be changed prior to rethrowing it.
- The exception object is always valid up to the end of the catch clause that last handles the exception.
- Templates and exceptions don't mix. Avoid using throw lists in function templates.
- `auto_ptr` is a class template that wraps a pointer variable. The pointer variable should be viewing a heap-allocated object. When the `auto_ptr` is destroyed, its destructor will `delete` the object it is wrapping if the `auto_ptr` still enjoys ownership. Ownership is transferred if the `auto_ptr` is copied into another `auto_ptr`.
- Avoid using `auto_ptr` objects in container classes such as `vector`.

Exercises

1. Describe the semantics of `abort` and `exit`.
2. What does `assert` do?
3. List some standard C++ exceptions.

4. What does a missing throw list mean?

5. What objects can be thrown as exceptions?

6. How is an exception rethrown?

7. How can you catch all exceptions?

8. Why are exceptions never caught using call-by-value?

9. What is an `auto_ptr`?

10. How long is the exception object valid?

11. Why is it dangerous to include a throw specifier in a method template?

12. What happens if an exception that is not listed in the throw list is thrown?

13. Implement the `auto_ptr` class template. For an implementation that allows compatibility between derived and base class `auto_ptr`s, you should use member templates.

Input and Output

9

Chapter Outline

In Java, I/O is supported by a large library that resides mostly in package `java.io`. The package makes use of inheritance by defining four abstract classes (`InputStream`, `OutputStream`, `Reader`, and `Writer`), which can then be extended to target different sources of data (files, sockets, and arrays) and can be wrapped in a classic decorator pattern to achieve different functionality (buffering, compression, encryption, serialization, pushback operators, and so on). In

C++, inheritance is also used to define a hierarchy, although the C++ hierarchy is considerably smaller and use of the decorator pattern is not adopted.

In this chapter, we begin by discussing the I/O hierarchy in C++. Because exceptions are not part of I/O, we see how the error state is encoded in a stream. Then we look at basic output and input, and see an equivalent to the use of `StringTokenizer` that is seen in Java.

9.1 The Basic Hierarchy

The basic inheritance hierarchy is shown in Figure 9-1. At the root of the hierarchy is class `ios_base`. This class contains operations and information that is independent of whether the I/O operations are intended to work in ASCII (`char`), Unicode (`wchar_t`), or some other unspecified character type. It contains data members that represent the state of the stream, and constants that can control whether a file is opened in binary or nonbinary mode and whether reading/writing begins at the start, end, or some specific point inside a file. Such information does not depend on whether operations are input or output, nor does it depend on the type of characters being used, so it makes sense to factor it out into a common superclass.

Subclasses of `ios_base` are all templates that are instantiated with the type of characters that are used in the implementation. Standard instantiations include one for `char` and another for the wide character type `wchar_t`.

The `basic_ios` class encapsulates some information that is common to both input and output. The instantiation `basic_ios<char>` is defined with a `typedef` as `ios`. Similarly, instantiation `basic_ios<wchar_t>` is defined with a `typedef` as `wios`. In other words, we have

```
template <typename chartype>
class basic_ios : public ios_base { ... }

typedef basic_ios<char>    ios;
typedef basic_ios<wchar_t> wios;
```

Subclasses of `basic_ios` are `basic_istream` and `basic_ostream`; a typical simplified implementation of `istream` is

```
template <typename chartype>
class basic_istream : virtual public basic_ios<chartype> { ... }

typedef basic_istream<char>    istream;
typedef basic_istream<wchar_t> wistream;
```

Note the use of virtual inheritance since `basic_iostream` uses multiple inheritance. In the remainder of this chapter, we will ignore the fact that these are class templates and, instead, refer directly to the instantiations with `char`.

Subclasses of `istream` include `ifstream`, for input from files and `istringstream` for input from a string. `istringstream` is like `StringReader` in that it implements

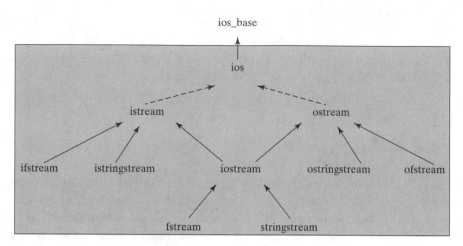

Figure 9-1   Basic inheritance hierarchy of streams. Any class c in the shaded area is really a template instantiation `basic_c<char>`; there is a similar instantiation for `wchar_t` (e.g., `wifstream` is used for wide characters)

all of the `istream` operations, taking its data from a `string`. `istringstream` also is like `StringTokenizer`, in that `StringReader` has little more than the ability to read one character, while `StringTokenizer` can separate its string into tokens.

C++ does not define a `socketistream` class, but there are third-party implementations such as the GNU library that do, and such classes easily fit into the inheritance hierarchy.

The `iostream` class extends both `istream` and `ostream`, and allows reading and writing to a stream simultaneously. Often doing so is fairly tricky, so we recommend following the Java style of having each stream do reading or writing exclusively. The declaration is interesting, at least so much as it provides a practical example of multiple inheritance:

```
template <typename chartype>
class basic_iostream : public basic_istream<chartype>,
                       public basic_ostream<chartype>
{ ... }
```

Eight streams are predefined. `cin`, `cout`, `cerr`, and `clog`, which are, in order, standard input, output, error, and an error stream that is automatically flushed. Also predefined are the wide character counterparts `wcin`, `wcout`, `wcerr`, and `wclog`.

 ## 9.2   Error States

A stream can interrogate its state by invoking one of `eof`, `fail`, `bad`, or `good`. If an I/O operation fails because of `eof`, the stream state will be set to indicate `eof`. For instance,

```
cin >> x;
if( cin.eof( ) )
    cout << "Oops ... eof was reached" << endl;
```

Note carefully that

```
while( !cin.eof( ) )
{
    cin >> x;
    cout << "Read " << x << endl;
}
```

does not work, because the end-of-file stream state is not set until an I/O operation actually fails. Thus the loop above goes around one time too many, printing the last successfully read value twice (since x won't change on the unsuccessful read). This is an extremely common error that could never happen in Java, because an exception would cause the flow to leave prior to the cout. However, in C++, if you do not test the stream state, flow continues as if nothing happened.

If the stream is in an error state, then the expression cin, when used as a condition of an if or loop, returns false. Thus, commonly seen code is

```
while( cin >> x )
    cout << "Read " << x << endl;
```

which correctly outputs all successfully read data. However, if the read fails (for instance, x is an int and there is a noninteger character on the input), this loop terminates at that point, rather than attempting error recovery.

For more robust code, a test that attempts recovery could be used. An example of this strategy is shown in Figure 9-2. Here we have a routine that reads items, separated by white space, of arbitrary type (as long as the type has correctly overloaded operator<<).

```
1    template <typename Object>
2    void readData( istream & in, vector<Object> & items )
3    {
4        items.resize( 0 );
5        Object x;
6        string junk;    // to skip over bad data
7
8        while( !( in >> x ).eof( ) )
9        {
10            if( in.fail( ) )
11            {
12                in.clear( );        // clear the error state
13                in >> junk;         // skip over junk
14                cerr << "Skipping " << junk << endl;
15            }
16            else
17                items.push_back( x );
18        }
19    }
```

Figure 9-2   Function template to read data, with error checking

Method	Result is true ...
eof	If the stream has ALREADY encounted end-of-file
bad	For an invalid operation; stream is probably corrupt
fail	For an unsuccessful operation, such as reading data in the wrong format
good	If none of the other conditions is true

Figure 9-3   Methods to test the stream error state

This code illustrates three important points. First, `fail` will be true if the I/O operation has failed for some reason, but that the stream is still in good shape and so the error is correctable. If, for instance, we are trying to read an integer, `fail` could indicate that noninteger data, such as the word `"Joe"`, was found on the input stream. Second, we could solve the problem by skipping over the next token. However, third, whenever the stream is in an error state, all I/O on the stream will continue to fail. So before we attempt to read the string that we will discard, we must first clear the error state by invoking `clear`. (The read of the string cannot normally fail, since there must be data and the stream is in good shape otherwise, but critical code would check an error state after the read also.)

A technical point about this example is not related to I/O, but instead deals with templates. The code can be invoked as

```
vector<int> arr;
readData( cin, arr );
```

If the call `readData` returns the `vector` instead of using it as a parameter, then the instantiation of the function template must be explicit, as in

```
vector<int> arr = readData<int>( cin );
```

since a function template's return type is not considered in determining a template expansion and, thus, the compiler would have no way to deduce what `Object` should be.

The method `good` returns true if the stream is not in an error state. The method `bad` is like `fail`, except it is more severe: the stream has been corrupted for some reason and so it is not worth attempting recovery. Figure 9-3 summarizes the methods that can test the state of a stream.

9.3   Output

As we have already seen, the vast majority of output statements simply overload `operator<<`. In addition to `operator<<`, single characters can be output by invoking the `put` member function. The most interesting part of output in C++ is probably the technique that is used to finely tune how the output is formatted, especially since we might not be happy with the defaults.

For instance, if we run the code in Figure 9-4, the output that is produced is

```
Pat 40000.1
Sandy 125443
```

```
1    class Person
2    {
3      public:
4        Person( const string & n = "", double s = 0.0 )
5          : name( n ), salary( s ) { }
6
7        void print( ostream & out = cout ) const
8          { out << name << " " << salary; }
9
10     private:
11       string name;
12       double salary;
13   };
14
15   ostream & operator<< ( ostream & out, const Person & p )
16   {
17       p.print( out );
18       return out;
19   }
20
21   int main( )
22   {
23       vector<Person> arr;
24       arr.push_back( Person( "Pat", 40000.11 ) );
25       arr.push_back( Person( "Sandy", 125443.10 ) );
26
27       for( int i = 0; i < arr.size( ); i++ )
28           cout << arr[ i ] << endl;
29       return 0;
30   }
```

Figure 9-4   Stream output defaults are not pretty

Here we see two deficiencies. First, by default, doubles are output to at most six significant digits. Second, integer and string types print only the minimum number of characters needed, making it hard to align output. We would prefer output such as

```
Pat                 40000.11
Sandy               125443.10
```

in which we force two decimal places and require that both the string and double be padded with at least a few spaces: strings should be placed on the left, followed with padding, while doubles should be placed on the right, preceded with padding.

The number of significant digits and digits after the decimal point, as well as how much and where padding of output is done, is part of the state of a stream. Specifically, it is part of the format state. Thus we can invoke methods on the stream to examine and possibly change the format state on a stream-by-stream basis.

```
1        void print( ostream & out = cout ) const
2        {
3            out << left << setw( 15 ) << name << " "
4                << right << fixed
5                << setprecision( 2 ) << setw( 12 ) << salary;
6        }
```

Figure 9-5   Revised print that uses manipulators

The easiest way to do this is to use *manipulators*. For instance, some of the manipulators of concern to us, with examples of their use on a specific output stream cout, could include

```
cout << setw( 15 );          // set next field width to 15
cout << left;                // field on left, padding on right
cout << right;               // field on right, padding on left
cout << setprecision( 2 );   // two decimal places
cout << scientific:          // output double w/ scientific notation
cout << fixed;               // output double no scientific notation
```

Most of these change the format state for all subsequent operations (until overridden by a contradictory manipulator), except for setw, which only applies to the next field. The manipulators that accept a parameter are available by including the standard header file iomanip. Figure 9-5 shows how we can use these manipulators to generate aligned, nicely formatted output. A host of manipulators are available.

Manipulators boolalpha and noboolalpha are used to control whether bools are printed as false and true or 0 and 1. The latter is the default (for backward compatibility). Thus

```
cout << boolalpha << true << " " << noboolalpha << true << endl;
```
prints

```
true 1
```

oct, dec, and hex are manipulators used to control how numbers are output. Alternatively, setbase(b) can be used. The base by default is not printed, but this can be changed by manipulator showbase; the default is noshowbase. Thus,

```
cout << 37 << " " << oct << 37 << " "
    << hex << 37 << " " << setbase( 10 ) << 37 << endl;
```
prints

```
37 45 25 37
```
If we have

```
cout << showbase;
cout << 37 << " " << oct << 37 << " "
    << hex << 37 << " " << setbase( 10 ) << 37 << endl;
```
then the output is

```
37 045 0x25 37
```

uppercase and nouppercase controls whether the x in 0x and e in scientific notation are printed in lowercase or uppercase. left and right control the positioning of the data relative to the padding. internal puts fill characters between the sign and the value. setprecision(n) sets the floating point precision. setw(w) sets the width of the next output only to w. fixed and scientific control whether scientific notation is output.

setfill(ch) sets the fill white space to ch. For instance, setfill('*') can be used to fill with *, as is commonly done on cashier's checks to prevent fraud. The following code

```
cout << setprecision( 2 ) << setfill( '*' ) << fixed << right;
cout << setw( 8 ) << 12.49 << endl;
cout << setw( 8 ) << 3.1 << endl;
```

outputs

```
***12.49
****3.10
```

showpoint and noshowpoint control whether or not a decimal point is printed if there are no digits following the decimal point. showpos and noshowpos control whether or not a leading + is printed in nonnegative numbers.

flush flushes an output stream, causing any pending writes to be completed. endl inserts a newline and flushes an ostream. ends inserts a null (this is used for null-terminating primitive strings) and flushes an ostream. skipws and noskipws control whether leading white space is skipped on input operators. ws on an input stream skips leading white space for the next read only.

 ## 9.4 Input

We have already seen that input streams make use of overloaded sets of operator<< to do significant work, and in Section 9.2, we saw how the error state of a stream can be accessed and cleared. In this section we discuss some additional input operations.

Often we want to perform character at a time input. Although operator<< is overloaded to accept a character, using it can be tedious because operator<< skips white space by default. Although the manipulator skipws can change this setting for future reads and ws can change the state for the next read, at best this is tedious and at worse it potentially is time-consuming if we repeatedly have to set the format state and then reset because the character-at-a-time input is interspersed with other input.

For this reason, istreams provide a get method. There are several versions of get, but the easiest to use is the one with the signature

```
istream & get( char & ch );
```

Thus, in

```
char ch;
if( cin.get( ch ) )
    cout << "Read " << ch << endl;
else
    cout << "Read error" << endl;
```

or, for wide characters,

```
wchar_t ch;
if( wcin.get( ch ) )
    wcout << L"Read " << ch << endl;
else
    wcout << L"Read error" << endl;
```

a single character is read, and if the read fails, the stream is put in a bad state. The `unget` method is used to undo a `get`. The `peek` method is used to examine the next character in the input stream without digesting it. The declarations of these methods are

```
istream & unget( );
int peek( );
```

The return type of `peek` is an `int`, in much the same way as the `read` method in `java.io.Reader` returns a `char` in an `int` variable. If `peek` sees the end of input, it returns EOF. Unlike Java, if the return value of `peek` is assigned to a variable of type `char` prior to checking if it is EOF, the compiler will not complain and the code is likely in error, particularly for unformatted data streams.

The function `getline`, which is not a member of `istream`, can be used to read a line of input. The signature is

```
istream & getline( istream & in, string & str, char delim = '\n' );
```

`getline` reads characters from an input stream and forms a string `str`. Reading stops when either `delim` is encountered or the end-of-file is reached. The `delim` character is not included in the string, but is removed from the input stream. Some older compilers have broken implementations of `getline`. The implementation in Figure 9-6 shows a plausible implementation of `getline` (and not being a template, one that should get preferential consideration by the compiler) and serves to illustrate the use of `get`.

Finally, member function `ignore` is used to skip characters. `ignore`'s signature is

```
istream & ignore( int n = 1, int delim = EOF );
```

`ignore` reads and discards n characters from the `istream`, or all characters up to and including the `delim`, or until the end-of-file is encountered.

```
1   istream & getline( istream & in, string & str, char delim )
2   {
3       char ch;
4       str = "";      // empty string, will build one char at-a-time
5
6       while( in.get( ch ) && ch != delim )
7           str += ch;
8
9       return in;
10  }
```

Figure 9-6   `getline` routine implementation

9.5 Files

Files are modelled by either an ifstream for input or an ofstream for output (again there are corresponding class template expansions for wide-character implementations). An fstream can be used for both input and output, but we do not recommend it. To perform file I/O, the standard header fstream should be included.

File streams can be constructed with a primitive string (either a string constant, null-terminated array of characters, or a result of c_str on a string object) and an optional *mode* that describes how the file is to be used. Some examples include

```
ifstream file1( "data.txt" );

char name2[ 100 ];
get( name2, 100 );        // reads a whole line or 99 chars
ofstream file2( name2 );

string name3
cin >> name3;
ofstream file3( name3.c_str( ), ios_base::out | ios_base::trunc );

string name4;
getline( cin, name4 );
ofstream file4( name4.c_str( ), ios_base::out | ios_base::app );
```

In these examples, first we see that an ifstream can be constructed with a filename. The second example constructs an ofstream with a primitive string (an array of character) and the default output mode of truncation. Note that although cin>>name2 compiles, using it is very dangerous, since it can lead to a buffer overflow. Invoking an overloaded version of get that works with character arrays is a much safer solution. Option number 3 uses a string class object, and we see that we can invoke c_str to obtain the primitive string that the ofstream constructor requires. Also, we see an explicit use of a mode in which we bitwise-or out and trunc. This is the default. Finally we see a constructor that opens a file for appending. (Older versions of C++ use ios instead of ios_base.) Alternatively, we can simply declare the stream object and use the member function open later. The state of the stream should be tested after it is opened, as in

```
if( file4 )
  // ok
else
  // not ok
```

When a stream goes out of scope, it is guaranteed that its destructor is called, thereby closing the stream automatically. The user can invoke close if it is desired to close the stream sooner, perhaps to reopen a different file with the same stream object.

9.6   Random Access

Both the istream and ostream classes allow random access in the stream. This is most useful for file streams. The member function tellg (tellp for ostreams) returns the current position in the stream, measured in characters. seekg and seekp allow the current position to be changed.

seekg is used for istreams, and seekp is used for ostreams (g stands for get, p for put, and we can presume that the different names are to avoid ambiguity in the case of multiple inheritance from both istream and ostream). The declaration for member function seekg is

        istream & seekg(int offset, int whence = ios_base::beg);

As a result of seekg, the current position in the stream is changed to one of three states:

1. offset characters from the beginning of the stream, if whence is ios_base::beg
2. offset characters from the current position in the stream, if whence is ios_base::cur
3. offset characters from the end position in the stream, if whence is ios_base::end

offset may be negative. Generally, it is an error to attempt to seekg before the beginning of the stream. On some systems, notably Unix, a seekg past the end of the file is supported by extending the file with undefined contents.

As an example, the routine in Figure 9-7 prints the last howMany characters in the (binary) file fileName. After opening the file for reading and checking for errors, we invoke seekg at line 9 to go to the end. We then back up howMany characters, taking care to avoid backing up to before the beginning. We do this by calling tellg at line 10 to see how large the file is and use

```
1    void lastChars( const string & fileName, int howMany )
2    {
3        ifstream fin( fileName.c_str( ), ios_base::binary );
4        if( !fin )
5            throw io_exception( );    // made this one up
6        else if( howMany <= 0 )
7            throw invalid_argument( "howMany is negative" );
8
9        fin.seekg( 0, ios_base::end );
10       int fileSize = fin.tellg( );
11       if( fileSize < howMany )
12           howMany = fileSize;
13       fin.seekg( -howMany, ios_base::cur );
14
15       char ch;
16       while( fin.get( ch ) )
17           cout.put( ch );
18   }
```

Figure 9-7   Routine that prints last howMany characters from fileName

the smaller of the file size and howMany as the new value of howMany. Then at line 13 we back up howMany characters and, finally, we can read characters with get and output them with put.

 ## 9.7   String Streams

The typical problem with operator>> for istreams is that all white space — blanks, tabs, and, in particular, newlines — are treated equally. So if we are expecting each line of a data file to have two integers and we write code such as

```
while( fin >> x >> y )
      ...
```

a file that had only one int on each of the first two lines would be processed without error. If we wanted to insist that every line had two and only two integers, we would need to do more work.

In Java, we would read one line at a time into a String. Once we had the string, we could parse it with a StringTokenizer, using code such as Figure 9-8.

```java
 1   public static void twoInts( BufferedReader fin )
 2                                           throws IOException
 3   {
 4       String oneLine = null;
 5       while( ( oneLine = fin.readLine( ) ) != null )
 6       {
 7           int x = 0, y = 0;
 8
 9           StringTokenizer st = new StringTokenizer( oneLine );
10           if( st.countTokens( ) != 2 )
11           {
12               System.err.println( "Skipping line: " + oneLine );
13               continue;
14           }
15           try
16           {
17               x = Integer.parseInt( st.nextToken( ) );
18               y = Integer.parseInt( st.nextToken( ) );
19           }
20           catch( NumberFormatException e )
21           {
22               System.err.println( "Skipping line: " + oneLine );
23               continue;
24           }
25           System.out.println( "Successfully read " + x + " " + y );
26       }
27   }
```

Figure 9-8   Java code to distinguish lines that contain exactly two integers

This is exactly the behavior that can be implemented with an istringstream, which like its companion ostringstream, is available by including the standard header sstream. An istringstream is constructed by passing a string as a parameter. At that point, all of the basic istream operators, including operator>> and testing of error states, are available. Note that the error states apply to the istringstream, and not the fstream.

Figure 9-9 shows the C++ implementation of twoInts, which is only cosmetically different from the Java code. Observe, first, that fin is a reference to an istream instead of an ifstream. As with Java, it is always best to use the most generic type. Once we have the istringstream at line 6, we can do two input operations and then test the error state, skipping a line. Since there is no equivalent to countTokens to check if there are exactly two tokens, we attempt to read a string, which should fail. If it succeeds, we print an error message and go on to the next line. Note carefully that in this code, each iteration of the loop creates a new istringstream object (on the runtime stack), destroying the original.

Declaring istringstream inside the while loop has the advantage that since each iteration creates a fresh istringstream, we do not have to clear the error state. The obvious disadvantage is the repeated calls to constructors and destructors. An alternative is to use the str method of istringstream to change str. Then we can put the istringstream object outside

```
1    void twoInts( istream & fin ) throw( io_exception )
2    {
3        string oneLine;
4        while( getline( fin, oneLine ) )
5        {
6            istringstream st( oneLine );
7            int x, y;
8            st >> x;
9            st >> y;
10           if( st.fail( ) )
11           {
12               cerr << "Skipping line " << oneLine << endl;
13               continue;
14           }
15           string junk;
16           if( st >> junk )
17           {
18               cerr << "Skipping line " << oneLine << endl;
19               continue;
20           }
21
22           cout << "Successfully read " << x << " " << y << endl;
23       }
24       if( !fin.eof( ) )
25           throw io_exception( );
26   }
```

Figure 9-9   C++ code to distinguish lines that contain exactly two integers

```
1    void twoInts( istream & fin ) throw( io_exception )
2    {
3        string oneLine;
4        istringstream st;
5
6        while( getline( fin, oneLine ) )
7        {
8            st.str( oneLine );
9            st.clear( );
10               ...
11       }
12   }
```

Figure 9-10   Revised code avoids excessive creation of `istringstream` objects

the loop, uninitialized, and set its `string` each time around the loop. However, now we must clear the error state. Figure 9-10 shows this approach.

For `ostringstream`, writes can be directed to a string instead of standard output, files, or other places. To extract the string from the `ostringstream`, invoke the `str` method. A classic example is the conversion of any (printable) type to a string as shown in Figure 9-11.

 ## 9.8   endl

Because `endl` writes a newline and flushes the stream, using `endl` can be time-consuming when there is significant disk-bound (or network-bound) I/O. In such a case, writing the "\n" character directly can be more efficient.

On one of our machines, we copied from one file to another a line at a time and measured the time spent writing. In this program which is almost exclusively I/O, we observed that using `endl` is four times slower for writing. The files were approximately 2,000,000 lines, with 78,000,000 characters. When each line was written using `endl`, the time spent writing was approximately 40 seconds. Ending the line with "\n" reduced the time to 10 seconds. Using the character '\n' instead of a string "\n" did not affect the running time.

Needless to say, this consideration is important only if a significant portion of the running time is spent performing I/O.

```
1    template <typename Object>
2    string toString( const Object & x )
3    {
4        ostringstream os;
5        os << x;
6        return os.str( );
7    }
```

Figure 9-11   Generic `toString`

9.9   Serialization

Serialization is not part of standard C++. Each implementation might provide some customized support for serialization, but certainly objects written by the implementation could only be read in the same implementation.

Key Points

- The C++ I/O library combines inheritance and templates. The templates are used to specify the underlying implementation of characters.
- Four standard streams are defined for each character type: `cin`, `cout`, `cerr`, and `clog` for `char`; `wcin`, `wcout`, `wcerr`, and `wclog` for `wchar_t`.
- `ifstream` and `istringstream` are subclasses of `istream`.
- `ofstream` and `ostringstream` are subclasses of `ostream`.
- `iostream` extends both `istream` and `ostream`.
- Error handling is performed by checking the state of the stream.
- The most common I/O operations involve `operator<<` and `operator>>`.
- Manipulators are used to control formatting options for output and digestion of white space for input.
- To repair an `istream` error, typically the stream state must be cleared first and then some input must be digested (perhaps by reading a string).
- The `istream` and `ostream` hierarchies allow for random access in the stream. Most often this is used for file streams.
- Files are closed automatically by destructors.
- An `istringstream` can be used in the same way as a Java `StringTokenizer`.
- An `ostringstream` can be used to print data to a `string`.
- Sockets are not part of standard C++, but there is a GNU socket class that contains `TCPstream`, which is part of the stream hierarchy.
- Serialization is not part of standard C++.

Exercises

1. Describe the I/O hierarchy in C++.
2. What are the standard predefined I/O streams?

3. How are errors handled in the C++ I/O library?
4. What is wrong with the `while(!fin.eof())` idiom?
5. What happens if a file is not closed by the user?
6. List some of the I/O manipulators.
7. What are `istringstream` and `ostringstream`?
8. Using Figure 9-11, implement a function template

   ```
   string operator+( const string & lhs, const Object & rhs );
   ```

   that mimics Java's string concatenation.
9. Write a routine that gives the character that is in the middle of a file (if the file has an even size, return the character in position `fileLength/2`).
10. Suppose a data file consists of lines in which each line stores a `string`, another `string`, and an integer. Write a routine that reads the file and returns a vector of objects (each object is a class type representing a line). Any ill-formatted lines will generate an error message and will be skipped.
11. Write a program that processes include directives. Since an included file may itself contain include directives, the basic algorithm is recursive.
12. Write a method that takes the name of a file as a parameter and reverses the contents of the file.

Collections: The Standard Template Library

10

Chapter Outline

In Java, the Collections API in package `java.util` implements standard data structures such as lists, sets, and maps. C++ has a package that provides similar functionality, namely the Standard

Template Library, which is known simply as the STL. As the name suggests, the STL makes heavy use of templates.

In this chapter, we describe how the STL is organized, and cover the basic containers and iterators, as well as a small collection of algorithms such as sorting and searching.

 ## 10.1 Containers and Iterators

In Java, the Collections API makes heavy use of inheritance. Recall that the Collections API defines an interface, `Collection`, and then subinterfaces `List` and `Set`, and `Set` itself has sub-interface `SortedSet`. These interfaces have various implementations. The Collections API also defines an interface, `Iterator`, that can be used to traverse any collection. Each collection class is responsible for defining an appropriate iterator class. The Java idiom is that the iterator class is declared as a private inner class of the collection, and that each container provides a factory method, `iterator`, that returns, using the `Iterator` interface type, a newly created and initial-ized instance of the iterator it has defined. The `Iterator` interface in Java is limited in that it contains only three methods: `next`, `hasNext`, and `remove`.

C++ has the same ideas of collections and iterators. However, the specific methods are slightly different. C++ iterators are more flexible than Java iterators, and not surprisingly, opera-tor overloading is used to replace named methods with operators.

10.1.1 Containers

C++ defines several container templates. Like Java, some collections are unordered; others are ordered. Some collections allow duplicates; others do not. All containers support the following operations:

```
int size( ) const;
void clear( );
bool empty( ) const;
```

`size` returns the number of elements in the container; `empty` returns true if the container con-tains no elements and returns false otherwise.

Unlike Java, there is no universal `add` method; different containers use different names. Some of the container class templates are `vector`, `deque`, `list`, `set`, `multiset`, `map`, `multimap`, and `priority_queue`.

`vector` is the equivalent of an `ArrayList`. The `add` operation for `vector` is named `push_back`. `vector` supports `operator[]`. `list` is the equivalent of `LinkedList`. Its `add` operation is also named `push_back`, but `list` does not support `operator[]`. However, `list` does support `push_front`. `deque` is an array-based data structure that supports efficient indexing with `operator[]`, and both `push_front` and `push_back`, all in constant time per operation.

`set` is the equivalent of `TreeSet`. The `add` operator for `set` is `insert`. `multiset` allows duplicates, whereas `set` does not. `map` is the equivalent of `TreeMap`. The `add` opera-tion is `insert`, but one must pass the key and value in a single pair object. However, `map` also provides an overloaded `operator[]` that makes the `map` look just like an array. A `multimap` allows duplicate keys.

The STL also contains a `priority_queue` class. Its operation is known as `push`. Comparing these collections with Java, we see that STL supports sets and maps that contain duplicates, as well as the priority queue, but does not support searching with hash tables.

10.1.2 Iterators

In Java, each container defines an internal iterator type, but exports it through the `Iterator` interface type. In C++, each container defines several iterator types, and these specific iterator types are used by the programmer instead of an abstract type.

For instance, if we have a `vector<int>`, the basic iterator type is `vector<int>::iterator`. Another iterator type, `vector<int>::const_iterator`, does not allow changes to the container on which the iterator is operating. This implies that the basic iterator can be used to change the container.

All iterators are guaranteed to have at least the following set of operations:

- `++itr` and `itr++` advance the iterator `itr` to the next location. Both the prefix and postfix forms are available. This does not cause any change to the container. Some iterators support `--itr` and `itr--`, and are called *bidirectional iterators*. Some iterators support both `itr+=k` and `itr+k`, and are called *random-access iterators*. `itr+=k` advances the iterator k positions; `itr+k` returns a new iterator that is k positions ahead of `itr`.
- `*itr` returns a reference to the container object that `itr` is currently representing. The reference that is returned is modifiable for basic iterators, but is not modifiable (i.e., a constant reference) for `const_iterators`.
- `itr1==itr2` returns true if iterators `itr1` and `itr2` refer to the same position in the same container and returns false otherwise. `itr1!=itr2` returns true if iterators `itr1` and `itr2` refer to different positions or different containers and returns false otherwise.

To use an iterator, we must obtain one from a container. The way this is done in C++ is that the container has two methods, `begin` and `end`, that return iterators. Each collection defines four methods:

```
iterator begin( );
const_iterator begin( ) const;
iterator end( );
const_iterator end( ) const;
```

`begin` returns an iterator that is positioned at the first item in the container. `end` returns an iterator that is position at the *endmarker*, which represents a position one past the last element in the container. For instance, on an empty container, `begin` and `end` return the same position.

`begin` and `end` both make use of the fact that identical-looking methods can be overloaded if one is an accessor and one is a mutator. So if `begin` is invoked on a constant container, we will get a `const_iterator`, which won't support any changes to the container. If `begin` is invoked on a mutable container, we will get an `iterator`, which can be used to change the container.

```
1   template <typename Container>
2   void print( const Container & c, ostream & out = cout )
3   {
4       typename Container::const_iterator itr;
5       for( itr = c.begin( ); itr != c.end( ); ++itr )
6           out << *itr << " ";
7       out << endl;
8   }
```

Figure 10-1   Routine to print any container

Typically we initialize a local iterator to be a copy of the `begin` iterator and have it step through the container, stopping as soon as it hits the endmarker. As an example, Figure 10-1 shows a `print` function that prints the elements of any container, provided that the elements in the container have provided an `operator<<`. If the container is a `set`, its elements are output in sorted order. Figure 10-2 illustrates four different containers that invoke the `print` function, along

```
1   #include <iostream>
2   #include <vector>
3   #include <list>
4   #include <set>
5   #include <string>
6   using namespace std;
7
8   int main( )
9   {
10      vector<int> vec;
11      vec.push_back( 3 ); vec.push_back( 4 );
12
13      list<double> lst;
14      lst.push_back( 3.14 ); lst.push_front( 6.28 );
15
16      set<string> s;
17      s.insert( "foo" ); s.insert( "bar" ); s.insert( "foo" );
18
19      multiset<string> ms;
20      ms.insert( "foo" ); ms.insert( "bar" ); ms.insert( "foo" );
21
22      print( vec );       // 3 4
23      print( lst );       // 6.28 3.14
24      print( s );         // bar foo
25      print( ms );        // bar foo foo
26
27      return 0;
28  }
```

Figure 10-2   Example of invoking `print` with four different containers

```
1   #include <iostream>
2   #include <map>
3   using namespace std;
4
5   template <typename Type1, typename Type2>
6   ostream & operator<<( ostream & out, const pair<Type1,Type2> & p )
7   {
8       return out << "[" << p.first << "," << p.second << "]";
9   }
```

Figure 10-3 Overloading operator<< for pairs

with the expected output (in comments). Observe that both set and multiset output in sorted order, with multiset allowing the second insertion of foo.

10.1.3 Pairs

If we try to print a map, the program will not compile immediately because the elements of a map are pairs of keys and values. If operator<< is overloaded for pair, then we can, in fact, use the print routine. Figure 10-3 illustrates the general strategy.

As expected, pair is a class template and it stores two data members, first and second, which can be directly accessed without invoking methods. So we can easily overload operator<< to output a pair, assuming its components first and second have done so too.

In Figure 10-4 we can create a map that stores the names of cities and their zip codes, both as strings. (The zip code cannot be an int, since many zip codes begin with 0.) Lines 10 and 11 show that a map stores pair objects; the pair objects can be added by calling insert. Line 12

```
1    #include <iostream>
2    #include <map>
3    #include <string>
4    using namespace std;
5
6    int main( )
7    {
8        map<string,string> zip;
9
10       zip.insert( pair<string,string>( "Miami", "33199" ) );
11       zip.insert( pair<string,string>( "Princeton", "08544" ) );
12       zip[ "Boston" ] = "02134";
13
14         // Prints: [Boston,02134] [Miami,33199] [Princeton,08544]
15       print( zip );
16
17       return 0;
18   }
```

Figure 10-4 Example of invoking print with maps

shows the much more natural equivalent that makes use of operator overloading. We describe maps in more detail in Section 10.7.

10.1.4 Inheritance and Containers

Recall that because of slicing, derived class objects cannot be copied into base class objects. Unlike Java, the STL stores copies of objects, not simply references to the objects. Thus, heterogeneous containers that store multiple types of compatible objects should store pointers to the objects, rather than the objects themselves.

Figure 10-5 shows a `vector` that stores pointers to both `Student` and `Person` (these classes were defined in Figures 6-2 and 6-4, respectively). Observe that we must again overload `operator<<`, because if we do not, the existing `operator<<` that outputs the value of the pointer (the memory address of the object it is pointing at) will be used. By providing our own pointer, with the base class type as a parameter, we have a better match than the existing version that accepts a generic `void *` as a parameter.

It is tempting to make `operator<<` a function template, as in

```
template <typename Object>
ostream & operator<< ( ostream & out, const Object *p )
    { return out << *p; }
```

However, doing so is dangerous because `operator<<` is already a template, so ambiguities (for instance, with `char *`, the primitive string) may result.

10.1.5 Constructors

All containers can be constructed from other containers. However, instead of a constructor that accepts another container, the constructors will accept a pair of iterators that represent the first

```
 1   ostream & operator<< ( ostream & out, const Person *p )
 2   {
 3       return out << *p;
 4   }
 5
 6   int main( )
 7   {
 8       vector<Person *> vec;
 9
10       vec.push_back( new Person( 987654321, "Bob" ) );
11       vec.push_back( new Student( 123456789, "Jane", 4.0 ) );
12       print( vec );
13
14       return 0;
15   }
```

Figure 10-5   Heterogeneous containers

item from the other container and the first nonincluded item from the other container. Thus, for instance,

```
vector<int> clone( original.begin( ), original.end( ) );
```

constructs a new `vector` `clone` with the same elements as any container (of `int`s) `original`.

10.2 Sequence Containers: `vector` and `list`

The `vector` is the STL equivalent of `ArrayList`, and `list` is the STL equivalent of `LinkedList`. `deque` has no Java counterpart and stores items in an array that appears to grow in both directions (several plausible implementations are known to accomplish this, one of which maintains the `deque` as a pair of `vector`s that grow in opposite directions and which reallocates the elements evenly if removal causes one of the `vector`s to empty).

One of the issues that we consider in C++ is that although expansion of an array is relatively cheap when it needs to occur, in Java, references are relocated to a larger array, whereas in C++ entire objects are relocated. If these are large objects rather than pointers, this can be more costly than expected. Thus `list`s in C++ have the additional C++ advantage of generally requiring less data movement compared to arrays when objects are large and a reasonable estimate of the `vector` capacity is not available at the start.

The basic operations that are supported by both containers are

```
void push_back( const Object & x );
Object & back( );
void pop_back( );
Object & front( );
iterator insert( iterator pos, const Object & x );
iterator erase( iterator pos );
iterator erase( iterator start, iterator end );
```

`push_back` adds `x` to the end of the container. `back` returns the object at the end of the container; an accessor is also defined that returns a constant reference. `pop_back` removes the object at the end of the container. `front` returns the object at the front of the container. `insert` adds `x` into the container prior to the position given by the iterator. This is a constant time operation for `list`, but not for `vector` or `deque`. `insert` returns an iterator representing the position of the inserted item.

Adding `x` to the front of `c` could be implemented as

```
c.insert( c.begin( ), x );
```

Adding `x` to the back of `c` could be implemented as

```
c.insert( c.end( ), x );
```

since `end` returns the endmarker.

The one-parameter `erase` removes the object at the position given by the iterator and takes in constant time for `list`, but not `vector` or `deque`. It returns the position of the element that followed `pos` prior to the call to `erase`. Most importantly, this operation invalidates `pos`, which is now stale. Typically `pos` is reset to the return value of `erase`. Removing the first and last elements of container `c` can be done with

```
c.erase( c.begin( ) );
c.erase( --c.end( ) );
```

In the second call, observe that the return value from `c.end()` is an unnamed temporary whose position represents the endmarker. Thus the `--` operator changes the state of the unnamed temporary to view the last item in the container. After the `erase` method is called, the unnamed temporary's destructor is invoked.

Two-parameter `erase` removes all items beginning at position `start`, up to but not including `end`. The idea of a range being half-open-ended is similar to substring operations in `java.util.String`. It means that an entire container can be erased by the call

```
c.erase( c.begin( ), c.end( ) );
```

A possible implementation of `erase` is

```
template <typename Object>
list<Object>::iterator list<Object>::erase( iterator from,
                                                     iterator to )
{
    for( iterator itr = from; itr != to; )
        itr = erase( itr );
    return to;
}
```

This implementation is inefficient for `vector`, in which it is better to remove elements in reverse order. For instance, in the worst case, this algorithm applied to empty the entire `vector` would consume quadratic time. An alternate algorithm is

```
template <typename Object>
list<Object>::iterator list<Object>::erase( iterator from,
                                                     iterator to )
{
    --from;
    for( iterator itr = --to; itr != from; )
        itr = --erase( itr );
    return ++from;
}
```

This code makes use of the fact that corresponding to the endmarker is the beginmarker, which is a valid position, but whose contents should not be accessed. One can see that traversing in reverse order is messy. We will revisit this in Section 10.4.

For `deque` and `list`, two additional operations are available with expected semantics:

```
void push_front( const Object & x );
void pop_front( );
```

The `list` also provides a `splice` operation that allows the transfer of a sublist to somewhere else.

For `vector` and `deque`, additional operations include

```
Object & operator[] ( int idx );
Object & at( int idx );
int capacity( ) const;
void reserve( int newCapacity );   // vector only
```

`operator[]` and `at` come in both accessor and mutator versions, and support array indexing. `at` does bounds checking, `capacity` returns the internal capacity, and `reserve` can be used to set the new capacity. `reserve` is only available for `vector`. If a good estimate is available, it can be used to avoid array expansion.

In addition to the usual set of constructors, a `vector` can be constructed with either an initial size, or an initial size and an initial value for all the elements. For instance,

```
vector<int> v1( 20 );        // 20 ints
vector<int> v2( 30, 37 );    // 30 ints, all with value 37
```

10.3 Error Checks in the STL

The compiler does significant type-checking because of the template expansion mechanism. Thus, many type errors that are detected only at runtime in the Java Collections API (bad downcasts, etc.) are detected at compile time in C++.

However, except for member function `at`, virtually no other STL members do any kind of error checking at runtime. Thus, applying * to an iterator that is out of bounds (for instance at the beginmarker or endmarker) or is stale can have dire consequences or fail in an undetectable manner (which is probably worse!). Comparing iterators that are in different containers will always produce false, rather than throwing an exception. Finally, certain mutating operations on containers cause the associated iterators to become invalid.

Java's rule is that any structural modification by a container method invalidates all iterators that view the container, any structural modification by the iterator invalidates all other iterators, and a `ConcurrentModificationException` will be thrown on an attempt to use an invalidated iterator.

C++'s rule is that some, but not all, operations invalidate an iterator, but the result is simply that the iterator is stale. For instance, `push_back` on a `list` does not invalidate any iterators. `push_back` on a `vector` invalidates all iterators. `erase` on a `list` invalidates all iterators that were viewing erased elements. `erase` on a `vector` invalidates all iterators that were at or past any erased element. The logic in both cases is that an iterator may be implemented internally as a pointer variable. In the case of a `list`, it is a pointer to a list node. In the case of the `vector`, it is a pointer into the underlying primitive array at the particular item. Because adding to an array could cause a resize (thus creating a different array), the pointer could become stale. On the other hand, adding to a linked list would never invalidate the pointer to a list node. In C++, you must be extremely careful when using iterators, since the runtime system will not provide much of a safety net.

10.4 Other Iterators

Two types of iterations get special treatment in C++. First, as we saw in Section 10.2, often we want to traverse a container backwards. This is usually awkward, because of the asymmetry between begin and end: begin is the first element, but end is the endmarker. Another type of iteration concerns the idea of repeatedly reading or writing to a file. We briefly discuss some C++ goodies to handle both reverse iteration and stream iterations.

10.4.1 Reverse Iterators

Suppose we want to print any collection backwards. Using iterators, the code is surprisingly messy, as shown in Figure 10-6, and uses a bidirectional iterator. At line 7, we initialize itr to the last position in the container (the position prior to the endmarker) and we loop until we are at the first position. Then we print the item in the first position (if there is one). What a mess.

A *reverse iterator*, as shown in Figure 10-7, allows us to do reverse traversal more naturally. First, each of the standard containers defines member function rbegin and rend that return reverse iterators that represent the last position (not the endmarker) and the beginmarker (not the first position), respectively. The reverse iterator is reverse_iterator or const_reverse_iterator, as appropriate. For a reverse iterator, ++ moves toward the front, while -- moves toward the rear, which is opposite to normal iterator semantics.

10.4.2 Stream Iterators

A *stream iterator* allows us to repeatedly read items or write items. Outputting items is discussed in Section 10.10 in conjunction with the copy algorithm. Use of the input stream iterator is best done with an example.

Suppose we want to read words from a file "dict.txt" into a set. Assume we are not concerned with errors. Then we already know we can use the code

```
1    // Print the contents of Container c in reverse
2    template <typename Container>
3    void printReverse( const Container & c, ostream & out = cout )
4    {
5        typename Container::const_iterator itr;
6
7        for( itr = c.end( ), --itr; itr != c.begin( ); --itr )
8            out << *itr << " ";
9        if( !c.empty( ) )
10           out << *c.begin( );
11       out << endl;
12   }
```

Figure 10-6 Awkward routine to print a container in reverse with a normal iterator

```
1   // Print the contents of Container c in reverse
2   template <typename Container>
3   void printReverse( const Container & c, ostream & out = cout )
4   {
5       typename Container::const_reverse_iterator itr;
6
7       for( itr = c.rbegin( ); itr != c.rend( ); ++itr )
8           out << *itr << " ";
9       out << endl;
10  }
```

Figure 10-7   Routine to print a container in reverse with a reverse iterator

```
ifstream fin( "dict.txt" );
string x;
set<string> s;
while( fin >> x )
    s.insert( x );
```

Recall that the containers have constructors that take two iterators. The stream iterator allows us to rewrite this code, passing to it a pair of `istream_iterator<string>` objects. The first object represents the start of the file and the second object represents the end-of-file marker. The code becomes

```
ifstream fin( "dict.txt" )
set<string> s( istream_iterator<string>( fin ),
               istream_iterator<string>( ) );
```

 ## 10.5 Stacks and Queues

The STL contains class templates named `stack` and `queue`. Clearly these are not needed, since `vector`, `list`, and `deque` all implement `stack` operations with `push_back`, `back`, and `pop_back`, while `list` and `deque` implement `queue` operations with `push_back`, `front`, and `pop_front`.

Thus what the STL provides are adapters that add nicer names to the interface. For `stack`, the member functions are `push`, `pop`, and `top`. For `queue`, we get `push`, `front`, and `pop` (which are not clear improvements).

The `stack` and `queue` templates require the user to specify the type of objects and the underlying representation. By default, a `vector` is used for `stack` and a `deque` is used for `queue`. The standard header `stack` must be included for `stacks`, while the standard header `queue` must be included for `queues`. Figure 10-8 shows how to use the `queue` adapter.

 ## 10.6 Sets

The `set` class template in C++ behaves in the same manner as Java. A `set` does not allow duplicates and, by default, iteration of a `set` views items in the default order. However, `sets` can use a function object to override the default ordering.

```
1   #include <queue>
2   #include <iostream>
3   #include <list>
4   using namespace std;
5
6   int main( )
7   {
8       queue<int,list<int> > q;
9       q.push( 37 ); q.push( 111 );
10      for( ; !q.empty( ); q.pop( ) )
11          cout << q.front( ) << endl;
12
13      return 0;
14  }
```

Figure 10-8   Using the queue adapter

10.6.1 Standard Function Objects

C++ defines several class templates in the standard header functional that implement function objects. These function object templates are less, greater, equal_to, not_equal_to, great_equal, and less_equal. The default for a set is an appropriately instantiated less template. The less template is easy to code, as shown in Figure 10-9, and illustrates that by default, a set expects to have an operator< available.

10.6.2 set Operations

The set provides several member functions in addition to the usual suspects, including

```
pair<iterator,bool> insert( const Object & x );
pair<iterator,bool> insert( iterator hint, const Object & x );
iterator find( const Object & x ) const;
int erase( const Object & x );
iterator erase( iterator itr );
iterator erase( iterator start, iterator end );
iterator lower_bound( const Object & x );
iterator upper_bound( const Object & x );
pair<iterator,iterator> equal_range( const Object & x );
```

```
1   template <typename Object>
2   class less
3   {
4     public:
5       bool operator( ) ( const Object & lhs,
6                          const Object & rhs ) const
7         { return lhs < rhs; }
8   };
```

Figure 10-9   Implementation of the less function template

insert adds x to the set. Since duplicates are not allowed, if x is not present, the returned pair will contain the iterator that represents the already contained x and false. Otherwise, it will contain the iterator that represents the newly inserted x and true. The two-parameter insert allows specification of a hint, which represents the position where x should go. If the hint is accurate, the insertion is fast. If not, the insertion still performs comparably to the one-parameter insert. For instance, the following code might be faster using the two-parameter insert than the one-parameter insert:

```
set<int> s;
for( int i = 0; i < 1000000; i++ )
    s.insert( s.end( ), i );
```

find returns an iterator that represents the position of x in the set. If x is not found, the endmarker is returned. The various erase routines behave in the same manner as for the sequence containers in Section 10.2, except that erase that takes Object x returns the number of items removed. In a set this is 0 or 1, but could be larger in a multiset.

lower_bound returns an iterator to the first element in the set with a key that is greater than or equal to x. upper_bound returns an iterator to the first element in the set with a key that is greater than x. equal_range returns a pair of iterators that represents lower_bound and upper_bound. These routines are typically most useful in multisets.

10.6.3 multisets

A multiset is like a set except that duplicates are allowed. The return type of insert is modified to indicate that the insert always succeeds. As a result, we no longer need a pair, but can simply return an iterator that represents the newly inserted x:

```
iterator insert( const Object & x );
iterator insert( iterator hint, const Object & x );
```

For the multiset, the erase member function that takes an Object x removes all occurrences of x. To simply remove one occurrence, use the erase member function that takes an iterator. To find all occurrences of x, we cannot simply call find; that returns an iterator that references one occurrence (if there is one), but which specific occurrence is returned is not guaranteed. Instead, the range returned by lower_bound and upper_bound (with upper_bound not included) contains all of the occurrences of x. Typically this is obtained by a call to equal_range.

10.6.4 Using Function Objects to Change Default Ordering

Just as a Java TreeSet can be specified to use either the default ordering or an ordering given by a comparator, a C++ set uses either a default ordering (operator<) or an ordering provided by a function object. Recall from Section 7.6.3 that the function object idiom in C++ is implemented by providing a class that contains an overloaded operator() and then instantiating a template with the class name as a template parameter. Figure 10-10 illustrates the idiom by adapting the code seen earlier in Figure 10-5 to use a set instead of a vector.

```
1    class PtrToPersonLess
2    {
3      public:
4        bool operator() ( const Person *lhs,
5                          const Person *rhs ) const
6          { return lhs->getSsn( ) < rhs->getSsn( ); }
7    };
8
9    int main( )
10   {
11       set<Person *, PtrToPersonLess> s;
12
13       s.insert( new Person( 987654321, "Bob" ) );
14       s.insert( new Student( 123456789, "Jane", 4.0 ) );
15
16       print( s );
17
18       return 0;
19   }
```

Figure 10-10 Heterogeneous set

 ## 10.7 Maps

As we have already seen, a map behaves like a set instantiated with a pair that represents a key and value, with a comparison function that refers only to the key. Thus it supports all of the set operations, including insert, but as we saw in Figure 10-4, we must insert a properly instantiated pair. The find operation for maps requires only a key, but the iterator that it returns references a pair. Similarly, erase requires only a key, and otherwise behaves like the set's erase.

Most importantly, the map overloads the array indexing operator[]:

```
ValueType & operator[] ( const KeyType & key )
```

The semantics of operator[] are as follows. If the key is present in the map, a reference to the value is returned. If the key is not present in the map, it is inserted with a default value into the map and then a reference to the inserted default value is returned. The default value is obtained by applying a zero-parameter constructor or is zero for the primitive types. These semantics do not allow an accessor version of operator[], so operator[] cannot be used on a map that is constant. For instance, if a map is passed by constant reference, inside the routine, operator[] is unusable. This could be a case where casting away const-ness is useful.

The code snippet in Figure 10-11 illustrates two techniques to access items in a map. First observe that at line 3, the left-hand side invokes operator[], thus inserting "Pat" and a double of value 0 into the map, and returning a reference to that double. Then the assignment changes that double inside the map to 75000. Line 4 outputs 75000. Unfortunately, line 5 inserts "Jan" and a salary of 0.0 into the map, and then prints it. This may or may not be the

```
1      map<string,double> salaries;
2
3      salaries[ "Pat" ] = 75000.00;
4      cout << salaries[ "Pat" ] << endl;
5      cout << salaries[ "Jan" ] << endl;
6
7      map<string,double>::const_iterator itr;
8      itr = salaries.find( "Chris" );
9      if( itr == salaries.end( ) )
10         cout << "Not an employee of this company!" << endl;
11     else
12         cout << itr->second << endl;
```

Figure 10-11 Accessing values in a map

proper thing to do, depending on the application. If it is important to distinguish between items that are in the map and are not in the map or if it is important to not insert into the map (because it is immutable), then an alternate approach shown at lines 7 to 12 can be used. There we see a call to find. If the key is not found, the iterator is the endmarker and can be tested. If the key is found, we can access the second item in pair referenced by the iterator, which is the value for the key. We could also assign to itr->second if, instead of a const_iterator, itr is an iterator.

10.7.1 Multimaps

A multimap is a map in which duplicate keys are allowed. Multimaps behave like maps, but do not support operator[]. In Java, the effect of a multimap is achieved by using a map whose values are Lists.

 ## 10.8 STL Example

As an example of the use of STL, we write a function that reads a sequence of words from an istream and outputs onto an ostream the list of words along with the line numbers on which the words occur. Thus the call

```
printConcordance( ifstream( "data.txt" ), cout );
```

will read from file data.txt and send the list of words to standard output. For simplicity, we assume that a word is any sequence of non-white-space characters and, thus, can easily be extracted by operator>>.

The idea is to use a map, in which the keys are the words and the line numbers are stored in a vector<int> or list<int>. We'll use vector<int>, but typedef vector<int> as LList, so we can change it later without much effort. When we see an existing word, we add its line number to the list that is stored in the map. If the word is new, we add its line number to the empty list that is created when the word is inserted into the map. After all the words have been read, we can iterate through the map, and output the words and their line numbers, and, since the keys are sorted, the output will be sorted by words. The line numbers themselves are output with an iterator.

Complete code is shown in Figure 10-12. The previously mentioned `typedef` is shown at line 10. We discuss `printConcordance` first. The loop from lines 26 to 33 populates the map. We read one line at a time and then create an `istreamstring` object at line 28. The loop at lines 31 and 32 steps through each word on the line and adds it to the map. The tricky code is clearly line 32. If the word already has been seen, then `operator[]` returns a reference to the list that is in the map and, thus, `push_back` simply adds a new line number to the end of the list.

```
1    #include <iostream>
2    #include <fstream>
3    #include <sstream>
4    #include <map>
5    #include <string>
6    #include <vector>
7    #include <iomanip>
8    using namespace std;
9
10   typedef vector<int> LList;
11
12   ostream & operator<<( ostream & out,
13                         const pair<string,LList> & rhs )
14   {
15       out << left << setw( 20 ) << rhs.first;
16       print( rhs.second, out );    // Figure 10-1
17       return out;
18   }
19
20   void printConcordance( istream & in, ostream & out )
21   {
22       string            oneLine;
23       map<string,LList>  wordMap;
24
25           // Read the words; add them to wordMap
26       for( int lineNum = 1; getline( in, oneLine ); lineNum++ )
27       {
28           istringstream st( oneLine );
29           string word;
30
31           while( st >> word )
32               wordMap[ word ].push_back( lineNum );
33       }
34
35       map<string,LList>::iterator itr;
36       for( itr = wordMap.begin( ); itr != wordMap.end( ); ++itr )
37           out << *itr << endl;
38   }
```

Figure 10-12 The concordance routine

If the word is new, `operator[]` adds it into the map with an empty list and returns a reference to the empty list that is now in the map. `push_back` makes this a one-element list.

We can then step through the map with the standard loop at lines 35 to 37. `operator<<` for the `pair` that is in the map is overloaded at lines 11 to 17. First, we print the word that is the `first` data member; second, we output the list of line numbers, which is the `second` data member.

 ## 10.9 Priority Queue

The `priority_queue` template, found in the standard header `queue`, contains several member functions, most importantly

```
void push( const Object & x );
const Object & top( ) const;
void pop( );
```

`push` adds x to the priority queue, `top` returns the largest element in the priority queue, and `pop` removes the largest element from the priority queue. Duplicates are allowed; if there are several largest elements, only one of them is removed.

Sometimes priority queues are set up to remove and access the smallest item instead of the largest item. In such a case, the priority queue can be instantiated with an appropriate `greater` function object to override the default ordering.

The priority queue template is instantiated with an item type, the container type (as in `stack` and `queue`), and the comparator; defaults are allowed for the last two parameters. In the following, the first line shows the default instantiation of `priority_queue` that allows access to the largest item while the second line shows an instantiation that allows access to the smallest item:

```
priority_queue<int>                               maxpq;
priority_queue<int,vector<int>,greater<int> > minpq;
```

 ## 10.10 Generic Algorithms

The Standard Library includes a rich set of functions that can be applied to the standard containers. These are called *generic algorithms* and are used by including the standard header `algorithm`. Some of the algorithms include routines for sorting, searching, and copying (possibly with substitutions). In all, there are over 60 generic algorithms. In this section we highlight a few of the most useful algorithms.

10.10.1 Sorting

Sorting in C++ is accomplished by use of function template `sort`. The parameters to `sort` represent the start and endmarker of a (range in a) container, and an optional comparator:

```
void sort( Iterator begin, Iterator end );
void sort( Iterator begin, Iterator end, Comparator cmp );
```

The iterators must support random access. The `sort` algorithm does not guarantee that equal items retain their original order. For that, we can use `stable_sort` instead of `sort`.

As an example, in

```
sort( v.begin( ), v.end( ) );
sort( v.begin( ), v.end( ), greater<int>( ) );
sort( v.begin( ), v.begin( ) + ( v.end( ) - v.begin( ) ) / 2 );
```

the first call sorts the entire container, v, in nondecreasing order. The second call sorts the entire container in nonincreasing order. The third call sorts the first half of the container in non decreasing order. Note that `(v.begin()+v.end())/2` is not allowed; instead we can compute a separation distance, halve it, and add it to the `begin` iterator.

The sorting algorithm is generally quicksort, which yields an $O(N \log N)$ algorithm, on average. However, $O(N \log N)$ worst-case performance is not guaranteed. In addition to sorting, there are also algorithms for selection, shuffling, partitioning, partial sorting, reversing, rotating, and merging.

10.10.2 Searching

Several generic searching algorithms are available for containers. The two most basic are

```
Iterator find( Iterator begin, Iterator end, const Object & x );
Iterator find_if( Iterator begin, Iterator end, Predicate pred );
```

`find` returns an iterator that represents the first occurrence of x in the range specified by `begin` and `end`, or `end` if x is not found. `find_if` returns an iterator that represents the first occurrence of an object for which the function object `pred` would return true or represents `end` if no match is found.

For instance, suppose we want to find the first occurrence of a string of length exactly 9 in a `vector<string>`. First, we define a function object that expresses this condition:

```
class StringLengthComp
{
  public:
    bool operator() ( const string & s ) const
      { return s.length( ) == 9; }
};
```

However, for additional code reuse, a class template might be better:

```
template <int len>
class StringLength
{
  public:
    bool operator() ( const string & s ) const
      { return s.length( ) == len; }
};
```

Then, at the end of the following code fragment, in which v is of type `vector<string>` and `itr` is of type `vector<string>::const_iterator`, `itr` will be either `v.end()` or will be located at a string of length 9:

```
itr = find_if( v.begin( ), v.end( ), StringLength<9>( ) );
```

Thus, find is implemented as a call to find_if with an appropriately instantiated equal_to as the third parameter.

A host of generic algorithms are available. We list a few of the common ones.

binary_search is used to search a sorted range for an object. A comparator can be provided or the default ordering can be used. equal_range, lower_bound, and upper_bound search sorted ranges and behave with the same semantics as the identically named member functions in set. min_element can be used to find the smallest item in a range and can be invoked with or without a comparator. count returns the number of occurrences of an object in a range delimited by a pair of iterators. count_if returns the number of objects in a range delimited by a pair of iterators that are true according to a predicate.

adjacent_find returns an iterator that refers to the first element such that a predicate returns true when applied to the element and its predecessor. The default predicate is equal_to, in which case adjacent_find finds the first occurrence of an element that equals the next element.

find_first_of takes four iterators that represent two sequences (the first sequence and the second sequence). It returns an iterator that represents the first occurrence in the first sequence of any of the elements in the second sequence. For instance,

```
vector<int> wins;   // store winning numbers
wins.push_back( 37337 );
wins.push_back( 46521 ),
wins.push_back( 53810 );

vector<int> myNumbers;
    ...        // populate myNumbers
vector<int>::const_iterator itr;
itr = find_first_of( myNumbers.begin( ), myNumbers.end( ),
                     wins.begin( ), wins.end( ) );
```

searches the vector myNumbers for any of the numbers in wins and returns an iterator that represents the first occurrence of such a number in myNumbers.

A fifth parameter, a predicate, can be used to decide if an item in the second sequence is a match for an item in the first sequence. Of course, the default is equal_to.

10.10.3 Unary Binder Adapters

The find_if algorithm requires that we pass a function object that returns a Boolean. This is called a *predicate*. As we know, the library defines several templates that are predicates: less, equal_to, and so forth. However, these predicates are not directly suitable for find_if, because their operator() requires two parameters. find_if requires *unary predicates*, which are predicates that take only one parameter.

A *unary binder adapter* is a function that takes a binary predicate, such as less (appropriately instantiated) and a value, and constructs a unary predicate in which the value is used as one of the two parameters to the binary predicate. This is called *binding a parameter*. We can bind the first parameter with bind1st or we can bind the second parameter with bind2nd.

For instance, the result of `bind2nd(less<int>(),0)` is a new unary predicate. If this new function object is `f1`, then any call `f1(x)` is interpreted as `less<int>()(x,0)`. Similarly, if `f2` represents the function object given by `bind1st(0,less<int>())`, then any call `f2(x)` is interpreted as `less<int>()(0,x)`.

If we want to find the first negative number in a `vector`, `v`, of `int`s, we can use

```
itr = find_if( v.begin( ), v.end( ), bind2nd( less<int>( ), 0 ) ),
```

10.10.4 Copying

There are several algorithms that deal with copying. These include `copy`, `copy_backwards`, `remove`, `remove_copy`, `remove_if`, `remove_copy_if`, `replace`, `replace_copy`, `replace_if`, `replace_copy_if`, `unique`, and `unique_copy`. Method names that have copy and noncopy versions differ in whether they change the original or leave the original unchanged and produce a new sequence. A typical routine is `copy`:

```
Iterator copy( Iterator begin, Iterator end, Iterator target );
```

The copy algorithm copies the range specified by `begin` and `end` to the target. The target must be modifiable and be large enough to store the result. For instance, the code

```
vector<int> source( 10, 37 );
vector<int> target( 10 );
ostream_iterator<int> out( cout, "\n" );

copy( source.begin( ), source.end( ), target.begin( ) );
copy( source.begin( ), source.end( ), out );
```

copies the contents of `source` to `target`, changing all those values to 37, and then copies the contents to the standard output stream, printing newlines after each item.

On the other hand, if we had

```
vector<int> smallArray;    // size is 0
copy( source.begin( ), source.end( ), smallArray.begin( ) );
```

the call to `copy` generates difficulties at runtime because the target array is not large enough.

10.10.5 Inserter Adapters

The last example in Section 10.10.4 illustrates a problem with copying. Often, we want the target of a copy (for instance, `replace_copy_if`) to be an initially empty container. Rather than providing another set of functions, C++ provides *inserter adapters*. The idea of an inserter adapter is that we create an iterator, whose `operator=` is altered.

The most common adapter is the `back_inserter`. The `back_inserter` is constructed with a sequence container and generates an iterator whose assignment operator is replaced by a `push_back` operation. As a result, the effect of

```
copy( source.begin( ), source.end( ), back_inserter( target ) );
```

is to copy the contents of `source` to the end of `target`, lengthening `target`.

Two other adapters are `front_inserter`, which not surprisingly causes a call to `push_front` (and cannot be used for `vector`), and `inserter`, which causes a call to `insert` and must be constructed with both a container and an iterator that specifies the insertion point. Thus, an equivalent call to the most recent copy above is

```
copy( source.begin( ), source.end( ),
                        inserter( target, target.end( ) ) );
```

10.11 bitsets

Like Java, C++ has bitwise operators that can manipulate a set of bits stored in a primitive type and a `bitset` class template. The class template, which is declared in the standard header `bitset`, is instantiated with the number of bits to be stored (this must be a compile-time constant) and indexing starts at 0. Bits can be accessed with `test` or, alternatively, with the array indexing `operator[]`. `set` and `unset` can be used to turn on or off a particular bit; with no parameters, these methods affect all bits. Alternatively, `operator[]` can be used on the left-hand side of an assignment. Also overloaded are the standard bitwise operators that allow bitwise operations on `bitset` types. The `bitset`s involved in those operations must have identical sizes.

The `bitset` has a look and feel that is similar to both `vector` and `map`, but it can be expected to be more efficient than `vector`, `set`, or `map`. However, a `set` or `map` could be space-efficient for cases where there are many bits, but only a few are ever set to be on.

Key Points

- Standard STL containers include the sequence containers `vector`, `list`, and `deque`, and also `set`, `multiset`, `map`, `multimap`, and `priority_queue`. `multiset`s allow duplicates and `multimap`s allow duplicate keys.
- `map`s store keys and values. `operator[]` returns the value associated with a key; if the key is not present, it is inserted with a default value that is then returned.
- Containers can be accessed by iterators, which are more powerful than their Java counterparts.
- Significant compile-time type checking is performed by the STL.
- Little runtime error checking is performed by the STL.
- There are several general types of iterators: Forward iterators, bidirectional iterators, random access iterators, and stream iterators are the most common. Additionally, there are `const_iterators`, `reverse_iterators`, and `const_reverse_iterators`.
- Iterators use operator overloading extensively. The common operators are ++, *, =, ==, and !=. Bidirectional iterators allow --. Random access iterators allow -, +, -=, and +=.
- Stream iterators allow repeated iteration over an input or output stream.

- Each container has a `begin` and `end` member function that yields iterators that represent the beginning of the container and the endmarker of the container, respectively. There are both accessor and mutator versions of `begin` and `end`.
- `pair` is a class template that stores the first item and the second item as public data. The `pair` is used in the `map`, which is a set of `pairs`, and also in the return type of some `set` member functions.
- If a standard container stores a heterogeneous collection, it should store pointers to the objects.
- Six function objects are defined as class templates in the standard header `functional`. These are `less`, `greater`, `equal_to`, `not_equal_to`, `great_equal`, and `less_equal`.
- Unary adapters allow the conversion of standard binary predicates to unary predicates by supplying one of the parameters to the binary predicate.
- Inserter adapters allow copying into empty containers by converting the assignment operator of an iterator into an insertion operation on the container.
- The standard library includes over 60 function templates for sorting, searching, copying, and many other generic algorithms.
- C++ has a `bitset` class template. To use it, the number of bits must be known at compile time. If this is not possible, alternatives such as `vector<bool>`, `set<int>` (containing only the true bits), or `map<int,bool>` can be used, but might not be as fast.

Exercises

1. How does the STL differ from the Java Collections API?
2. Describe the functionality of iterators in C++.
3. What are the different types of iterators?
4. What does `end` return?
5. What kind of error checks are performed by STL routines?
6. What is a `const_iterator` and how is it used?
7. What is a reverse iterator and how is it used?
8. What is a stream iterator and how is it used?
9. What is the difference between a `set` and a `multiset`?
10. Why is there no `operator[]` accessor for `map`?
11. What is a unary binder adapter?
12. What is an inserter adapter?
13. Describe the general categories of STL algorithms and give an example or an algorithm in each category.

14. In Exercise 6.19, make two modifications. First, in the Employee class, add operator<
    that orders employees by name. Then change the implementation of Roster to use a
    multiset of Employee * (ordered by name). Part of the multiset template instantia-
    tion includes an appropriate function object. The multiset print routine should output
    employees in sorted order (by name).

15. Implement a spelling checker. Prompt the user for the name of a file that stores a dictio-
    nary of words. Then prompt for the name of a file that you want to spell-check. Any word
    that is not in the dictionary is considered to be misspelled. Output, in sorted order, each
    misspelled word and the line number(s) on which it occurs. If a word is misspelled more
    than once, it is listed once, but with several line numbers. Of course you should verify that
    files open correctly. Use the following rule to determine what a word is: The input is con-
    sidered to be a sequence of tokens separated by white space. Any token that ends with a
    single period, question mark, comma, semicolon, or colon should have the punctuation
    removed. After doing this, any token that contains letters only is considered a word. Con-
    vert this word to lowercase.

16. Implement the sort template that takes a pair of iterators and a comparator, using any
    simple sorting algorithm. Then implement the sort template that takes a pair of iterators.
    To do this and reuse the three-parameter sort, you will need to define a phantom four-
    parameter sort template that takes an object of the type to be sorted as the fourth param-
    eter. The two-parameter sort will invoke the four-parameter sort, which in turn will
    invoke a three-parameter sort, with less<Object>() as the third parameter.

Primitive Arrays and Strings

11

Chapter Outline

In a perfect world, all array and string manipulations in C++ would be done with the `vector` class template and the `string` class that is part of the standard library, but life is not perfect. Many programs written prior to the standardization of `vector` and `string` make use of primitive arrays and strings, and some library routines interface with primitive arrays and strings instead of the library classes. Parameters to `main`, for instance, are a primitive array of primitive strings.

In this chapter, we discuss primitive arrays and strings in C++. We will see the relationship between the primitive array and pointer variables, and how this relationship influences the design of the STL. We will also discuss command-line arguments and briefly mention multi-dimensional arrays.

11.1 Primitive Arrays

An array is declared by giving it a name and by telling the compiler what type the elements are. If we are defining an array (creating a new array object), a size must also be provided. The size can be omitted if an initialization is present; the compiler will then count the number of initializers and take that as the array size. Either of the following declarations

```
int a[ 3 ];   // Three int objects: a[0], a[1], and a[2]
int a[ ] = { 37, 45, 61 };   // with initialization
```

has the compiler allocate space to store three integers, namely a[0], a[1], and a[2]. No index range checking is performed in C++, so an access out of the array index bounds is not caught by the compiler or runtime system. Instead, undefined and occasionally mysterious behavior occurs. Furthermore, if the array is passed as an actual argument to a function, the function has no idea how large the array is unless an additional parameter is passed. Finally, arrays cannot be copied by the = operator. In this section we will stick with the core language features of arrays and pointers, and discuss why these restrictions come into play.

11.1.1 The C++ Implementation: An Array Name Is a Pointer

When a new array is allocated, the compiler multiplies the size in bytes of the type in the declaration by the array size (the integer constant between the []) to decide how much memory it needs to set aside. This is essentially the only use for the size component. In fact, after the array is allocated, with minor exceptions, the size is irrelevant because the name of the array represents a pointer to the beginning of allocated memory for that array. This is illustrated in Figure 11-1.

Suppose we have the declarations

```
int a[ 3 ];
int i;
```

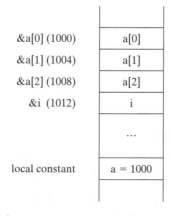

Figure 11-1   Memory model for arrays (assumes 4 byte `int`); declaration is `int a[3];`
`int i;`

The compiler allocates memory as follows: First, three integers are set aside for the array object. These are referenced by a[0], a[1], and a[2]. The objects in the array are guaranteed to be stored in one contiguous block of memory. Thus, if a[0] is stored at memory location 1000 and integers require four bytes, it is guaranteed that a[1] is located at memory location 1004 and a[2] is located at memory location 1008. (Java does not make this guarantee, so as to allow the garbage collector the option of storing parts of the array separately if needed to minimize memory fragmentation.) Finally, the compiler allocates storage for the object i. One possibility is shown in Figure 11-1, where i is allocated the next available memory slot.

For any i, we can deduce that a[i] would be stored at memory location 1000 + 4i. The value stored in a is exactly equal to &a[0]; this equivalence is always guaranteed and tells us that a is actually a pointer. Now we can see that to access the item a[i], the compiler needs only to fetch the value of a and add to it 4i.

Now that we have seen how arrays are manipulated in C++, we can see why some of the limitations discussed earlier occur. We can also see how arrays are passed as function parameters. First we have the problem of checking that the index is in range. Performing the bounds check would require that we store the array size in an additional parameter. Certainly this is feasible, but it does incur both time and space overhead. In a common application of arrays (short strings), the overhead could be significant. As we mentioned in Section 2.2.1 and illustrated in Section 8.1, the lack of range checking can cause serious problems such as off-by-1 errors in array indexing that can lead to bugs that are very difficult to spot. (If index range checking is crucial, use the vector's at member function.)

The second limitation of the basic array (is solved by vector) is array copying. Suppose that a and b are arrays of the same type. In many languages, if the arrays are also the same size, the statement a=b would perform an element-by-element copy of the array b into the array a. In C++, this statement is illegal because a and b represent constant pointers to the start of their respective arrays, specifically &a[0] and &b[0]. Then a=b is an attempt to change where a points, rather than to copy the contents of array b into array a. What makes the statement illegal, rather than legal but wrong, is that a cannot be reassigned to point somewhere else because it is essentially a constant object. The only way to copy two arrays is to do it element by element; there is no shorthand. A similar argument shows that the expression a==b does not evaluate to true if and only if each element of a matches the corresponding element of b. Instead, this expression is legal. It evaluates to true if and only if a and b represent the same memory location (that is, they refer to the same array).

Finally, an array can be used as a parameter to a function; the rules follow logically from our understanding that an array name is little more than a pointer. Suppose we have a function functionCall that accepts one array of int as its parameter. The caller/callee views are

```
functionCall( actualArray );        // Function Call
functionCall( int formalArray[ ] )  // Function Declaration
```

Note that in the function declaration, the brackets serve only as a type declaration, in the same way that int does. Note that the [] must follow the formal parameter, unlike Java where it can either follow or precede the formal parameter. In the function call, only the name of the array is passed; there are no brackets. In accordance with the call-by-value conventions of C++, the value of `actualArray` is copied into `formalArray`. Because `actualArray` represents the memory location where the entire array `actualArray` is stored, `formalArray[i]` accesses `actualArray[i]`. This means that the variables represented by the indexed array are modifiable. Thus, an array, when *considered as an aggregate*, is passed *by reference*. Furthermore, any size component in the `formalArray` declaration is ignored and the size of the actual array is unknown. If the size is needed, it must be passed as an additional parameter.

Note that passing the aggregate by reference means that `functionCall` can change elements in the array. We can use the `const` directive to attempt to disallow this (but this technique is not foolproof because of the ability to cast away `const`-ness):

```
functionCall( const int formalArray[ ] );
```

11.1.2 Dynamic Allocation of Arrays

Suppose we want to read a sequence of numbers and store them in an array for processing. The fundamental property of an array requires us to declare a size so that the compiler can allocate the correct amount of memory, and we must make this declaration prior to the first access of the array. If we have no idea how many items to expect, then it is difficult to make a reasonable choice for the array size. In this section, we show how to allocate our arrays dynamically and expand them if our initial estimate is too small. This technique, *dynamic array allocation*, allows us to allocate arbitrary-sized arrays and make them larger or smaller as the program runs. This is what goes on behind the scenes in `vector` and in the Java `ArrayList`.

The allocation method for arrays that we have seen thus far is

```
int a1[ SIZE ];       // SIZE is a compile-time constant
```

We also know we can use

```
int *a2;
```

like an array, except that no memory is allocated by the compiler for the array. We know that the `new` operator allows us to obtain memory from the memory heap as the program runs. An alternative form is the *array new operator*, `new[]`, which causes the creation of an array of objects from the memory heap, invoking a zero-parameter constructor for each array item (unfortunately, for `int`s, this does not always guarantee any initial value). Thus, the expression

```
new int [ SIZE ]
```

allocates the array. The expression evaluates to the address where the start of that memory resides. It may be assigned only to an `int *` object, as in

```
int *a2 = new int [ SIZE ];
```

As a result, a2 is virtually indistinguishable from a1. The `new` operator is type-safe, meaning that

```
int *a2 = new char[ SIZE ];
```

would be detected at compile time as a type mismatch error.

So what is the difference, if any, between the two forms of array memory allocation? A minor difference is that a1 cannot appear on the left side of an assignment operator, because the

```
1   void f( int i )
2   {
3       int a1[ 10 ];
4       int *a2 = new int [ 10 ];
5
6       ...
7       g( a1 );
8       g( a2 );
9
10      // On return, all memory associated with a1 is freed
11      // On return, only the pointer a2 is freed;
12      // 10 ints have leaked
13      // delete [ ] a2;    // This would fix the leak
14  }
```

Figure 11-2   Two ways to allocate arrays; one leaks memory

array name is a constant, while a2 can. This is a relatively minor difference, since if we declared

```
int * const a2 = new int [ SIZE ];
```

there is no difference with respect to what can appear on the left-hand side. A more important difference is that SIZE does not have to be a compile-time constant when we use new.

The most important difference is that the memory for a1 is taken from a different source than a2, which is allocated from the memory heap and eventually must be released to avoid a memory leak. The source of the memory, however, is otherwise transparent to the user.

Thus, when a1 is a local variable and the function in which it is declared returns (that is, when a1 exits scope), the memory associated with the array is reclaimed automatically by the system. a1 exits scope when the block in which it is declared is exited. For example, in Figure 11-2, a1 is a local variable in a function f. When f returns, the entire contents of the a1 object, including the memory associated with the array, is freed. In contrast, when a2 exits scope, only the memory associated with the pointer is freed; the memory allocated by new is now unreferenced and we have a memory leak. The memory is claimed as used, but is unreferenced and will not be used to satisfy future new requests, and if the array contains class type objects, those object's destructors will not have been invoked. The situation is shown graphically in Figure 11-3.

To recycle the memory, we must use the delete[] operator. The syntax is

```
delete [ ] a2;
```

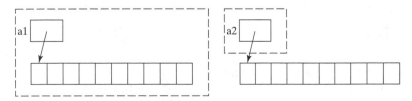

Figure 11-3   Memory reclamation in Figure 11-2

The [] is absolutely necessary here to ensure that all of the objects in the allocated array have their destructors called prior to reclaiming the memory for array a2. Without the [], it is possible that only a2[0]'s destructor is called and the remaining items in the array do not have their destructors called. In addition, a2's memory will not be reclaimed, which is hardly what we intended.

With new and delete, we have to manage the memory ourselves rather than allow the compiler to do it for us. Why then, would we be interested in this? The answer is that by managing memory ourselves, we can build expanding arrays. Suppose, for example, that in Figure 11-2 we decide, after the declarations but before the calls to g at lines 7 and 8, that we really wanted 12 ints instead of 10. In the case of a1, we are stuck and the call at line 7 cannot work. However, with a2 we have an alternative, as illustrated by the maneuver

```
int *original = a2;      // 1. Save pointer to the original
a2 = new int [ 12 ];     // 2. Have a2 point at more memory
for( int i = 0; i < 10; i++ ) // 3. Copy the old data over
    a2[ i ] = original[ i ];
delete [ ] original;     // 4. Recycle the original array
```

Figure 11-4 shows the changes that result. A moment's thought will convince you that this is an expensive operation, because we copy all of the elements from original to a1. If, for instance,

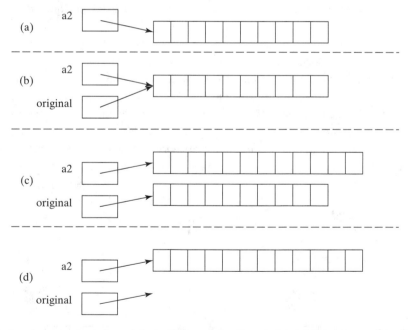

Figure 11-4 Array expansion: (a) starting point: a2 points at 10 integers; (b) after step 1, original points at the 10 integers; (c) after steps 2 and 3, a2 points at 12 integers, the first 10 of which are copied from original; (d) after step 4, the 10 integers are freed

this array expansion is in response to reading input, it would be inefficient to reexpand every time we read a few elements. Thus, when array expansion is implemented, we always make it some multiplicative constant times as large. For instance, we might expand to make it twice as large. In this way, when we expand the array from N items to $2N$ items, the cost of the N copies can be amortized over the next N items that can be inserted into the array without an expansion. This is exactly how `vector` is implemented.

To make things more concrete, Figure 11-5 shows a program that reads an unlimited number of integers from the standard input and stores the result in a dynamically expanding array. The function declaration for `getInts` tells us that it returns the address where the array will reside and it sets a reference parameter `itemsRead` to indicate how many items were actually read.

At the start of `getInts`, `itemsRead` is set to 0, as is the initial `arraySize`. We repeatedly read new items at line 15. If the array is full, as indicated by a successful test at line 17, then the array is expanded. Lines 19 to 23 perform the array doubling. At line 19 we save a pointer to the currently allocated block of memory. We have to remember that the first time through the loop, the pointer will be NULL. At line 20 we allocate a new block of memory, roughly twice the size of the old. We add 1 so that the initial doubling converts a zero-sized array to an array of size 1. At line 24 we set the new array size. At line 26, the actual input item is assigned to the array and the number of items read is incremented. When the input fails (for whatever reason), we merely return the pointer to the dynamically allocated memory. Note the following statements carefully:

- We do not `delete[]` the array.
- The memory returned is somewhat larger than is actually needed. This can be easily fixed.

The `main` routine calls `getInts`, assigning the return value to a pointer.

As you can see, this is lots of work. That's why modern C++ programmers use `vector`.

 ## 11.2 Primitive Strings

An important use of pointers and arrays is the C++ implementation of strings. The C++ base language provides some minimal support for strings; it is based entirely on the conventions of C and the C library. The result is too minimal to be useful in a modern language, so as they do with arrays, sane C++ programmers rely on the `string` class type rather than the predefined language features. Nonetheless, it is still important to know how strings are implemented in the basic C library, because they often occur in older code and are occasionally needed even in newer code.

In C++ as well as C, a primitive string is an array of characters. As a result, when passed to a function, the string has type `char *` or `const char *`. At first glance we might assume that the string `"Jill"` is an array of four characters: `'J'`, `'i'`, `'l'`, and `'l'`. The problem with this

```
1   #include <iostream>
2   #include <cstdlib>
3   using namespace std;
4
5   // Read an unlimited number of ints with no attempts at error
6   // recovery; return a pointer to the data, and set ItemsRead
7   int * getInts( int & itemsRead )
8   {
9       int arraySize = 0;
10      int inputVal;
11      int *array = NULL;    // Initialize to NULL pointer
12
13      itemsRead = 0;
14      cout << "Enter any number of integers: ";
15      while( cin >> inputVal )
16      {
17          if( itemsRead == arraySize )
18          {     // Array doubling code
19              int *original = array;
20              array = new int[ arraySize * 2 + 1 ];
21              for( int i = 0; i < arraySize; i++ )
22                  array[ i ] = original[ i ];
23              delete [ ] original; // Safe if Original is NULL
24              arraySize = arraySize * 2 + 1;
25          }
26          array[ itemsRead++ ] = inputVal;
27      }
28      return array;
29  }
30
31  int main( )
32  {
33      int *array;
34      int numItems;
35
36      array = getInts( numItems );
37      for( int i = 0; i < numItems; i++ )
38          cout << array[ i ] << endl;
39
40      return 0;
41  }
```

Figure 11-5   Code to read an unlimited number of ints and write them out

assumption is that if we pass this array to any routine, that routine would not know how many characters are in the array, because, as we have seen, a function that receives an array only receives a pointer and thus has no idea how large the actual array is. One solution to this problem is to use a slightly larger array with an endmarker.

For instance, we can declare an array of five elements, placing a blank in the last spot to signal that only the first four positions represent significant characters. If all routines are written to reflect this convention, we have a solution to our problem that requires little alteration of the language. Because we might actually want to use a blank in the string (e.g., to store a street address), we need to pick an endmarker that is not likely to appear elsewhere in the string. In C++, this special character is the *null terminator* '\0'. The escape sequence indicates that the null terminator is always represented internally as zero, which, as we shall see, leads to some shorthand when the controlling expression is written in an if statement or a loop. (A common error is to forget the \; this leaves '0', which is the character representation for the digit 0.) Therefore, if an array of six characters has 'J', 'i', 'l', 'l', and '\0', it represents the string "Jill", no matter what is in the sixth character.

So far, what has C++ provided in the way of string support? The answer is absolutely nothing! Furthermore, there are some things it does not directly provide in the language. Suppose we declare two strings str1 and str2:

```
char str1[ 10 ]; // Max length is nine
char str2[ 10 ]; // Max length is nine
```

Then the following statements cannot be correct:

```
str1 = str2;                  // Wrong!
bool cond = ( str1 == str2 );  // Wrong!
```

This follows directly from the facts that str1 and str2 are arrays, and array assignment and comparison are not supported directly by the language. Almost all of the support, in fact, is provided by the C++ library, which specifies routines that work for null-terminated strings. The prototypes for these routines are given in the standard header cstring. Some routines of interest are shown in Figure 11-6.

strlen(str) gives the length of the string represented by str (not including the null terminator); the length of "Jill" is 4. In this and all routines, if a NULL pointer is passed, you can expect a program crash. Notice that this is different from passing a pointer to a memory cell that contains the '\0' character, which represents the empty string of length 0. strcpy(lhs,rhs) performs the assignment of strings; characters in the array given by rhs are copied into the array given by lhs until the null terminator is copied. If the string represented by lhs is not large enough to store the copy, then somebody else's memory gets overwritten.

The statement

```
strcpy( lhs, rhs )
```

```
1  size_t strlen( const char *str );
2  char * strcpy(        char *lhs, const char *rhs );
3  char * strcat(        char *lhs, const char *rhs );
4  int    strcmp( const char *lhs, const char *rhs );
```

Figure 11-6   Some of the string routines in <cstring>

is meant to mimic the statement

    lhs = rhs;

The return type char * allows strcpy calls to be chained in the same way as assignments: strcpy(a,strcpy(b,c)) is much like a=b=c. strcat(lhs,rhs) appends a copy of the string represented by rhs to the end of lhs. As with strcpy, it is the programmer's responsibility to assure that lhs is pointing at sufficient memory to store the result. strcmp compares two strings and returns a negative number, zero, or a positive number, depending on whether the first string is lexicographically less than, equal to, or greater than the second. The compareTo method in java.lang.String stole this convention from C++.

C++, as described so far, provides library routines for strings, but no language support. In fact, the only language support is provided by a *string constant*. A string constant provides a shorthand mechanism for specifying a sequence of characters. It automatically includes the null terminator as an invisible last character. Any character except the null terminator (specified with an escape sequence if necessary) may sensibly appear in the string constant. Thus "Jill" represents a five-character array. Additionally, a string constant can be used as an initializer for a character array. Thus,

```
char name1[   ] = "Jill"; // name1 is an array of five char
char name2[ 9 ] = "Jill"; // name2 is an array of nine char
char name3[ 4 ] = "Jill"; // name3 is an array of four char
```

In the first case, the size of the array allocated for name1 is determined implicitly, while in the second case we have overallocated (which is necessary if we intend later to copy a longer string into name2). The third case is wrong because we have not allocated enough memory for the null terminator. Initialization by a string constant is a special exemption. We cannot say

```
char name4[ 8 ] = name1;   // ILLEGAL!
```

A string constant can be used in any place where both a string and a constant string can be used. For instance, it may be used as the second parameter to strcpy, but not as the first parameter. This is because the declaration for strcpy does not disallow the possibility that the first parameter might be altered (indeed, we know that it will). Because a string constant can be stored in read-only memory, allowing it to be used as a target of strcpy could result in a hardware error. Note carefully that we can always send a nonconstant string to a parameter that expects a constant string. Thus we have

```
strcpy( name2, "Mark" );   // LEGAL
strcpy( "Mark", name2 );   // ILLEGAL!
strcpy( name2, name1 );    // LEGAL
```

The declarations for the string routines indicate that the parameters are pointers. This follows from the fact that the name of an array is a pointer. The second parameter to strcpy is a constant string, meaning that any string can be passed and it is guaranteed to be unchanged. The first parameter is a nonconstant string and might be changed. Consequently, a constant string cannot be passed; this includes string constants.

Beginners tend to take the equivalence of arrays and pointers one step too far. Recall that the fundamental difference between an array and a pointer is that an array definition allocates enough memory to store the array, while a pointer points to memory that is allocated elsewhere. Because strings are arrays of characters, this distinction applies to strings. A common error is declaring a pointer when an array is needed. As examples, consider the declarations

```
char name[ ] = "Jill";
char *name1  = "Jill";
char *name2;
```

The first declaration allocates five bytes for `name`, initializing it to a copy of the string constant `"Jill"` (including the null terminator). The second declaration states merely that `name1` points at the zeroth character of the string constant `"Jill"`. In fact, the declaration is wrong because we are mixing pointer types: the right side is a `const char *`, while the left side is merely a `char *`. Some compilers will complain. The reason for this is that a subsequent

```
name1[ 0 ] = 'H';
```

is an attempt to alter the string constant. Since a string constant is supposed to be constant, this action should not be allowed. The easiest way for the compiler to do this is to follow the convention that if `a` is a constant array, then `a[i]` is a constant also and cannot be assigned to. If the statement

```
char *name1  = "Jill";
```

were allowed, this would be hard to enforce. By enforcing `const`-ness at each assignment, the problem becomes manageable. It is legal to use

```
const char *name1 = "Jill";
```

but that is hardly the same as declaring an array to store a copy of the actual string. Furthermore, `name1[0]='H'` is easily seen by the compiler to be illegal in this case. A common example where this would be used is

```
const char *message = "Welcome to FIU!";
```

Another common consequence of declaring a pointer instead of an array object is the statement (in which we assume that `name2` is declared as above)

```
strcpy( name2, name );
```

Here the programmer expects to copy `name` into `name2`, but is fooled because the declaration for `strcpy` indicates that two pointers are to be passed. The call fails because `name2` is just a pointer rather than a pointer to sufficient memory to hold a copy of `name`. If `name2` is a NULL pointer, points at a string constant stored in read-only memory, or points at an illegal random location, `strcpy` is certain to attempt to dereference it, generating an error. If `name2` points at a modifiable array (for instance, `name2=name` is executed), there is no problem.

All these considerations tell us that using the C++ `string` is a better option than primitive strings, in most cases, to safely hide all new uses of primitive strings inside of a `string`.

A `string` can be constructed from a `const char *`, and a `const char *` can be extracted from a `string` via the member function `c_str`. So when you are interacting with older code that expects `char *` and produces `char *`, one strategy is to create a `string` as soon as possible, do the string manipulations safely with the `string` class, extract a `const` char * by using c_str, and pass that to the older code. The return value from the older code can be immediately converted into a string. For instance, suppose there is a routine

```
const char *getenv( const char *prop );
```

that expects a primitive string and returns a primitive string. We can pass it a string prop and assign the result to a string val, as

```
string val = getenv( prop.c_str( ) );
```

making use of the automatic implicit conversion from const char * to string.

11.3 Pointer Hopping

Many programmers spend lots of time attempting to hand-optimize their code. One common myth is that pointers can be used to access arrays more quickly than the usual indexing method. While this is occasionally true and sometimes leads to better or simpler code, in this section we will show that this is not universally true (and in fact is frequently false). This is interesting for two reasons. First, it illustrates that with modern compilers, the speedups obtained by low-level optimizations often do not justify the effort that is put into them. Instead, we should concentrate our optimizations on larger algorithmic issues. Second, although the tricks that we used reflect an old way of programming, it is the basis for many constructs in the STL. So when we wonder why things in the STL are the way they are, this section provides some of the answers and also shows that STL generic algorithms can be applied to primitive arrays.

Our discussion proceeds as follows: First we look at how arithmetic applies to pointers. We have two issues to consider. First, in an expression such as *x+10 or *x++, is the operator (+ or ++) being applied to x or *x? The answer to this question is determined by normal precedence rules. In the first case, 10 is added to *x, while in the second case, the increment is applied to x (after the value of *x is used). The second issue, then, is to decide what it means to increment or apply various operations to a pointer. Then we will see an application that shows how pointer math is typically used and whether or not it is a good idea.

11.3.1 Implications of the Precedence of *, &, and []

The dereferencing operator * and the address-of operator & are grouped together in a class of prefix operators. These operators include the unary minus (-), the not operator (!), the bitwise complement operator (~), and the prefix increment and decrement operators (++ and --), as well as new, delete, and sizeof. The prefix unary operators have higher precedence than almost all other operators, except for the scope operators and the postfix operators, such as the postfix increment and decrement operators (++ and --), the function call operator (), and the array access operator []. Consequently, the only arithmetic operators that have higher precedence than a dereferencing operator are the postfix increment and decrement operators. In all of the following expressions, the operator is applied to the dereferenced value:

```
*x + 5      // Adds 5 to *x
*x == 0     // True if *x is 0
*x / *y     // Divide *x by *y
```

Notice carefully that because of precedence rules, *x++ is interpreted as *(x++), not (*x)++. The precedence of the array indexing operator tells us that if x is a pointer, all of the following operators are applied to the indexed value of x:

```
5 + x[ 0 ]     // Add x[0] and 5
0 == x[ 0 ]    // True if x[0] is 0
++x[ 0 ]       // Increment x[0]. Same as ++*x (why?)
x++[ 0 ]       // Same as *x++ (why?)
x == &x[ 0 ]   // Always true
```

In the last example, we reiterated that x always stores the memory location of x[0]. The precedence rules are convenient here because we do not need to parenthesize, as in &(x[0]).

11.3.2 What Pointer Arithmetic Means

Suppose that x and y are pointer variables. Now that we have decided on precedence rules, we need to know what the interpretation is for arithmetic performed on pointers. For instance, what does it mean to multiply x by 2? The answer in most cases is that arithmetic on pointers is totally meaningless and is therefore illegal. Most other languages allow only comparison, assignment, and dereferencing of pointers. C++ is somewhat more lenient.

Looking at the various operators, we see that none of the multiplicative operators makes sense. Therefore, a pointer may not be involved in a multiplication. Note carefully that the dereferenced value can, of course, be multiplied, and that what we are restricting is computations that involve addresses.

Equality and logical operators all make sense for pointers, so they are allowed and have obvious meanings. Two pointers are equal if they both point to NULL or they both point to the same address. Assignment by = is allowed, as we have seen, but *=, /=, and %= are disallowed. Therefore, the questionable operators are the additive operators (including +=, -=, ++, --) and the relational operators (<, <=, >=, >). To make sense, all these operators need to be viewed in the context of an array.

Figure 11-7 shows an array a, a pointer ptr, and the assignment ptr=a. The figure reinforces the idea that the value stored in a is just the memory location where the zeroth element of the array is stored and that elements of an array are guaranteed to be stored in consecutive and increasing memory locations. If the array a is an array of characters, a[1] is stored in memory location a+1 because characters use 1 byte. Thus the expression ++ptr would increase ptr by 1, which would equal the memory location of a[1].

We see from this example that adding an integer to a pointer variable can make sense in an array of characters. If a was an array of 4 byte integers, adding 1 to ptr would make only partial sense under our current interpretation. This is because ptr would not really be pointing at an integer, but somewhere in the middle, and would be misaligned, generally leading to a hardware fault. Since that interpretation would give erroneous results, C++ uses the following interpretation: ++ptr adds the size of the pointed at object to the address stored in ptr.

This interpretation carries over to other pointer operations. The expression x=&a[3] makes x point at a[3]. Parentheses are not needed, as mentioned earlier. The expression y=x+4

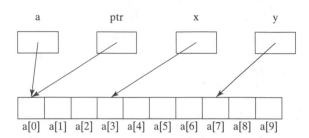

Figure 11-7   Pointer arithmetic: x=&a[3]; y=x+4;

makes y point at a[7]. We could thus use a pointer to traverse an array instead of using the usual index iteration method. We will discuss this in Sections 11.3.3 and 11.3.4.

Although it makes sense to add or subtract an integer type from a pointer type, it does not make sense to add two pointers. It does, however, make sense to subtract two pointers: y-x evaluates to 4 in the example above (since subtraction is the inverse of addition), this result is known as the *separation difference*. Thus pointers can be subtracted but not added.

Given two pointers x and y, x<y is true if the object x is pointing at is at a lower address than the object y is pointing at. Assuming that neither is pointing at NULL, this expression is almost always meaningless unless both are pointing at elements in the same array. In that case, x<y is true if x is pointing at a lower-indexed element than y because, as we have seen, the elements of an array are guaranteed to be stored in increasing and contiguous parts of memory. This is the only legitimate use of the relational operator on pointers; all other uses should be avoided. To summarize, we have the following pointer operations:

- Pointers may be assigned, compared for equality (and inequality), and dereferenced in C++, as well as almost all other languages. The operators are =, ==, !=, and *.
- We can apply the prefix or postfix increment operators to a pointer, can add an integer, and can subtract either an integer or a pointer. The operators are ++, --, +, -, +=, and -=.
- We can apply relational operators to pointers, but the result makes sense only if the pointers point to parts of the same array or one pointer points to NULL. The operators are <, <=, >, and >=.
- We can test against NULL by applying the ! operator (because the NULL pointer is 0).
- We can subscript and delete pointers via [], delete, and delete[].
- We can apply trivial operators, such as & and sizeof, to find out information about the pointer (not the object at which it is pointing).
- We can apply some other operators, such as ->.

11.3.3 A Pointer-Hopping Example

Figure 11-8 illustrates how pointers can be used to traverse arrays. We have written two versions of initialize. The first version, initialize1, uses the normal indexing mechanism to step

```
1    // initialize implemented with usual indexing mechanism
2    void initialize1( int arr[ ], int n, int val )
3    {
4        for( int i = 0; i < n; i++ )
5            arr[ i ] = val;
6    }
7
8    // initialize implemented with pointer hopping
9    void initialize2( int arr[ ], int n, int val )
10   {
11       int *endMarker = arr + n;
12       for( int *p = arr; p != endMarker; p++ )
13           *p = val;
14   }
```

Figure 11-8   Array initialization coded two ways: first by using indexing, second by using pointer hopping

through the array and is straightforward. The *pointer-hopping* version is `initialize2`. At line 11, we declare a pointer `endMarker` that is initialized to point 1 past the array portion we are trying to initialize; in STL jargon, it is the endmarker. A second pointer `p` repeatedly hops through the array initializing each entry until it hits the endmarker.

A crucial observation with respect to the discussion of the STL in Chapter 10 is that in `initialize2`, p is used to iterate over the collection of integers, and this is the basis for the selection of the particular operators such as * and ++ in the STL iterators. In particular, as we discuss in Section 11.4, this makes the generic algorithms in the Standard Library usable by primitive arrays.

11.3.4 Is Pointer Hopping Worthwhile?

Is the trickier code worth the time savings? The answer is that in most programs a few routines dominate the total running time. Historically, the use of trickier code for speed has been justified only in those routines that actually account for a significant portion of the program's running time or in routines used in enough different programs to make the optimization worthwhile. Thus in the old days, C programs that used pointer hopping judiciously had a large speed advantage over programs written in other high-level languages. However, good modern compilers can, in many cases, perform this optimization. Thus, the use of pointers to traverse arrays will help some compilers, will be neutral for others, or may even generate slower code than the typical index addressing mechanism.

The moral of the story is that, in many cases, it is best to leave minute coding details to the compiler and concentrate on the larger algorithmic issues and on writing the clearest code possible. Many systems have a *profiler* tool that will allow you to decide where a program is spending most of its running time. This will tell you where to apply algorithmic improvements, so it is important to learn how to use the optimizer and profiler on your system.

11.4 Primitive Arrays and the STL

A pointer variable that points at an array element satisfies all of the properties of a random access iterator. Thus by passing a pair of pointers, primitive arrays can be the subject of an STL generic algorithm. For instance, the two lines

```
int arr[ ] = { 3, 4, 1, 2, 5 };
sort( arr, arr + 4 );
```

sort the first four (not all five) elements of arr. This is because arr represents an iterator for the beginning of array arr, while arr+4 is an iterator that represents index 4 and since the second parameter in all STL ranges operations is an endmarker of the range, index 4 is the first item not to be included in the sort. Indeed, the iterator that is part of vector is often defined simply as a pointer variable, which helps explain why vector iterators do not have any bounds checking built in to them.

Functions such as copy work, but since primitive arrays do not have push_back operations, primitive arrays that are the target of a copy already need to have enough space to store the result.

11.5 Command-Line Arguments

In Java, command-line arguments are available in an array of strings passed as the mandatory parameter to main. In C++, we can access command-line arguments if we provide additional parameters to main. However, there are two relatively minor differences.

First, the command that invokes the executable is considered a command-line argument. Thus, the 0th command-line argument is often skipped when processing command-line arguments. Second, the command-line arguments are passed as a primitive array of primitive strings. Because primitive arrays do not know how large they are, an additional parameter, the number of command-line arguments (including the executable name) is passed.

The number of command-line arguments is the first parameter to main and is commonly named argc. The second parameter, which is an array of strings, is historically named argv. Note the type, array of char *, and this gives a typical signature of

```
int main( int argc, char *argv[ ] );
```

As an example, the echo command, shown in Figure 11-9, prints out its command-line arguments. Alternatively, we sometimes see

```
int main( int argc, char **argv );
```

making use of the fact that the array variable is simply a pointer. However,

```
int main( int argc, char argv[ ][ ] );
```

is not an acceptable alternative, because it signals, illegally, a two-dimensional array (see Section 11.6).

In addition to command-line arguments, some systems invoke C++ with *environment variables*. An environment variable can be used to indicate, for instance, the location of a directory

```
1   #include <iostream>
2   using namespace std;
3
4   int main( int argc, char *argv[ ] )
5   {
6       cout << "Invoking command: " << argv[ 0 ] << endl;
7       for( int i = 1; i < argc; i++ )
8           cout << argv[ i ] << " ";
9       cout << endl;
10
11      return 0;
12  }
```

Figure 11-9   The echo command (a little more verbose than normal)

suitable for the placement of temporary files. If a C++ program is being used as a server-side script (e.g., a script to handle submitted forms), information about the client and the request will be stored in a host of environment variables.

Environment variables are stored as a list of entries in the form name=value. The variable name is typically uppercase. Some systems provide this list as a third parameter to main. Like argv, the environment list is represented as an array of char *. The end of the environment list is marked with a NULL pointer, so an additional parameter is not needed. (This scenario could have been used for command-line arguments; the use of argc and argv is retained for backward compatibility.) Typically the environment list parameter name is envp.

The environment parameter to main is not part of the C++ standard. Some systems maintain a global variable environ, which is an equivalent representation of envp. If only one environment variable needs to be examined, that standard library provides getenv (standard header cstdlib needs to be included), which has the signature previously discussed in Section 11.2:

```
const char *getenv( const char *prop );
```

Figure 11-10 shows how we list all the environment variables, assuming that the third parameter to main is being supported.

```
1   #include <iostream>
2   using namespace std;
3
4   int main( int argc, char *argv[ ], char *envp[ ] )
5   {
6       for( int i = 0; envp[ i ] != NULL; i++ )
7           cout << envp[ i ] << endl;
8
9       return 0;
10  }
```

Figure 11-10 List of all the environment variables

11.6 Primitive Multidimensional Arrays

Sometimes arrays need to be accessed based on more than one index. A common example of this is a matrix. A *multidimensional array* is an array that is accessed by more than one index. It is allocated by specifying the size of its indices, and each element is accessed by placing each index in its own pair of brackets. As an example, the declaration

```
int m[ 2 ][ 3 ];        // x has two rows and three columns
```

defines the two-dimensional array m, with the first index ranging from 0 to 1 and the second index ranging from 0 to 2 (for a total of six objects). The compiler sets aside six memory locations for these objects.

An alternate form allows initialization, in a manner similar to Java,

```
int m[ ][ ] = { { 1, 2, 3 }, { 4, 5, 6 } };
```

which defines a two-dimensional array m, as before with 1, 2, 3 in row 0, and 4, 5, 6, in row 1.

Figure 11-11 shows the memory layout of either declaration and helps explain why using primitive multidimensional arrays is hard to do in C++. In Java, a two-dimensional array is implemented as an array of arrays. Similarly, the Matrix class in Section 7.3 is implemented as a vector of vectors. However, when a multidimensional array is created, we do not get an array of arrays. Instead we get a single array, arranged in row-major order. This means that the array elements proceed from the lowest to the highest row.

Evidently, to access m[r][c], the compiler simply accesses the item in row-major index 3*r+c. Because of this, in a multidimensional array, the compiler must always know all the dimensions of the multidimensional array, except possibly the first dimension. Thus, to declare a routine to compute the sum of all the elements in the matrix, the following code works:

```
int sum1( int m[2][3] )
{
    int totalSum = 0;
    for( int r = 0; r < 2; r++ )
        for( int c = 0; c < 3; c++ )
            totalSum += m[ r ][ c ];
    return totalSum;
}
```

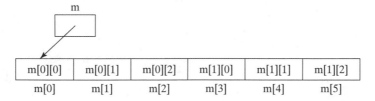

Figure 11-11 Memory layout of a multidimensional array

So does

```
int sum2( int m[ ][ 3 ], int rows )
{
    int totalSum = 0;
    for( int r = 0; r < rows; r++ )
        for( int c = 0; c < 3; c++ )
            totalSum += m[ r ][ c ];
    return totalSum;
}
```

However, this code does not work:

```
int sum3( int m[ ][ ], int rows, int cols )
{
    int totalSum = 0;
    for( int r = 0; r < rows; r++ )
        for( int c = 0; c < cols; c++ )
            totalSum += m[ r ][ c ];
    return totalSum;
}
```

Clearly, the compiler needs to know how many columns are in two-dimensional array m to do the double indexing, and this information is not available (the simple presence of a parameter named cols is hardly sufficient). If we want our routine to work for any two-dimensional array, with arbitrary numbers of rows and columns, we would have to write the nonsense

```
int sum4( int m[ ], int rows, int cols )
{
    int totalSum = 0;
    for( int r = 0; r < rows; r++ )
        for( int c = 0; c < cols; c++ )
            totalSum += m[ r * cols + c ];
    return totalSum;
}
```

and then pass &m[0][0] as a parameter, but once we do so, what's the point? We might as well declare a one-dimensional array from the start.

Although these problems can be avoided by creating a primitive array of primitive arrays, the memory management issues are even more challenging than for a single primitive array, and like one-dimensional arrays, memory management is required if we do not know the dimensions at compile time. Thus it is highly recommended that a matrix class be used.

Key Points

- Primitive arrays are represented by a pointer variable rather than a real array object.
- Heap-allocated arrays are created by invoking the array new operator, `new[]`.
- Heap-allocated arrays are reclaimed by invoking the array delete operator, `delete[]`. Do not simply invoke `delete`, because that may reclaim only the object in index 0 (if that object is itself a pointer variable).
- When a primitive array is passed as a parameter to a function, the array when viewed as an aggregate is being passed by reference.
- Primitive strings are implemented as a null-terminated array of characters.
- String copies are difficult to do correctly because there is no runtime check that the target string has enough memory to store the result (plus the null terminator).
- A common string error is simply to declare a `char*` and assume that a string is created. The `char*` has to point at memory that can store the characters.
- Avoid primitive string manipulations by using the library `string` class, the implicit conversion from `char*` to `string`, and the `c_str` member function.
- ++, when applied to a pointer variable that is pointing at an array element, advances the pointer variable to the next array element.
- Pointer hopping historically was widely used to increase program speed. Modern optimizing compilers reduce the need for pointer hopping.
- Pointers can be used as iterators for the STL generic algorithms.
- Command-line arguments are available through the `argv` parameter that can be provided to `main`. `argv` is an array of strings (`char *argv[]`) and the command itself is `argv[0]`. The number of command-line arguments is passed as the `argc` parameter to `main`.
- Environment variables can often be accessed by a third parameter to `main`.
- Avoid multidimensional arrays, which are simply stored as a flat one-dimensional array by the compiler. When a primitive multidimensional array is listed as a formal parameter, all but the first dimension must be provided.

Exercises

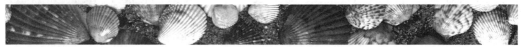

1. How are primitive arrays implemented in C++?
2. How are primitive strings implemented in C++?

3. How is a primitive array created from the memory heap?

4. How is a primitive array returned to the memory heap?

5. What is the difference between `delete[]` and `delete`?

6. What is the difference between the declarations `int a[3]` and `int *a`?

7. What happens when copying two primitive strings with = is attempted?

8. What is the result of using < on two primitive strings?

9. What is pointer hopping and why is it no longer as useful as it was in the past?

10. What is the result of adding a pointer and an integer?

11. How are command line arguments accessed in C++?

12. How are environment variables accessed in C++?

13. Write a program that reads a sequence of `doubles` into a primitive array and outputs them in sorted order. You may not use the `vector` class template.

14. Write a function that returns true if primitive string `str1` is a prefix of primitive string `str2`. Do not use any library routines.

15. Write a function that returns a `map<string,string>` that contains the environment variables.

C-Style C++

12

Chapter Outline

Because C++ is based on C and was designed to be compatible with most C programs, several C constructs that have much better C++ equivalents are still part of C++. We have already seen, for example, that C-style strings are part of the language and still are used as parameters to main. Some C constructs are required for third-party libraries that were intended to be used by C programs.

In this chapter, we describe C constructs that are commonly seen in C++ programs, particularly in older C++ code, even though better alternatives exist. These constructs include preprocessor macros, using pointers to simulate call-by-reference, and the C libraries that are part of Standard C++. Although it is a relatively rare occurrence, occasionally program speed can be improved by judiciously using C constructs in performance-critical sections of code.

12.1 Preprocessor Macros

The original C language included a phase that was executed prior to the compilation. This phase, known as the *preprocessor*, conceptually applied simple textual alterations to the input file, passing the result along to the compiler. The two most popular alterations were (and still are) the inclusion of header files, via #include, and the macro replacement of tokens via #define. The #define statement can also be used to implement parameterized macros, which look like, but are quite different from, functions. The preprocessor in current C and also C++ is now part of the compilation phase, although the apparent behavior is as if the preprocessor was executed prior to compilation.

We have already seen the preprocessor directives #include, #ifndef, and #endif. Additional preprocessor directives include #ifdef, #else, #elif, and #if, most of which are self-explanatory. Both #if and #elif can be used in code such as

```
#if !defined( __BORLANDC__ ) || __BORLANDC__ >= 0x0530
    // code for newer Borland compilers
#elif defined( __GNUC__ )
    // code for g++
#endif
```

defined is part of the preprocessor also; it returns true if the symbol has been the target of a #define. A symbol can also be undefined by using #undef.

12.1.1 Simple Textual Substitution

The most interesting (and dangerous if abused) preprocessor directive is #define. The directive

```
#define IDENTIFIER ReplacementText
```

causes the substitution of all occurrences of the token IDENTIFIER with the sequence of tokens given in ReplacementText. This form is commonly used to give symbolic meaning to constants. Typical usage is

```
#define MAX 50
```

All subsequent occurrences of MAX when seen as a separate token (characters inside a string constant do not count) are replaced by 50. Thus,

```
cout << "MAX is" << MAX << endl;
```

becomes

```
cout << "MAX is" << 50 << endl;
```

ReplacementText can be essentially anything, so theoretically, one could see uses that include variations of

```
#define FOREVER for( ; ; )
#define extends public :
```

On the other hand, simple errors in #define yield compilation errors, but the compiler will flag the error at the point of the expansion, often providing little hint that the problem was at the #define statement. For instance, the three #define statements

```
#define MAX 50;
```

```
#define MAX = 50
#define MAX 50    // the max
```

used in

```
if( i == MAX )
```

cause an expansion to, respectively,

```
if( i == 50; )
if( i == = 50 )
if( i == 50  // the max )
```

all of which have syntax errors. It's hard to get in serious trouble here, since the code doesn't compile. However, the following directive illustrates more dangerous problems:

```
#define RANGE_SIZE MAX - MIN
```

The directive is bad because if it is used in

```
int r2 = RANGE_SIZE * RANGE_SIZE;
```

the statement expands to

```
int r2 = MAX - MIN * MAX - MIN;
```

which is a problem because the precedence is wrong. This means that when using preprocessor definitions, it is important to parenthesize liberally, as in

```
#define RANGE_SIZE (MAX-MIN)
```

The use of `#define` to provide replacement text (rather than simply the fact that a symbol is defined for the ifndef/endif trick) is obsolete in C++, since symbolic constants can be declared with `const`, and textual substitution, such as replacing `:public` with `extends,` is probably bad style. It was needed in C because old C did not have a `const` and array sizes needed to be constants.

12.1.2 Parameterized Macros

Parameterized macros were used in C to avoid the overhead of function calls. For instance, rather than write a function to compute the absolute value, we define a macro

```
#define absoluteValue(x)  ( (x) >= 0 ? (x) : -(x) )
```

Of course we parenthesize liberally. There are various syntax rules. One rule is that the parenthesis that follows the macro name cannot be separated with white space, since otherwise it looks like a simple textual replacement.

Note here that the parameters are typeless, which is nice in a pretemplate world. Now, the statement

```
y = absoluteValue(a-3);
```

is expanded to

```
y = ( (a-3) >= 0 ? (a-3) : -(a-3) );
```

What happens is that the macro is expanded, with `a-3` replacing all occurrences of `x`. The macro can have several parameters. Also note the use of the `?:` operator, which seems to have been invented just for this, since substitution with a full if statement would not generate legal code.

```
1   #define printDebug( expr ) cout << __FILE__  << " [" <<    \
2        __LINE__ << "] (" << #expr << "): " << ( expr ) << endl;
3
4   int main( )
5   {
6       int x = 5, y = 7;
7
8       printDebug( x + y );
9
10      return 0;
11  }
```

Figure 12-1   Macro for debugging prints with file and line number included

Although the macro looks good here, it should not be necessary in the modern C++ world, because optimizing compilers are very good at doing this exact kind of inline optimization. They are so good at it, that whereas C++ has an inline directive, Java does not even bother, deciding that the compiler (and possibly the runtime system in the case of Java) doesn't need any hints. Other uses of the macros, such as writing a typeless routine or simulating call-by-reference (by putting the changes to the parameters in the substitution text), are better handled by templates or call-by-reference.

Not only are there better C++ alternatives to the macro, but, in general, macros are not semantically equivalent to a function call, as is demonstrated by

```
z = absoluteValue( ++a );
```

which is expanded to

```
z = ( (++a) >= 0 ? (++a) : -(++a) );
```

and produces the absolute value of a+2, and increments a twice.

There are some uses of macros that are reasonable. The `assert` mechanism is a macro. It takes advantage of some preprocessor symbols, such as __LINE__ and __FILE__, that expand to the current line number and source code file name, and the # operator that converts a parameter to a string. An example of similar macro code is shown in Figure 12-1, which uses \ to continue a line and which outputs

```
Fig12.1.cpp [8] (x + y): 12
```

Similarly, we could write a version of `assertWithException` that is similar to `assert`, but throws an exception instead of calling `abort`.

 ## 12.2 Unsafe Casts

In C, the only typecast is the Java-style cast, except that it is unchecked. Thus, as we saw in Section 6.7, to cast down an inheritance hierarchy, the `dynamic_cast` should be used. Sometimes we need to do totally bizarre casts. This is a very rare occurrence and usually means we are either writing totally bizarre code, or perhaps device drivers or other low-level code.

```
 1  void clear( char [ ] arr, int n )
 2  {
 3      int *iarr = reinterpret_cast<int *>( arr );
 4      int newn = n / sizeof( int );      // number of ints
 5      int extras = n % sizeof( int );    // extra chars leftover
 6
 7      for( int i = 0; i < newn; i++ )
 8          iarr[ i ] = 0;
 9
10      for( int j = n - extras; j < n; j++ )
11          arr[ j ] = 0;
12  }
```

Figure 12-2   Nonsense example of `reinterpret_cast`

In such a case, although the old-style cast works, it is better to use `reinterpret_cast`, since this cast stands out much more in the code. When you use a `reinterpret_cast`, all bets are off, since you are, in effect, disregarding the typing information of an object. All you can expect is that the result of a `reinterpret_cast` will have the new type with the same bits as the old. In the case of a pointer, it will be pointing at the same object, but the object will be viewed as a different type that might not make any sense at all.

Here's a poor example: We have a primitive array of `char` and we want to set all the entries to zero. We are unhappy with the compiler's performance (very unusual), so we decide to take matters into our own hands. The idea is to treat the array of `char` as an array of `int` and set the `int`s to zero. This reduces the number of assignments by a factor of 4, since typically an `int` is four `char`s. The resulting code is shown in Figure 12-2. This code is nonsense because it is unlikely to be useful in practice.

 12.3 C-Style Parameter Passing

Because C does not have call-by-reference, pointer variables are used to achieve the effect. The idea is identical to what happens in Java. Recall that in Java, when we pass to a method a reference to an object, call-by-value guarantees that the value of the reference (i.e., which object it references) cannot be changed by the method, but the method can change the state of the object.

So in C, we pass the address of an object to a function that expects a pointer to the object. Then the function can change the state of the object (by dereferencing the pointer) and we have simulated a call-by-reference. The typical idiom is shown in Figure 12-3. Here we see that function `swap3` swaps the values stored in the objects pointed at by `a` and `b`, and `main` passes the address of the two objects that are to be swapped.

We know that, in addition to call-by-reference, C++ uses call-by-constant reference to avoid the overhead that call-by-value imposes to copy large objects. Although C does not have classes, the `struct` in C can be large, especially if it stores a primitive array. Thus, `struct`s in C are almost always passed by sending the address of a `struct` to a routine that expects a pointer, putting a `const` in front if needed to signal that the `struct` is not to be altered.

```
1    void swap3( int *a, int *b )
2    {
3        int tmp = *a;
4        *a = *b;
5        *b = tmp;
6    }
7
8    int main( )
9    {
10       int x = 5, y = 7;
11
12       swap3( &x, &y );
13       cout << "x=" << x << " y=" << y << endl;
14
15       return 0;
16   }
```

Figure 12-3   Using pointers as parameters to simulate call-by-reference

Figure 12-4 shows some type declarations that C++ has inherited from C. All standard header files in C are part of C++ and are located in both the same `.h` file as in C and alternately, a file that does not end in `.h`, but starts with `c` and is in the `std` namespace.

The `tm struct` stores a host of `int`s that attempt to encapsulate a specific point in time. A `time_t` is a type that represents time; typically it is a 32 bit unsigned entity, storing the number of seconds since midnight January 1, 1970. This allows a `time_t` object to store time until roughly the year 2037.

```
1    struct tm
2    {
3       int      tm_sec;    /* seconds after the minute (0- 61) */
4       int      tm_min;    /* minutes after the hour   (0- 59) */
5       int      tm_hour;   /* hours after midnight      (0- 23) */
6       int      tm_mday;   /* day of the month          (1- 31) */
7       int      tm_mon;    /* month since January       (0- 11) */
8       int      tm_year;   /* years since 1900          (0-   ) */
9       int      tm_wday;   /* days since Sunday         (0-  6) */
10      int      tm_yday;   /* days since January 1      (0-365) */
11      int      tm_isdst;  /* daylight savings time flag       */
12   };
13
14   typedef unsigned long time_t;
15
16   /* Some functions */
17   char *asctime( const struct tm * );
18   time_t mktime( struct tm * );
```

Figure 12-4   `struct tm` as defined in `<ctime>` (and `<time.h>` for C systems)

```
1    // Find Friday the 13th birthdays for person born Oct 13, 1937
2
3    #include <ctime>
4    #include <iostream>
5    using namespace std;
6
7    int main( )
8    {
9        const int FRIDAY = 6 - 1;          // Sunday is 0, etc...
10       tm theTime = { 0 };                // Set all fields to 0
11
12       theTime.tm_mon = 10 - 1;           // January is 0, etc...
13       theTime.tm_mday = 13;              // 13th day of the month
14
15       for( int year = 1937; year < 2073; year++ )
16       {
17           theTime.tm_year = year - 1900;  // 1900 is 0, etc...
18           if( mktime( &theTime ) == -1 )
19           {
20               cerr << "mktime failed in " << year << endl;
21               continue;
22           }
23           if( theTime.tm_wday == FRIDAY )
24               cout << asctime( &theTime );
25       }
26       return 0;
27   }
```

Figure 12-5   Program to find all Friday the 13th birthdays for a friend

We see two functions in `time.h`. The function `asctime` takes a pointer to a `tm struct` and returns a primitive string that represents the time and date of the `tm struct` that is being pointed at. Note that the return type is a pointer. Looking at the documentation, we find that the returned string is static data and must be used prior to the next call to `asctime`. `mktime` takes a pointer to a `tm struct` and returns the `time_t` entity that corresponds to it or returns −1 if the `tm struct` is out of range. The `tm struct` is mutable because `mktime` also attempts to fill in fields such as `tm_wday` and `tm_yday`. Note that in both cases, the `tm` type includes the word `struct`. This is optional in C++, so we have never done it, but it is required in C. A person born on October 13, 1937 will naturally have a few birthdays fall on Friday the 13th. Figure 12-5 shows a simple program to calculate when this occurs.

12.4 C Library Routines

As we have mentioned, the C library is part of C++. This section described some of the library routines that you may run into; for most, you should run away.

12.4.1 `printf` and `scanf`

`printf` is the basic output function in C. It is surprising to see how many C++ programs still have calls to `printf`. The basic form of `printf` is

```
int printf( const char *control, val1, val2, ... );
```

The first parameter is the *control string* and is output, except that the additional parameters are substituted as appropriate into the control string in places marked by a % conversion sequence. For instance %d is used to print an integer in decimal, %o prints an integer in octal, %s prints a (primitive) string, %f prints a `float` or `double`, and %% prints a %.

The return value of `printf` is the number of characters actually written or −1 if there is an error. Hardly anybody ever bothers to check the return code. As an example,

```
int x = 5;
double y = 3.14;
printf( "x is %d, y is %f\n", x, y );
```

returns 18 (characters, newline included) and prints

```
x is 5, y is 3.14
```

After the % and before the character that specifies the type, a host of options control all of the same things that can be controlled by the `ostream` manipulators. For instance, in Figure 9-5 we had

```
out << left << setw( 15 ) << name << " "
    << right << fixed
    << setprecision( 2 ) << setw( 12 ) << salary;
```

The equivalent call to `printf` is

```
printf( "%-15s %12.2f", name, salary );
```

The most important thing to know about `printf` is that it is not type-safe. If the additional parameters do not match the conversion specifiers in the control string, you get gibberish.

Because C is not object-oriented, only the primitive types have conversion specifiers; even in C++, you cannot define new specifiers for user-defined class types, making `printf` vastly inferior to the C++ iostream library.

The C function that reads formatted input is `scanf`. The basic form is

```
int scanf( const char *control, void *obj1, void *obj2, ... );
```

The first parameter is the control string, as before, except that `double`s should use %lf instead of %f. Also, field width specifiers become maximums instead of minimums (this is useful for strings, because you want to make sure you don't read more characters than you have room for). The return value is the number of conversion specifiers that are actually matched, so if this is less than the number of conversion specifiers, something has gone wrong. As an example,

```
int x;
double y;
char name[ 100 ];
scanf( "%d %lf %99s", &x, &y, name );
```

reads an `int`, `double`, and primitive string, putting them in the objects specified, and hopefully returns 3. Note that `name` is already an address, so we don't need the &.

Like `printf`, `scanf` is not type-safe and errors are likely to result in an abnormal program termination, because pointer variables are involved. The most common mistake with `scanf` is to forget to pass an address, as in

```
scanf( "%d", x );
```

This attempts to put an integer in the memory location given by the integer stored in x. It is unlikely that this is a valid location; it certainly is not x's location.

`scanf` is a dangerous routine that has little use in a C++ program. If possible, you should replace existing calls to `print` and `scanf` with the `iostream` equivalents. You should avoid having a program use both libraries, since both libraries buffer and I/O can be interwoven unexpectedly.

Use of `printf`, `scanf`, and all file routines requires the standard header `cstdio` (or `stdio.h`).

12.4.2 File I/O

In C, file I/O is supported with the FILE* type and a set of functions. FILE is a typedef for a `struct`, and because in C `structs` have historically been passed and returned by pointers, all the I/O routines work with FILE* as the basic stream parameter. The FILE* type is used for both reading and writing. Three standard streams, `stdin`, `stdout`, and `stderr`, are already predefined as standard input, standard output, and standard error.

To use a file, we must obtain a stream for it by using `fopen`. When we are done, we close the file with `fclose`. The parameters to `fopen` are a primitive string that represents the filename and a primitive string that represents the mode. Typical modes are `"r"` for reading, `"w"` for writing, and `"a"` for appending. Also `"rb"`, `"wb"`, and `"ab"` are used for binary files on systems that distinguish between text and binary files. `fopen` returns a FILE* or NULL if there is an error. Thus the declarations for `fopen` and `fclose` are

```
FILE *fopen( const char *fileName, const char *mode );
int fclose( FILE *stream );
```

The calls `getc` and `putc` provide single-character input and output for files. Their declarations are

```
int getc( FILE *stream );
int putc( int ch, FILE *stream );
```

`getc` returns EOF if the end-of-file is seen. The return type of `getc` is an `int` for the same reason that method `java.io.Reader.read` returns an `int` that represents the `char` that has been read: A `char` is not sufficient to store all possible characters and the EOF symbol. Unfortunately, in C and C++, if the return value of `getc` is directly assigned to a `char`, the code will probably not work on files with full character sets (e.g., binary files). `putc` returns EOF if the write fails; otherwise it returns `ch`. Attempts to write on a stream open for reading or vice versa yields a bad return value, instead of the compile-time error that you get in C++.

Like `printf` and `scanf`, `fprintf` and `fscanf` can be used for formatted input and output. The first parameter is a FILE* and the remaining parameters are as described earlier.

```
1    // Copy files; return number of chars copied
2    int copy( const char *destFile, const char *sourceFile )
3    {
4        int charsCounted = 0
5        int ch;
6        FILE *sfp, *dfp;
7
8        if( strcmp( sourceFile, destFile ) == 0 )
9        {
10           fprintf( stderr, "Cannot copy to self\n" );
11           return -1;
12       }
13       if( ( sfp = fopen( sourceFile, "rb" ) ) == NULL )
14       {
15           fprintf( stderr, "Bad input file %s\n", sourceFile );
16           return -1;
17       }
18       if( ( dfp = fopen( destFile, "wb" ) ) == NULL )
19       {
20           fprintf( stderr, "Bad output file %s\n", destFile );
21           fclose( sfp );
22           return -1;
23       }
24
25       while( ( ch = getc( sfp ) ) != EOF )
26           if( putc( ch, dfp ) == EOF )
27           {
28               fprintf( stderr, "Unexpected write error.\n" );
29               break;
30           }
31           else
32               charsCounted++;
33
34       fclose( sfp );
35       fclose( dfp );
36       return charsCounted;
37   }
```

Figure 12-6   Copy files using `getc` and `putc`; return number of characters copied

Figure 12-6 shows a routine that copies from one file to another. We write it in C style, using primitive strings. Line 4 declares `charCounted` and line 5 declares `ch`, which will represent a character read by `fgetc`. Note that `ch` must have type `int`. If it is `char` and this program is applied to large binary files, the copy will most likely be short. At line 6, observe that `sfp` and `dfp` must BOTH be declared as pointer variables. The first * applies only to `sfp`. Line 8 is a simple alias test. The error messages at line 10 illustrate the use of the `stderr` stream. Lines 13 and 18 open the files as binary files. If the second open fails, we must remember to close the first file. The copying of files is performed at lines 25 to 32, and then the files are closed at lines 34 and 35. Failing to close the output file could result in some buffered data not being written out, especially if the program terminates abruptly. `fflush` can be used to force buffered data to be written out prior to closing the file.

Two similar looking functions are `fgetc` and `fputc`. Because `getc` and `putc` are preprocessor macros, they can be dangerous to use if the arguments involve side effects. In this extremely rare case, which is almost certainly poor programming practice, `fgetc` and `fputc`, which are guaranteed to be functions and not macros, can be safely used.

Another routine that is provided is `ungetc`, which allows a character to be put back onto the input stream:

```
int ungetc( int ch, FILE *stream );
```

To read and write lines at a time, we can use `fgets` and `fputs`:

```
char *fgets( char *str, int howMany, FILE *stream );
int fputs( const char *str, FILE *stream );
```

`fputs` outputs a string to an output stream. It does not supply a newline character unless one is already present. `fgets` reads characters from an input stream until one of the following three events occurs:

1. EOF is encountered.
2. A newline is encountered.
3. `howMany-1` characters are seen, before event 1 or 2 occurs.

After the characters are read, a null terminator is appended. A newline is stored only if it was encountered. `str` is returned on success; if no characters were read because of an EOF or any other error, a `NULL` pointer is returned.

As an example, suppose we want to read a large file one line at a time, using normal C++:

```
void processFile( const string & fileName )
{
    ifstream fin( fileName.c_str( ) );
    string oneLine;

    while( getline( fin, oneLine ) )
        ...
}
```

On one of our systems, processing a file of about 78 million bytes containing about 2 million lines takes about 7.5 seconds simply to do the I/O. The slowness seems to have to do with the fact that this form of `getline` deals with `strings`. However, there is a method in `istream` called `getline` that works somewhat like `fgets`, except that it does not retain the newline character.

Figure 12-7 shows a routine called `getlineFast` that uses this `getline` routine, presuming that no line is longer than `MAX_LINE_LEN`. At line 7, the call to `gcount` returns the number of characters read by `getline`. Presumably, if this count is 0, `getlineFast` should return false; otherwise, we copy the primitive string into `oneLine`. If we use `getlineFast`

```
1   bool getlineFast( istream & in, string & oneLine )
2   {
3       static const int MAX_LINE_LEN = 10000;
4       char str[ MAX_LINE_LEN + 2 ];
5
6       in.getline( str, MAX_LINE_LEN );
7       if( in.gcount( ) == 0 )
8           return false;
9
10      oneLine = str;
11      return true;
12  }
```

Figure 12-7   getlineFast: takes half the time of getline, but can fail

instead of getline, 7.5 seconds becomes 2.8 seconds! However, getlineFast only works if lines have less than MAX_LINE_LEN characters. If not, very long lines will be split into separate lines silently. Although there are some solutions available in the istream class, all of them will take longer than 2.8 seconds. It turns out that this is a great place to use fgets.

We can write a getline that takes a FILE* and then have the user create a FILE* instead of an istream. With reasonable care, we can localize these changes, so that the rest of the program doesn't have to change. Best of all, our routine will handle arbitrarily long lines and be faster than getlineFast, taking about 2.4 seconds. The additional getline is shown in Figure 12-8.

```
1   bool getline( FILE *fin, string & oneLine )
2   {
3       static const int MAX_LINE_LEN = 100;
4       char str[ MAX_LINE_LEN + 2 ];
5
6       for( oneLine.erase( ); ; oneLine += str )
7       {
8           char *result = fgets( str, MAX_LINE_LEN, fin );
9           if( result == NULL )
10              return oneLine.length( ) != 0;
11
12          int len = strlen( str );
13          if( str[ len - 1 ] == '\n' )
14          {
15              str[ len - 1 ] = '\0';
16              break;
17          }
18      }
19
20      oneLine += str;
21      return true;
22  }
```

Figure 12-8   Replacement for getline; even faster than getlineFast

```
1   void lastChars( const string & fileName, int howMany )
2   {
3       FILE *fin = fopen( fileName.c_str( ), "rb" );
4       if( fin == NULL )
5           throw io_exception( );    // made this one up
6       else if( howMany <= 0 )
7           throw invalid_argument( "howMany is negative" );
8
9       fseek( 0, SEEK_END, fin );
10      int fileSize = ftell( fin );
11      if(  fileSize < howMany )
12          howMany = fileSize;
13      fseek( -howMany, SEEK_END, fin );
14
15      int ch;
16      while( ( ch = getc( fin ) ) != EOF )
17          putc( ch, stdout );
18      if( !feof( fin ) )
19          throw io_exception( );
20  }
```

Figure 12-9   Routine that prints last howMany characters from fileName

We begin by clearing out oneLine at line 6. Note that assignment of "" to oneLine with = is significantly slower than calling erase, and since this is done on every line (2,000,000 times), this inefficiency is significant enough to be worth using erase. In the main loop, the idea is to keep calling fgets, concatenating the result to oneLine (also line 6) until we read characters that contain a terminating newline character (that test is performed at line 13). Those characters are also appended (at line 20 outside of the main loop) after the newline character is stripped out at line 15.

Other routines that are available include feof and the random access routines fseek and ftell that mimic the routines in istream, discussed in Section 9.6. (Actually the istream routines mimic these.) For fseek, the constants that specify beginning, current, and end are SEEK_SET, SEEK_CUR, and SEEK_END. The code in Figure 12-9 shows the direct correspondence between FILE* and istream routines by recoding Figure 9-7 line-for-line. (However, as we mention in Section 12.5, several aspects of this code that are legal in C++, such as exceptions, are not legal C.)

Finally, we mention sprintf and sscanf which allow printing and scanning from a primitive string. These signatures are

```
int sprintf( char *buffer, const char *control, val1, val2, ... );
int sscanf( const char *buffer, const char *control,
            void *obj1, void *obj2, ... );
```

For instance, if we have

```
int x1 = 37, x2;
double y1 = 3.14, y2;
```

```
char oneLine[ 100 ];
sprintf( oneLine, "%d %f", x1, y1 );
```

oneLine will contain "37 3.14". A subsequent

```
sscanf( oneLine, "%d %lf", &x2, &y2 );
```

populates x2 and y2 with 37 and 3.14, respectively. Note that

```
sscanf( oneLine, "%d", &x2);
sscanf( oneLine, "%lf", &y2 );
```

sets x2 to 37 and y2 to 37.0, because sscanf does not maintain a notion of previous parsing of the buffer string.

sprintf is dangerous because it is possible that buffer does not contain enough characters to hold the result. sscanf is dangerous, especially in the case where the target tokens are strings. The functionality of these functions is provided in ostringstream and istringstream, so there is little need to use them.

12.4.3 malloc, calloc, realloc, and free

In C, memory is allocated from the memory heap by calling a family of alloc functions, malloc, calloc, and realloc. The memory is released back to the memory heap by calling free. The declarations found in the standard headers cstdlib and stdlib.h are

```
void *malloc( size_t howManyBytes );
void *calloc( size_t objectSize, int numObjects );
void *realloc( void *original, size_t newSize );
void free( void *p );
```

The most important things to know about these routines are that they are not type-safe and they do not invoke constructors. Instead, they simply return a pointer to raw memory that can be cast to the appropriate type. In the case of malloc, the memory is not initialized. In the case of calloc, memory is initialized to all bits zero, but that might not be suitable for pointer types or doubles. realloc can be used to get more memory, which is initialized by using the original memory (and then freeing the original, which needs to have been heap-allocated). free returns the memory back to the heap, but does not invoke destructors.

It is important not to mix malloc and delete or new and free. Specifically, memory that was allocated by malloc should be released by free, not by delete. Memory that was allocated by new should be released by delete, not by free. Otherwise, havoc results.

C library routines that return heap-allocated memory get the memory from an alloc function. Thus their memory is returned to the heap by calling free. One such example is strdup.

12.4.4 atoi, atof, strtol, and strtod

atoi and atof are original C library routines that parse a primitive string, returning an int or a double, respectively. These routines handled errors poorly. Their replacements, strtol and strtod, which yield long and double, respectively, were added in a later version of C and do a better job. Although these are not needed in C++ since istringstream can be used to do the same thing, it is certainly possible that strtol and strtod could be more efficient than using an istringstream.

12.4.5 system

The system function, in standard header cstdlib or stdlib.h, is used to invoke a command. It takes a primitive string that represents the command; this string is passed to the operating system's command processor and is run. How this is done is highly system dependent and obviously nonportable, since few commands are available on all systems. For instance,

```
system( "dir" );
```

invokes the dir command (if one exists).

12.4.6 qsort

qsort is a generic sorting algorithm with declaration

```
void qsort( void *base, size_t numItems, size_t itemSize,
                 int cmp( const void *, const void * ) );
```

The parameters to qsort represent the following items:

1. base: the array being sorted.
2. numItems: the number of items being sorted.
3. itemSize: the size of the items being sorted.
4. cmp: a comparison function that takes pointers to two items and returns a negative number, zero, or a positive number when the first item is smaller than, equal to, or larger than the second item, respectively.

Figure 12-10 shows the call to qsort to sort an array of integers, along with the definition of an appropriate comparison function. The comparison function takes two generic pointers to the items. At line 3, we convert lhs to a pointer to a const int and then dereference it to get the int to which lhs is pointing. In C++, we would sensibly use reinterpret_cast rather than the old style, but of course in C++ we would use the STL sort algorithm in the first place.

qsort is not required to be efficient, and although it is typically implemented as quicksort, older versions are known to have deficiencies that can cause quadratic behavior on degenerate

```
1   int intCmp( const void *lhs, const void *rhs )
2   {
3       int lhint = *(const int *)lhs;
4       int rhint = *(const int *)rhs;
5       return lhint < rhint ? -1 : lhint > rhint;
6   }
7           ...
8       int arr[ ] = { 3, 5, 1, 2, 6 };
9       qsort( arr, 5, sizeof( int ), intCmp );
```

Figure 12-10 Parameters to qsort and a comparison function

inputs (such as arrays with only two unique items, repeatedly occurring randomly). Furthermore, because `qsort` is already compiled, it is unreasonable to expect any inline optimizations to be performed. So applying `qsort` on an array of `int`s is going to be significantly slower than using the STL `sort` algorithm or even any quicksort that can be found in a standard textbook.

12.4.7 Variable Number of Arguments

Some routines, such as `print` and `scanf`, require a variable number of arguments. Allowing a variable number of arguments is not a good thing for a type-safe language, which is why the feature is not part of Java. However, it has long been part of C and C++.

To declare an unspecified number of arguments, we use ellipses (. . .). The arguments can be processed by a set of macros in the standard header `stdarg.h` (or `cstdarg`). The macros are `va_start`, `va_end`, and `va_arg`. A function declares at least one fixed parameter and then uses ellipses to specify an unknown (possibly zero) number of additional parameters.

Macro `va_start` is used to initialize an object of type `va_list` with the last fixed argument. Then each call to `va_arg` returns the next argument. `va_arg` takes the `va_list` object and the type of the parameter that is expected. This type cannot be one that widens when passed as an argument; use `double`, `int`, or `unsigned int` in place of shorter alternatives such as `float` and `short`. Prior to returning, the function should call `va_end`.

As an example, the code in Figure 12-11 illustrates a function `printStrings` that prints an arbitrary number of primitive strings. At line 5, we see the ellipses used to specify additional

```
1   #include <iostream>
2   #include <cstdarg>
3   using namespace std;
4
5   void printStrings( const char *str1, ... )
6   {
7       const char *nextStr;
8       va_list argp;
9
10      cout << str1 << endl;
11      va_start( argp, str1 );
12      while( ( nextStr = va_arg( argp, const char * ) ) != NULL )
13          cout << nextStr << endl;
14
15      va_end( argp );
16  }
17
18  int main( )
19  {
20      printStrings( "This", "is", "it", (const char *) NULL );
21      return 0;
22  }
```

Figure 12-11 Illustration of variable arguments

parameters after the first. The `va_list` object is declared at line 8 and initialized at line 11. Then we repeatedly loop at lines 12 to 13, reading parameters of type `const char *`. There needs to be some way to signal the end. Alternatives include encoding this information in the first parameter (as is done in `printf` and `scanf`) or simply terminating the list with a NULL pointer. We use the second alternative. Thus we see at line 20 that the last parameter to `printStrings` is NULL. (We use a pointer for the technical reason that we want to ensure that the type is a pointer type. This would be automatic if we had a fixed parameter list, but not with variable parameter lists.) At the end, we call `va_end` at line 15.

12.5 C Programming

If you program in C instead of C++, you need to be aware that some C++ features are missing in C. The partial list, based on ANSI C (note that items 11 and 12 will behave the same in recently adopted C99 as in C++) includes:

1. C has no classes and does not even support object-based programming.
2. C has no `vector` or `string` type. You have to use pointers.
3. C has weaker type checking than C++. The compiler will catch fewer problems.
4. C does not have reference variables or call-by-reference. You will have to pass pointers to objects to simulate the effect.
5. C does not provide function overloading. Once you use a name, that's it.
6. C does not provide namespaces.
7. C does not provide operator overloading.
8. C does not have templates.
9. C does not have exceptions.
10. C does not allow default parameters to functions.
11. C requires that all local variables be declared together at the top of a function. You cannot declare variables once you have a nondeclaration statement unless you create a block.
12. C does not have the `//` comment, although some compilers support it.

Basically, what's left? Not much. It's a long way down to C from the C++ or Java world.

Key Points

- The standard C library is part of the C++ library. Header files such as `stdio.h` are available as both `stdio.h` and `cstdio`. The latter header file places all of the library in the `std` namespace; the older header file leaves the library in the global namespace.
- The preprocessor can be used to implement macros; however, macros can be dangerous if invoked with a parameter that contains side effects.

- C-style parameter passing is needed to interact with libraries that were written for C. To simulate call-by-reference or call-by-constant reference for large objects, we pass the address of the object instead of the object. The formal parameter is declared as a pointer (or a pointer to a constant).
- `printf` and `scanf` are not type-safe and their functionality is completely contained in `ostream` and `istream`.
- Files can be accessed by using `FILE*` to represent both input and output streams. Attempts to read from a file open for writing (or vice versa) results in a bad return code for the read, rather than a compile-time error. Most of the C-style I/O routines are cosmetically similar to their C++ counterparts.
- Sometimes I/O that uses `char*` instead of `string` can be more efficient. Occasionally, using `fgets` can help implement the more efficient I/O.
- Never call `free` on an object created with `new`; never call `delete` on an object created with `malloc`. Avoid using the `alloc` family because they allocate raw memory, without calling constructors, and are not type-safe.
- `strtol` and `strtod` can be used to extract a `long` or `double` (or smaller type) from a primitive string. Although `istringstream` can accomplish the same thing, it is reasonable to expect that `strtol` and `strtod` can be more efficient for this task.
- `system` can be used to invoke a system command.
- C and C++ support variable-length argument lists via the standard header `cstdarg` or `stdarg.h`.
- Programming exclusively in C requires abandoning lots of the comforts of Java and C++.

Exercises

1. Describe the basic functionality of the preprocessor.
2. What does `reinterpret_cast` do?
3. How do C programs simulate call-by-reference?
4. How do C programs pass large structures?
5. How can a function accept a variable number of arguments?
6. The majority function for booleans returns true if more than half of the parameters are true and returns false otherwise. Write the macro

   ```
   #define MAJORITY( x, y, z )
   ```

   which returns true if at least two of x, y, and z are true, and returns false otherwise.
7. Using one / and one % operator, implement the macro

   ```
   #define DIVIDE( numerator, denominator, quotient, remainder )
   ```

8. Write an iteration macro

   `#define ITERATE( i, low, high )`

   that generates the clause that directs a for loop running from `low` to `high`, inclusive.
9. Write a macro, `max4`, to find the maximum of four numbers.
10. A safe macro can be implemented by declaring a block and copying the macro parameters into block variables. Parameters thus become implicitly typed. Write the `max4` macro for `int`s as a safe macro.
11. Implement the macro

    `#define main( )`

    that prints the compilation date and time, and then starts execution of the program.
12. Write a function that takes a month, day, and year, and returns the day of the week. Implement your function by using the routines in standard header file `<ctime>`.
13. Write a program that uses `printf` to print out the following numbers in decimal, octal, and hexadecimal: 37, 037, 0x37.
14. Reimplement Exercise 9.9 using I/O routines in standard header file `<cstdio>`.
15. Reimplement Exercise 9.10 using I/O routines in standard header file `<cstdio>`.
16. Reimplement Exercise 9.11 using I/O routines in standard header file `<cstdio>`.
17. Reimplement Exercise 9.12 using I/O routines in standard header file `<cstdio>`.
18. Implement a version of `findMax` that takes a variable number of `int` arguments.

Using Java and C++: The JNI

13

Chapter Outline

A native method is a method that is implemented in another language, such as C or C++, and run in the Java Virtual Machine. The JDK provides a standard programming interface, called the Java Native Interface (JNI), that in theory allows the Virtual Machine to invoke C and C++ code somewhat portably.

247

In this chapter, we describe the Java Native Interface. We begin by explaining why one might want to implement some Java methods in an alternate language. Then we describe the basic layout of the JNI, provide an example that involves invoking a simple native method, and then write native methods that access Java objects. Finally, we briefly discuss the use of Java features, such as exceptions and object monitors in native code.

13.1 JNI Basics

A *native method* is a method that is specified in Java with the reserved word `native`, but is implemented in another language. Typically the other language is C or C++. We will use C++ in most of our examples. Using C involves slightly more syntax, but no additional concepts. We show a C example in Section 13.7. There are several common reasons to use native methods:

1. You already have significantly large and tricky code written in another language and you would rather not rewrite it in Java. Instead, you would like to use the existing code base.
2. You need to access system devices or perform some platform-specific task that is beyond the capability of Java. Many Java library routines eventually invoke private native methods for just this purpose. For instance, the I/O, threading, and networking packages all contain private native methods.
3. You think that Java might be too slow for your application and that performance can be enhanced by implementing time-critical code in C++.

Although Java used to be painfully slow, a modern Java implementation has performance that is comparable to C++ for many applications. Using JNI to achieve performance improvements is possible, but is no longer needed as much as it used to be.

Using JNI has significant downsides. First, you lose portability. A native implementation must be supplied for each platform. Given the large Java library that already makes use of native methods, if a new native method has identical C++ code that can be used on all platforms, then it is likely that the code could have been implemented in Java in the first place. Second, you lose safety. Native methods are not afforded the same protections as Java methods. Once you enter C++ code, all bets are off and any C++ bug, such as indexing an array out of bounds, using a stale pointer, and trashing memory, can occur. Third, the implementation of the native method is contained in a dynamic library (in a Windows environment, a `.dll`; in a Unix environment, a `.so` file). Any Java program that uses native methods must load dynamic libraries, and this is an operation that the Java security manager might object to, because of the safety concerns listed above. Lack of safety means lack of security, so, for instance, by default, user-defined native methods generally cannot be invoked inside an applet. Fourth, the code is cumbersome, it often compiles and often fails to run because of silly typing errors such as poor capitalization or missing semicolons inside of string constants.

Once we decide to use JNI, the basic procedure is relatively straightforward.

1. A Java class declares that some methods have non-Java implementations by marking the methods as `native`.
2. A C++ function is written that implements the native method using the JNI protocols.
3. The C++ function is compiled and placed into a dynamic library.
4. The Java Virtual Machine loads the dynamic library. Calls to the native method are handled by invoking the implementation in the dynamic library.

The devil, of course, is in the details, which are numerous, since the JNI is expected to work not only for C++, but also for C and other languages that are not object-oriented. For instance:

1. How are fields and methods of a Java object used, given that C has no classes?
2. How are parameters passed from Java to C/C++?
3. How is a value returned from C/C++?
4. What about function overloading, since C does not allow it?
5. How do we differentiate between static and nonstatic members?
6. What about strings and arrays?
7. How can the C/C++ code throw an exception and what happens if it invokes a Java method that throws an exception?

We begin our discussion by first implementing a single native method. To avoid all of the above complications, our method will be static, with no parameters and no return type, and simply print a string. Still, this is tricky, since it is the first use of various incantations that will be part of all JNI implementations. Then we will access fields and invoke methods of an object, discuss arrays and strings, have the native method return a value and throw an exception, and then quickly examine some of the JNI support for object monitors.

13.2 Implementing a Simple Parameterless, Returnless Method

We begin with the "easy" stuff. Figure 13-1 shows a class, `HelloNative`, that contains a single native method, `hello`. As we see at line 3, declaring a native method is trivial on the Java side. In the test program, at line 15, we invoke the native method, as we would any Java method.

Because the method is native, the Java Virtual Machine will look for it among the dynamic libraries that have been loaded prior to the call. Thus, at line 7, we load the library that will contain the implementation of the native method. If the dynamic library that contains the implementation of the native method has not been loaded prior to invoking the method, you will get an `UnsatisfiedLinkError`. You will also get this exception if you provide the wrong name for the library or if the library is not located in the directories specified in the Java property `java.library.path`. Because it is important that the dynamic library be loaded prior to invoking the native method, the library is typically loaded in the static initializer block of the class that declares the native method.

The code in Figure 13-1 compiles. It generates an `UnsatisfiedLinkError` because the dynamic link library does not yet exist.

```
1   class HelloNative
2   {
3       native public static void hello( );
4
5       static
6       {
7           System.loadLibrary( "HelloNative" );
8       }
9   }
10
11  class HelloNativeTest
12  {
13      public static void main( String[ ] args )
14      {
15          HelloNative.hello( );
16      }
17  }
```

Figure 13-1   Declaration of a native method

Next, we have to write the C++ code. Although the name of the method is `hello`, we cannot expect to implement a C++ function named `hello`. After all, there could be several methods named `hello` in different classes or packages, or even an overloaded `hello` (and not all languages support overloading). The JNI specifies a complex algorithm that generates a function name based on the complete class name, method name, and parameter types of the Java native method. The complete class name includes the package name if appropriate, and the parameter types are considered in the name only if there is function overloading in the same class.

Fortunately, you do not have to know what this complicated algorithm is. Instead, the `javah` utility can be used to generate a C++ header file from a Java class. Note that the Java class must already be compiled. The header file will list all of the function declarations that you must provide to implement the native methods declared in the class. In our example, we run

        javah HelloNative

The output is shown in Figure 13-2. We can see that the name of the method is `Java_HelloNative_hello`, which reflects the (default) package, class, and method name.

The C++ declaration lists two parameters. The first is a pointer to a `JNIEnv` object and will be used extensively to access fields and methods of objects. The second parameter is a `jclass` object, representing information about the `HelloNative` class. Java programmers who are familiar with the Reflection API will recognize this as being the equivalent of a `Class` object. A `jclass` object allows us to obtain information and use fields and methods for any Java class. This second parameter is passed for static methods only. For instance methods, the second parameter is a `jobject` object, representing the moral equivalent of the `this` reference. Given a `jobject`, one can always obtain the `jclass` object that represents the object's class type, and at that point, the object's fields can be manipulated and methods can be invoked. More on this is given in Section 13.4.

```
1   /* DO NOT EDIT THIS FILE - it is machine generated */
2   #include <jni.h>
3   /* Header for class HelloNative */
4
5   #ifndef _Included_HelloNative
6   #define _Included_HelloNative
7   #ifdef __cplusplus
8   extern "C" {
9   #endif
10  /*
11   * Class:      HelloNative
12   * Method:     hello
13   * Signature:  ()V
14   */
15  JNIEXPORT void JNICALL Java_HelloNative_hello( JNIEnv*, jclass );
16
17  #ifdef __cplusplus
18  }
19  #endif
20  #endif
```

Figure 13-2   Result of `javah` for `HelloNative` (yields `HelloNative.h`)

Since the native method takes no parameters, the C++ declaration lists no additional parameters after the first two. We can implement the method trivially, as shown in Figure 13-3.[1] You should make sure to include the header file generated by `javah` and to give names to the formal parameters. It is standard to name the first parameter env; the second parameter is often either `cls` or `ths`, depending on whether we are implementing a static or instance method. Do not use `class` or `this`, since these are C++ reserved words (avoid them if you are using C, too, in case you want to painlessly upgrade to C++ later on).

13.2.1 Compiling a Shared Library

All that is left to do is to compile the C++ code into a shared library. How this is done depends on your environment. Observe first that the header file has an include directive for `jni.h`. Thus it is not part of Standard C++, but instead is part of the JDK.

If the JDK is installed in directory JAVA_HOME, then the header file is in a subdirectory named `include` of JAVA_HOME. `jni.h` itself includes a second file, and this second file is found in a subdirectory of `include`. This is important, because compiler options must be provided to search for header files in these nonstandard places.

---

1. Note that printing to the standard output from a native method is a bad plan, because writing to standard output in both C++ and Java's `System.out.println` could yield intermixed output due to buffering.

```
1   #include <iostream>
2   using namespace std;
3   #include "HelloNative.h"
4
5   JNIEXPORT void JNICALL
6   Java_HelloNative_hello( JNIEnv *env, jclass cls )
7   {
8       cout << "Hello world" << endl;
9   }
```

Figure 13-3 Implementation of `HelloNative.cpp`

Under Windows, the shared library must end in `.dll`, but the extension is not part of the string passed to `System.loadLibrary`. Under Unix, the shared library must end with `.so` and begin with `lib`, but neither the extension nor prefix is part of the string passed to `System.loadLibrary`.

Using Visual Studio 6.0 or Visual Studio DotNet, we can compile the shared library into a DLL either by using a DLL project (with the include search path augmented as specified above and an option to specify the target directory for the DLL file) or by using the command-line tools. Visual Studio DotNet provides a command-line window; in Visual Studio 6.0, after opening a MS/DOS window, find and run `vcvars32.bat` to set up command-line compilation. Then command-line compilation can be used. The magic incantation for our example (all on one line, of course), assuming that the JDK is in `C:\jdk`, is

```
cl -GX /GR -IC:\jdk\include -IC:\jdk\include\win32
            HelloNative.cpp -LD -FeHelloNative.dll
```

The first two options suppress warnings about exception handling not being enabled and are not needed to compile C++ programs.

In a Unix world, we can use `g++`. For `g++`, we first compile the file into a single `.o` and then create the shared library. (We assume that `$JAVA_HOME` represents the location of the JDK.) Thus, we have two commands (of course the first two lines should be typed as one):

```
g++ -c -fPIC -I$JAVA_HOME/include
            -I$JAVA_HOME/include/linux HelloNative.cpp
g++ -shared -o libHelloNative.so HelloNative.o
```

Using `g++` on Solaris, replace `linux` with `solaris` in the first command.

If you are using the standard Sun C++ compiler, one command compiles into the shared library:

```
CC -G -I$JAVA_HOME/include -I$JAVA_HOME/include/solaris
            HelloNative.cpp -o libHelloNative.so
```

For other platforms, consult local documentation. Once we have compiled the shared library, the Java program should run as expected. If an `UnsatisfiedLinkedError` is still being reported, verify that the dynamic library is correctly named, as specified above, and that it is in a viewable directory. On Unix, make sure the dynamic library is located either in the "current directory" when the Virtual Machine is invoked or in a directory listed in environment variable LD_LIBRARY_PATH. On Windows, make sure the dynamic library is located either in the current directory when the Virtual Machine is invoked or in a directory listed in environment variable PATH.

13.3 JNI Types

The header file jni.h defines a host of types, all of which start with the letter j. Each of the eight Java primitive types has a corresponding C++ type. Thus, these types are jbyte, jshort, jint, jlong, jfloat, jdouble, jchar, and jboolean. Constants JNI_TRUE and JNI_FALSE are also defined. typedef statements are used to define these types. For instance, on a 64 bit machine, a jlong might very well be typedefed as an int. These types should be used in implementations of native methods instead of standard C++ types, such as int and double, to avoid writing code that depends on the particular representation of C++ types. The JNI also defines the type jsize, which is the equivalent of C++'s size_t, representing the type that can be used to index an array.

Two Java class types also have a C++ type. These C++ types are jstring and jobject, representing String and Object. The C++ programmer should not assume any underlying implementation of jstring; specifically, routines are provided to create a char * from a jstring object, and the char * can then be manipulated. Similarly, a jstring can be created from a const char * by invoking a JNI routine. Array objects in Java are represented by corresponding C++ JNI types. These types include arrays of all types of primitives, such as jintArray and also an array of class types, jobjectArray. As was the case with strings, routines are provided to create a jint * from a jintArray object. However, as we discuss in Section 13.5.2, we cannot create a jobject * from a jobjectArray.

Finally, two objects are used to represent information about a method and a field. These are jmethodId and jfieldID, which are the moral equivalents of Method and Field in the Reflection API.

13.4 Accessing Java Objects

To see how Java objects can be manipulated by native code, we provide a Date class in Figure 13-4 that is completely implemented except for a single method, printDate. Of course, printDate could easily be implemented in Java too, but instead, we have declared it as native.

Clearly an implementation of instance method printDate requires access to either the instance data or, possibly, an invocation of some of the Date instance methods. In this section we provide three implementations of printDate. The first implementation accesses the data members. The second implementation invokes the three accessors, getMonth, getDay, and getYear. The third implementation invokes the toString method and illustrates how a C-style string is extracted from a jstring. The test program that we use is shown in Figure 13-5, for completeness.

```
1   class Date
2   {
3       public Date( int m, int d, int y )
4         { month = m; day = d; year = y; }
5
6       static
7       {
8           System.loadLibrary( "Date" );
9       }
10
11      native public void printDate( );
12
13      public int getMonth( )
14        { return month; }
15      public int getDay( )
16        { return day; }
17      public int getYear( )
18        { return year; }
19
20      public String toString( )
21        { return month + "/" + day + "/" + year; }
22
23      private int month;
24      private int day;
25      private int year;
26  }
```

Figure 13-4   Date class with a native method for `printDate`

13.4.1 Accessing Fields

Figure 13-6 shows the header file that is obtained as a result of running `javah` on class `Date`. Observe that the second parameter at line 15 is of type `jobject`, signalling that we are implementing an instance method.

To access fields of a `jobject`, we need to follow the following steps:

1. Obtain a `jclass` that represents the class information for the object.
2. Obtain a `jfieldID` that represents field information for a particular field in the `jclass`. To do this, we need to know that name of the field and its type.
3. Invoke a get method, passing a `jfieldID` and the `jobject` to obtain the field for a particular object.

The trickiest step in the process is obtaining the `jfieldID`. The name of the field is easy enough, but the type is difficult, because it can be any arbitrary type, such as array of some other class type. Once again, JNI specifies a coding mechanism for types and also for method signatures. Although the algorithm is relatively short, it can be tedious to do by hand. Fortunately,

```
1   class TestDate
2   {
3       public static void main( String[ ] args )
4       {
5           Date d = new Date( 8, 23, 2003 );
6           d.printDate( );
7       }
8   }
```

Figure 13-5   Test program for Date class

Java provides a program to generate all the field types and method signatures for you. To do so, invoke javap with the name of the class in which you are interested. Once again, the class must already have been compiled. javap requires two options to get the complete listing, so the command for our example is

    javap -s -private Date

The output of javap is shown in Figure 13-7. As we can see, int is represented as I. On the other hand, String is Ljava/lang/String;, and omitting the L or the ; will give incomprehensible runtime errors. Thus it is best to use javap.

   The signature of a method is given by an open parenthesis, followed by a concatenated list of parameter type encodings, followed by a close parenthesis, and an encoding for the return type. Thus getYear is ()I, printDate is ()V (void return type), and toString is ()Ljava/lang/String;. Arrays of String are encoded as [Ljava/lang/String;.

```
1   /* DO NOT EDIT THIS FILE - it is machine generated */
2   #include <jni.h>
3   /* Header for class Date */
4
5   #ifndef _Included_Date
6   #define _Included_Date
7   #ifdef __cplusplus
8   extern "C" {
9   #endif
10  /*
11   * Class:      Date
12   * Method:     printDate
13   * Signature: ()V
14   */
15  JNIEXPORT void JNICALL Java_Date_printDate( JNIEnv *, jobject );
16
17  #ifdef __cplusplus
18  }
19  #endif
20  #endif
```

Figure 13-6   Date.h generated by javah

```
1   class Date extends java.lang.Object {
2       private int month;
3           /*    I    */
4       private int day;
5           /*    I    */
6       private int year;
7           /*    I    */
8       static {};
9           /*    ()V    */
10      public Date(int,int,int);
11          /*    (III)V    */
12      public int getDay();
13          /*    ()I    */
14      public int getMonth();
15          /*    ()I    */
16      public int getYear();
17          /*    ()I    */
18      public native void printDate();
19          /*    ()V    */
20      public java.lang.String toString();
21          /*    ()Ljava/lang/String;    */
22  }
```

Figure 13-7   Result of running `javap -s -private` on class `Date`

With these preliminaries out of the way, Figure 13-8 illustrates the native implementation of `printDate` that accesses the `Date` fields. The coding is straightforward, albeit torturous.

At line 8, we get the `jclass` entity that represents `ths`. This contains information about class `Date`. Throughout the code, we see invocation of member functions in `JNIEnv`. We call these the *environment member functions*. Almost every function that is provided by the JNI is invoked the same way, through the `env` pointer. Once we have a `jclass`, we can get `jfieldID`s for the three data fields at lines 10 to 12 by calling `GetFieldID`, passing the class, field name, and field type. Then at lines 14 to 16, we can access the field of an object by specifying the object and the `jfieldID`. Finally, we can print the date at line 18.

There are a host of `GetXXXField` methods for each of the eight primitive types and also `GetObjectField` for `Object`. Strings are accessed by `GetObjectField` and then downcast to a `jstring`. At that point, the `jstring` is manipulated using the technique we will discuss in Section 13.5. Fields (even final fields!) can also have their values changed by invoking `SetXXXField` methods.

Static fields are treated differently from instance fields. We use `GetStaticFieldID` instead of `GetFieldID` and we call `GetStaticXXXField`, passing a `jclass` entity `cls` instead of the `jobject` entity `ths`. This is needed because some languages, such as C, do not support overloading, so they cannot have identically named functions where one accepts a `jclass` and the other accepts a `jobject`. Similarly, `SetStaticXXXField` changes the value of a static field.

```
1   #include "Date.h"
2   #include <iostream>
3   using namespace std;
4
5   JNIEXPORT void JNICALL
6   Java_Date_printDate( JNIEnv * env, jobject ths )
7   {
8       jclass cls = env->GetObjectClass( ths );
9
10      jfieldID monthID = env->GetFieldID( cls, "month", "I" );
11      jfieldID dayID =   env->GetFieldID( cls, "day", "I" );
12      jfieldID yearID =  env->GetFieldID( cls, "year", "I" );
13
14      jint m = env->GetIntField( ths, monthID );
15      jint d = env->GetIntField( ths, dayID );
16      jint y = env->GetIntField( ths, yearID );
17
18      cout << m << "/" << d << "/" << y << endl;
19  }
```

Figure 13-8   Implementation #1 of `printDate`: access fields

We remark that accessing `String` fields is done with `GetObjectField`, and the resulting `jobject` must be typecast to a `jstring`. In modern C++, one would expect that this could be done with `dynamic_cast`. However, to save space, in C++, `jobject` does not declare any virtual methods, so `dynamic_cast` does not work. An alternate is to use `reinterpret_cast`, but we will use the old-style cast, mostly to avoid excessive typing in these examples.

13.4.2 Invoking Methods

Invoking a method is done in a manner that is similar to accessing (or setting) fields. First, we need the `jclass` entity that represents the class of which the method is part. Then we get a `jmethodID`, representing the method. To obtain a `jmethodID`, we need the `jclass` entity, the name of the method, and the signature. Thus, this step is logically the same as obtaining a `jfieldID`. Finally, we can invoke the method. As in the case of the `GetXXXField` methods, there are a host of different versions of functions to invoke methods,

```
XXX CallXXXMethod( jobject ths, jmethodID m, ... );
XXX CallStaticXXXMethod( jclass cls, jmethodID m, ... );
```

where `...` represents the parameters to the method. In these calls, XXX represents the (Java) return type of the method.

Figure 13-9 provides our second implementation of `printDate` and shows how instance methods are invoked. As before, we get a `jclass` entity. Then at lines 11 to 13, we obtain the `jmethodID`s for each of the methods that we want to invoke (the `jmethodID` variable declarations are all together on line 9 simply to avoid making lines 11 to 13 too long). Once we have the `jmethodID`s, we can use them to invoke the method, as shown at lines 15 to 17. As with

```
1   #include "Date.h"
2   #include <iostream>
3   using namespace std;
4
5   JNIEXPORT void JNICALL
6   Java_Date_printDate( JNIEnv * env, jobject ths )
7   {
8       jclass cls = env->GetObjectClass( ths );
9       jmethodID getMonthID, getDayID, getYearID;
10
11      getMonthID = env->GetMethodID( cls, "getMonth", "()I" );
12      getDayID   = env->GetMethodID( cls, "getDay", "()I" );
13      getYearID  = env->GetMethodID( cls, "getYear", "()I" );
14
15      jint m = env->CallIntMethod( ths, getMonthID );
16      jint d = env->CallIntMethod( ths, getDayID );
17      jint y = env->CallIntMethod( ths, getYearID );
18
19      cout << m << "/" << d << "/" << y << endl;
20  }
```

Figure 13-9   Implementation #2 of `printDate`: invoke instance methods

accessing instance fields, the first parameter is the object on which the method is to be invoked. If this method took additional parameters, they would follow the `jmethodID`s in the parameter list.

Invocation of `CallXXXMethod` uses dynamic dispatch. An alternative is

```
XXX CallNonvirtualXXXMethod( jobject ths, jmethodID m, ... );
```

that does not use dynamic dispatch, but that is hardly ever something you would want to do.

13.4.3 Invoking Constructors

A constructor can be invoked by using environment method `NewObject` and passing the `jclass`, `jmethodID`, and parameters. If you already have a `jclass` entity, you can get a `jclass` by invoking `FindClass`, passing the name. The `jmethodID` uses `"<init>"` as the name of the method. As an example, to create a `Date` inside of a native method, use

```
jclass dateClass = env->FindClass( "Date" );
jmethodID ctor = env->GetMethodID( dateClass, "<init>", "(III)V" );
jobject d1 = env->NewObject( dateClass, ctor, 8, 23, 2004 );
```

 ## 13.5 Strings and Arrays

The `jstring` and various array objects such as `jintArray` cannot be used directly by C++ code. Instead, environment functions must be used to create a primitive string or array from the appropriate JNI type. Once this is done, we must remember to release the memory prior to returning. Strings and arrays behave similarly, so we discuss strings first.

13.5.1 Strings

To obtain a primitive `const char *` from a `jstring`, we invoke environment function `GetStringUTFChars`. The parameters to `GetStringUTFChars` are the `jstring` and the address of a `jboolean` variable. If this address is not NULL, the Boolean variable will be set to true if the `char *` is a copy of the original (which is to be expected, since Java uses 16 bit Unicode and the `char *` is an 8 bit UTF) and set to false if somehow a copy was not made. Since it rarely matters whether or not a copy was made, usually NULL is passed as a second parameter.

When we are done with the `const char *` that has been produced by `GetStringUTFChars` by allocation from the memory heap, we must release it by invoking `ReleaseStringUTFChars`. Failure to do so leads to a memory leak.

Figure 13-10, which is our third implementation of `printDate`, illustrates how we can access a `String`. Here `printDate` invokes the `toString` method, extracts the primitive string from the `jstring` that is returned by `toString`, and then prints it. Lines 10 and 11 get the `jmethodID` for `toString` and then lines 13 and 14 invoke the method (again with the old-style cast, to save typing). Simply printing the `jstring` does not work. If we try it on a Windows platform, we get 008D9E3C; other nonsense is produced on Unix machines. In fact, we are lucky not to crash the Virtual Machine. Instead, at line 16 we get a null-terminated primitive string, print it, and then free the C-style string at line 18.

A new `jstring` object can be created (mostly for the purposes of returning it) by invoking `NewStringUTF`. As an example, the code in Figure 13-11 shows a routine that implements a string concatenation in native code. Once again, this is a silly example, but it illustrates the syntax.

```
1   #include "Date.h"
2   #include <iostream>
3   using namespace std;
4
5   JNIEXPORT void JNICALL
6   Java_Date_printDate( JNIEnv * env, jobject ths )
7   {
8       jclass cls = env->GetObjectClass( ths );
9
10      jmethodID toStringID = env->GetMethodID( cls, "toString",
11                                       "()Ljava/lang/String;" );
12
13      jstring str = (jstring) env->CallObjectMethod( ths,
14                                               toStringID );
15
16      const char *c_ret = env->GetStringUTFChars( str, NULL );
17      cout << "(calling toString) " << c_ret << endl;
18      env->ReleaseStringUTFChars( str, c_ret );
19  }
```

Figure 13-10 Implementation #3 of `printDate`: invoke `toString` method

```
1   JNIEXPORT jstring JNICALL Java_StringAdd_add
2     ( JNIEnv *env, jclass cls, jstring a, jstring b )
3   {
4       const char *a1 = env->GetStringUTFChars( a, NULL );
5       const char *b1 = env->GetStringUTFChars( b, NULL );
6       char *c = new char[ strlen( a1 ) + strlen( b1 ) + 1 ];
7
8       strcpy( c, a1 );
9       strcat( c, b1 );
10      jstring result = env->NewStringUTF( c );
11
12      env->ReleaseStringUTFChars( a, a1 );
13      env->ReleaseStringUTFChars( b, b1 );
14      delete [] c;
15
16      return result;
17  }
```

Figure 13-11 Using strings (primitive style) for the static native method `StringAdd.add`

As we can see by lines 1 and 2, we are implementing method `add` in class `StringAdd`. This is a static method, since the second parameter is a `jclass`. The two parameters are both `String`, and the return type is `String`. At lines 4 and 5, we obtain the UTF strings, and at line 6, we allocate an array that will store the result of the concatenation. The +1 is needed to provide space for the null terminator. At lines 8 and 9, we compute the result of concatenation by first copying `a1` to `c` and then appending `b1` to `c`. Then we call `NewStringUTF` at line 10 to form a `jstring` that can be returned at line 16. Prior to returning, we must clean up memory. Lines 12 and 13 show the calls to `ReleaseStringUTFChars`, and line 14 cleans up the call to `new[]` with a matching `delete[]`.

A cleaner alternate that avoids the calls to `new[]` and `delete[]` by using the C++ `string` library type is shown in Figure 13-12.

13.5.2 Arrays

The JNI defines eight array types for the primitives. A typical example is `jintArray`. Additionally, `jobjectArray` is used to represent an array of `Object`. The environment function `GetArrayLength` can be used to get the length of any array object, passed as a parameter. To access individual items in the array, we have to use one strategy for primitives and another for objects.

To access an array of primitive types, we can obtain a primitive array using the same idioms as were seen for strings. As an example, Figure 13-13 declares a native method, `sum`, that returns the sum of the elements in an array of `double`. It also contains a test program.

When we run `javah`, we obtain the header file shown in Figure 13-14. There we see that the `double[]` parameter in the Java native declarations becomes a `jdoubleArray`. Implementation of `sum` is shown in Figure 13-15. The sum is declared as a `jdouble` (rather than a `double`) and is initialized at line 6. At line 7, we obtain the length of the array by calling `GetArrayLength`.

```
1    JNIEXPORT jstring JNICALL Java_StringAdd_add
2      ( JNIEnv *env, jclass cls, jstring a, jstring b )
3    {
4        const char *a1 = env->GetStringUTFChars( a, NULL );
5        const char *b1 = env->GetStringUTFChars( b, NULL );
6
7        string c = a1;
8        c += b1;
9        jstring result = env->NewStringUTF( c.c_str( ) );
10
11       env->ReleaseStringUTFChars( a, a1 );
12       env->ReleaseStringUTFChars( b, b1 );
13
14       return result;
15   }
```

Figure 13-12 Using the C++ string library for the static native method `StringAdd.add`

Line 10 gets a C-style array from the `jdoubleArray`. As was the case with strings, this array could be a copy or it could be the original, depending mostly on the implementation of the Virtual Machine. With arrays, if `double` and `jdouble` have identical representations and if the Java array is stored contiguously (which is not guaranteed, since the garbage collector may elect to move parts of the array to reduce fragmentation), then it is possible that the pointer variable is actually pointing to the memory that stores the original `double[]` inside the virtual machine. In such a case, no copy is made. However, once this pointer is handed out, the garbage collector cannot safely move parts of the array without invalidating the pointer. Thus, if no copy is made, the original array is *pinned* and cannot relocate until the pointer is released.

```
1    class NativeSumDemo
2    {
3        native public static double sum( double [ ] arr );
4
5        static
6        {
7            System.loadLibrary( "Sum" );
8        }
9
10       public static void main( String [ ] args )
11       {
12           double [ ] arr = { 3.0, 6.5, 7.5, 9.5 };
13           System.out.println( sum( arr ) );
14       }
15   }
```

Figure 13-13 Declaration of a native method that accepts an array as a parameter

```
1   /* DO NOT EDIT THIS FILE - it is machine generated */
2   #include <jni.h>
3   /* Header for class NativeSumDemo */
4
5   #ifndef _Included_NativeSumDemo
6   #define _Included_NativeSumDemo
7   #ifdef __cplusplus
8   extern "C" {
9   #endif
10  /*
11   * Class:     NativeSumDemo
12   * Method:    sum
13   * Signature: ([D)D
14   */
15  JNIEXPORT jdouble JNICALL Java_NativeSumDemo_sum
16    (JNIEnv *, jclass, jdoubleArray);
17
18  #ifdef __cplusplus
19  }
20  #endif
21  #endif
```

Figure 13-14 Result of `javah` for `NativeSumDemo` (yields `NativeSumDemo.h`)

Once we have the C-style array, we can compute its sum. Prior to returning, we must release the array, as shown at line 16. When we were working with strings, releasing the string returned the memory back to the system. With arrays, there are two independent issues.

```
1   #include "NativeSumDemo.h"
2
3   JNIEXPORT jdouble JNICALL Java_NativeSumDemo_sum
4     ( JNIEanv *env, jclass cls, jdoubleArray arr )
5   {
6       jdouble sum = 0;
7       jsize len = env->GetArrayLength( arr );
8
9         // Get the elements; don't care to know if copied or not
10      jdouble *a = env->GetDoubleArrayElements( arr, NULL );
11
12      for( jsize i = 0; i < len; i++ )
13          sum += a[ i ];
14
15        // Release elements; no need to flush back
16      env->ReleaseDoubleArrayElements( arr, a, JNI_ABORT );
17
18      return sum;
19  }
```

Figure 13-15 Implementation of `NativeSumDemo.sum` native method

First, if the array is a copy, we must copy any changes back to the original; otherwise, they are not reflected. Second, if the array is a copy, we must have memory reclaimed. As a result, the last parameter to `ReleaseXXXArrayElements` can be either 0, `JNI_COMMIT`, or `JNI_ABORT`. If the parameter is 0, we flush the contents back to the original, thus reflecting all changes, and then reclaim the memory if needed. `JNI_COMMIT` flushes the contents, but does not reclaim the memory. This can be useful if changes need to be reflected immediately, but would not be needed if no copy was made (hence the second parameter to `GetXXXArrayElements` could be useful to decide if this call should be made). `JNI_ABORT` does not flush the contents, but reclaims the memory if needed. `JNI_ABORT` would be useful if no changes were made to the array, because then we would avoid the flushing that would be done with a parameter of 0. In fact, this is exactly the case we have, so we call `ReleaseXXXArrayElements` with `JNI_ABORT` as the parameter.

Accessing elements in a `jobjectArray` is more difficult because we cannot obtain the C-style equivalent. Instead, we must call

```
GetObjectArrayElement( array, idx );
SetObjectArrayElement( array, idx, val );
```

through the `env` pointer. Clearly this makes accessing arrays of objects fairly slow.

New arrays can be created by using

```
NewObjectArray( jclass cls, int len, jobject default );
NewXXXArray( int len, XXX default );
```

through the `env` pointer; the return type is the appropriate `jarray` type.

13.6 Using Java Exceptions

Java exceptions come into play in two basic ways.

First, the native method might have a throws list, so that the native code can "throw" an exception if things go wrong. So how does a native method throw an exception?

Second, the native method might call a Java method, and the Java method throws an exception. Can the native method determine that an exception has occurred and either handle it or let it propagate cleanly?

Both problems have relatively simple solutions in the JNI. Keep in mind that we cannot assume that the target language has support for exceptions. In fact, C does not, and although C++ has exceptions, the exception handling mechanism in C++ is not currently compatible with Java exceptions.

Instead, an exception is signalled in native code simply by setting a flag. If a native method calls a Java method and the Java method throws an exception, then when the Java method returns back to the native method, and then by invoking an environment function `ExceptionOccurred`, the native method can determine if an exception is pending. If so, it can either return, in which case the Virtual Machine will propagate the exception, or it can call `ExceptionClear` to clear the exception, if it has a reasonable way of handling it.

The first case is most typical, resulting in code such as

```
    ...
jthrowable e = env->ExceptionOccurred( );
if( e != NULL )
    return;    // give up
    ...
```

If the native code does neither and, instead, continues executing native code, even though an exception is pending, then the behavior when other environment functions are called is undefined and dangerous.

If the native method needs to throw an exception on its own, then it can do so using the environment functions Throw or ThrowNew. The result of calling either function is that an exception is now pending; however, as before, the pending exception does not terminate the native method. Instead, a return statement should immediately follow and certainly other environment functions should not be called. So if it is important to release array elements, do so before invoking Throw or ThrowNew.

ThrowNew is much easier to use than Throw because you can simply give the complete name of the exception class and the parameter that is passed to its constructor. We illustrate how a native method can throw an exception in Figure 13-16, which provides a main, and Figure 13-17, which implements the native method itself.

```
 1   class NativeSumDemo
 2   {
 3       native public static double sum( double [] arr )
 4                                               throws Exception;
 5
 6       static
 7       {
 8           System.loadLibrary( "Sum" );
 9       }
10
11       public static void main( String[] args )
12       {
13           double [ ] arr1 = { 3.0, 6.5, 7.5, 9.5 };
14           double [ ] arr2 = { };
15
16           try
17           {
18               System.out.println( sum( arr1 ) );
19               System.out.println( sum( arr2 ) );
20           }
21           catch( Exception e )
22           {
23               System.out.println( "Caught the exception!" );
24               e.printStackTrace( );
25           }
26       }
27   }
```

Figure 13-16 Same main that illustrates an exception being thrown by a native call

```
1    #include <iostream>
2    using namespace std;
3
4    #include "NativeSumDemo.h"
5
6    JNIEXPORT jdouble JNICALL Java_NativeSumDemo_sum
7      ( JNIEnv *env, jclass cls, jdoubleArray arr)
8    {
9        jdouble sum = 0;
10       jsize len = env->GetArrayLength( arr );
11
12       if( len == 0 )
13       {
14           env->ThrowNew( env->FindClass( "java/lang/Exception" ),
15                                           "Empty array" );
16           cout << "Throwing an exception, but should exit" << endl;
17           return 0.0;
18       }
19
20       // Get the elements; don't care to know if copied or not
21       jdouble *a = env->GetDoubleArrayElements( arr, NULL );
22
23       for( jsize i = 0; i < len; i++ )
24           sum += a[ i ];
25
26       // Release elements; no need to flush back
27       env->ReleaseDoubleArrayElements( arr, a, JNI_ABORT );
28
29       return sum;
30   }
```

Figure 13-17 Implementation of `NativeSumDemo.sum` native method that throws an exception

In Figure 13-16, we see that the method `sum` might throw an `Exception`; the exception is thrown if the array has length 0. (This is terrible style; a better exception should be used, in general. However, using `Exception` illustrates a point as we will see when the native method is implemented.) Note also that the library loaded at line 8 is `Sum`, rather than `NativeSumDemo`. When you compile the example, make sure the appropriate link library is created. The rest of the code is standard fare and we expect that the second call to `sum` triggers the catch block.

Figure 13-17 illustrates the implementation of the native method. First, note that the throws list declared in Java is not part of the native function name at line 6. The additional code at lines 12 to 18 shows the test for the case of a zero-length array. When this test succeeds, a new exception is created and marked as pending at lines 14 and 15 by the call to `ThrowNew`. Note that the name of the exception must reflect the complete class name, including package name.

However, `ThrowNew` does not cause an immediate return, so the print statement at line 16 will be executed.

The return value at line 17 is required to avoid warnings from the C++ compiler, but is never used by the caller, because the return immediately causes the Virtual Machine to throw a Java exception.

 ## 13.7 Using C Instead of C++

All of our examples use C++, but C can be used with only minor cosmetic changes. There are two main differences. Probably most importantly, you must code in C. See Section 12.5 for reasons why this is a big deal; in part, you will have a harder time dealing with memory and you must declare all your local variables up front, instead of at first use.

The JNI difference is that all environment functions of the form

```
env->EnvFunction( ... );
```

are rewritten as

```
(*env)->EnvFunction( env, ... );
```

which does get ugly after a while, but is a relatively minor difference. Finally, make sure you place your source code in a `.c` file, since many C compilers also compile C++ code and make their decisions based on the suffix of the source file name.

Figure 13-18 shows a C implementation of the `add` method in class `StringAdd` that was previously written in Figure 13-11. The difference is mostly cosmetic.

```
1   JNIEXPORT jstring JNICALL Java_StringAdd_add
2     ( JNIEnv *env, jclass cls, jstring a, jstring b )
3   {
4       const char *a1 = (*env)->GetStringUTFChars( env, a, NULL );
5       const char *b1 = (*env)->GetStringUTFChars( env, b, NULL );
6       char *c = (char *) malloc( strlen(a1) + strlen(b1) + 1 );
7       jstring result;
8
9       strcpy( c, a1 );
10      strcat( c, b1 );
11      result = (*env)->NewStringUTF( env, c );
12
13      (*env)->ReleaseStringUTFChars( env, a, a1 );
14      (*env)->ReleaseStringUTFChars( env, b, b1 );
15      free( c );
16
17      return result;
18  }
```

Figure 13-18 Using C to implement a native method

13.8 JNI References

Data types such as `jobject`, `jclass`, `jstring`, `jmethodID`, and `jclassID`, and the array types all represent references to Java objects (whereas `jint`, `jdouble`, etc. do not). When these references are created, they are called *local references* and are valid under the following circumstances:

1. Only in the thread in which the native method is invoked.
2. Only for the duration of the native method.

This means that you cannot cache local references or pass them to other threads. If you do so and try to use them later on, you may find that the garbage collector has reclaimed the objects.

A *global reference* is a wrapper around a local reference. Unlike local references, global references are valid across multiple threads and multiple native calls, until a call to `DeleteGlobalRef`. If there is no call to `DeleteGlobalRef`, the global reference is valid for the entire duration of the Virtual Machine, which could be a problem for general objects and arrays, but is probably reasonable behavior for `jclass` references.

From this discussion, we also know that local references are valid for the duration of the native method call. However, if the native method makes a time-consuming function call, it might be worth releasing local references prior to making the function call. Alternatively, if the native method call creates many local references to large objects, it might be prudent to release some of the references when they are no longer needed. As an example, if we are iterating through a `jobjectArray`, each call to `GetObjectArrayElement` creates a `jobject`. It may be worth reclaiming it as we advance to the next array element. This is done with `DeleteLocalRef`. Figure 13-19 illustrates this with an example in a native routine that counts the total string length in an array of strings. We use `DeleteLocalRef` after accessing each string and prior to proceeding to the next string. Depending on the underlying implementation of the JNI, the number of strings, and the size of the string objects, this could help performance or simply have no noticeable effect.

 ## 13.9 Java Monitors

If a native method is declared as `synchronized`, then the usual monitor [`this` for instance methods; `getClass()` for static methods] is obtained prior to its invocation and released on its return. If the method is not synchronized or is insufficiently synchronized, you may need to obtain a monitor. The environment functions `MonitorEnter` and `MonitorExit`, which take a `jobject` can be used to delimit a synchronized block in native code. Thus

```
env->MonitorEnter( obj );
    /* synchronized block */
env->MonitorExit( obj );
```

is equivalent to

```
synchronized( obj )
{
    /* synchronized block */
}
```

```
1   JNIEXPORT jint JNICALL Java_StringStuff_totalChars
2     ( JNIEnv *env, jclass cls, jobjectArray arr )
3   {
4       jint totalChars = 0;
5       jsize len = env->GetArrayLength( arr );
6
7       for( jint i = 0; i < len; i++ )
8       {
9           jstring jstr = (jstring)
10                          env->GetObjectArrayElement( arr, i );
11          if( jstr == NULL )
12              continue;
13          const char *cstr = env->GetStringUTFChars( jstr, NULL );
14          totalChars += strlen( cstr );
15
16          env->ReleaseStringUTFChars( jstr, cstr );
17          env->DeleteLocalRef( jstr );
18      }
19
20      return totalChars;
21  }
```

Figure 13-19 Illustration of `DeleteLocalRef`

Don't forget to invoke `MonitorExit`. Although there are no environment functions to invoke `wait` and `notifyAll`, these can be called by obtaining a `jmethodID` and calling the appropriate function using the normal JNI mechanism.

13.10 Invocation API

The Invocation API allows the C++ programmer to create a Virtual Machine from inside a C++ program. Once the Virtual Machine is created, the normal mechanism can be used to invoke the `main` method of any class.

The code to do so is boilerplate and is shown in Figure 13-20. Clearly it can be generalized to allow any class and to allow command-line arguments to `main`. The hard part of this code is the compilation. In short, in addition to providing options to specify the include directories, you must make sure that library `jvm.lib` (for Windows) or `jvm` (for Unix) is used in the compilation. For Unix this involves using two options: `-L` to specify the search path for libraries and `-l` to specify the library itself. Using the Visual Studio products, the complete library name is included with the compilation command, and the `PATH` environment variable is set to include that hotspot compiler `C:\jdk\jre\bin\hotspot`. The online code contains more specific compilation instructions.

```
1    // Invoke the main method of Hello
2    #include <iostream>
3    #include <jni.h>
4    using namespace std;
5
6    const char *CLASS_NAME = "Hello";
7
8    int main( int argc, char *argv[] )
9    {
10       JavaVMInitArgs vm_args;
11       JavaVMOption options[ 1 ];
12       JavaVM *vm;
13       JNIEnv *env;
14
15       options[ 0 ].optionString = "-Djava.class.path=.";
16       vm_args.options = options;
17       vm_args.nOptions = 1;
18       vm_args.version = JNI_VERSION_1_2;
19
20       int res = JNI_CreateJavaVM( &vm, (void **)&env, &vm_args );
21       if( res < 0 )
22       {
23           cerr << "Failed to create VM (" << res << ")" << endl;
24           return -1;
25       }
26
27       jclass cls = env->FindClass( CLASS_NAME );
28
29         // Now try to call main
30       jmethodID mainMethodID = env->GetStaticMethodID( cls, "main",
31                                       "([Ljava/lang/String;)V" );
32       jclass classString = env->FindClass( "java.lang.String" );
33       jobjectArray argsToMain =
34                           env->NewObjectArray(0, classString, NULL);
35       env->CallStaticVoidMethod( cls, mainMethodID, argsToMain );
36
37       vm->DestroyJavaVM( );
38
39       return 0;
40   }
```

Figure 13-20 Creating a Java Virtual Machine from C++ main; invokes Hello with no
             parameters

Key Points

- Java native methods are specified with the `native` reserved word.
- After the class is compiled, we can run `javah` to generate a C/C++ header file.
- After the implementation is written in the native language, it must be compiled into a dynamic library.
- The library should be loaded by `System.loadLibrary`, typically invoked from the static initializer of the native method's class.
- The eight Java primitives have corresponding native types, such as `jint`.
- `JNI_TRUE` and `JNI_FALSE` are defined to represent true and false, respectively.
- `jstring` and `jobject` represent `String` and `Object`.
- `jXXXArray` is used to represent the eight primitive Java arrays.
- `jobjectArray` represents an array of `Object`.
- `jclass` represents a Java class type.
- `jmethodID` represents a method.
- `jfieldID` represents a field.
- The Java native method is implemented by a native function whose name incorporates the package name, the class name, and possibly the signature of the Java native method.
- The first parameter to a native function is the environment pointer.
- The second parameter is a `jclass`, representing the class type for static methods, or a `jobject`, representing `this` for instance methods.
- Additional parameters will be listed in the native function, as declared in the Java native method.
- `javap` is used to obtain a list of encoded field-type signatures and method signatures.
- An instance field of an object is accessed by getting a `jfieldID` from the class type, field name, and (encoded) field type, and then invoking `GetXXXField`, with a `jobject` and `jfieldID`. Static fields can be accessed by `GetStaticFieldID` and `GetStaticXXXField`, with a `jclass` in place of a `jobject`. Fields can also be changed with `SetXXXField` and `SetStaticXXXField`.
- An instance method of an object is invoked using dynamic dispatch by getting a `jmethodID` from the class type, method name, and (encoded) method signature, and then invoking `CallXXXMethod`, with a `jobject`, `jmethodID`, and parameters to the method. Static methods can be invoked by `GetStaticMethodID` and `CallStaticXXXMethod`, with a `jclass` in place of a `jobject`. Methods can also be invoked without dynamic dispatch by using `CallNonvirtualXXXMethod`.

- A C-style string (`const char *`) can be extracted from a `jstring` by invoking the environment function `GetStringUTFChars`. `ReleaseStringUTFChars` should be called when the C-style string is no longer needed.
- A C-style primitive array of primitive types, such as `jint *`, can be extracted from a `jarray` (such as `jintArray`) by invoking the environment function `GetXXXArrayElements`. The corresponding `ReleaseXXXArrayElements` should be called when the array is no longer needed and also if flushing of data back to the Java Virtual Machine is required.
- Elements in a `jobjectArray` can only be accessed individually through environment functions `GetObjectArrayElement` and `SetObjectArrayElement`.
- Environment function `ThrowNew` can be used to signal an exception from native code that can be sent back to the Virtual Machine. The exception is marked only in the native code and control does not automatically exit the native method.
- Environment function `ExceptionOccurred` can be used to test if an exception is active. If so, it is best to leave the native method as soon as possible.
- C can be used instead of C++, with mostly cosmetic differences in coding required.
- A local reference is valid only for the duration of the native method and only in the thread of the invoking native method.
- A global reference is created by environment function `NewGlobalRef` and wraps an existing (local) reference. It is valid until a `DeleteGlobalRef` is invoked on it.
- `MonitorEnter` and `MonitorExit` are environment functions that can be used to create a synchronized block in native code.
- The Invocation API is boilerplate code that allows the creation of a Virtual Machine from inside C++ code. Once the Virtual Machine is running, the `main` method of a class can be invoked using the usual techniques.

Exercises

1. Why would it make sense to write a native method?
2. On the Java side, how is a native method declared?
3. On the Java side, how is the library that contains the native method implementation loaded?
4. For a class that contains native methods, how is the corresponding C++ header file generated?
5. A C++ method is already implemented in a library and we want to be able to invoke it from Java. What is the typical strategy that is used?
6. What is a `jclass`?
7. What is a `jobject`?
8. What are the JNI primitive types?

9. What are the first two parameters in the signature of a C++ native method implementation?
10. Explain how an instance field of a Java object is accessed in C++ code. How are static fields accessed?
11. Explain how an instance method of a Java object is invoked in native code. How are static methods invoked?
12. How are constructors for new Java objects invoked in C++ code?
13. Why can't a jstring be safely typecast to a const char *? What is the correct way to obtain a const char * from a jstring? What memory issues must be dealt with?
14. How is a jstring created from a const char *?
15. Explain how Java arrays are accessed in C++ code.
16. What does it mean for an array to be pinned? How can you tell if an array is pinned?
17. What does the last parameter to ReleaseXXXArrayElements do?
18. How can a C++ native method signal an exception?
19. How can a C++ native method tell if invoking a Java method caused an exception to be raised? Can a C++ native method handle an exception?
20. How does C native code differ from C++ native code?
21. What is a local reference and how long are local references valid?
22. What is a global reference and how long are global references valid?
23. How can a C++ native method obtain and release a monitor?
24. What is the Invocation API?
25. Can a native method make changes to a final field? Find out by writing a program that attempts to do so.
26. Can a native method invoke a private method of another class? Find out by writing a program that attempts to do so.
27. Class CIO, defined below is intented to allow the output of a single int, double, or String, using C-style sprintf formatting. Each of the native methods returns a String in which the escape sequence in the control string is replaced by the second parameter. The native methods are implemented by calling the C library routine sprintf. In the call to sprintf, provide a large buffer for the first parameter (and hope for the best), and then pass control and var as parameters to the C library sprintf.

```
class CIO
{
  native public static String sprintf( String control, String var );
  native public static String sprintf( String control, int var );
  native public static String sprintf( String control, double var );
}
```

28. Implement the standard matrix multiplication algorithm using a native method, throwing an exception if the matrices have incompatible sizes. The signature of your method is

```
native public static double [][] multiply( double [][] a,
                                           double [][] b );
```

Bibliography

The thinking behind C++ is described in [13]. The two 1,000-page gorrillas that describe C++ are [12] and [5] (with answers to the latter title provided in [15]). The books [8] and [9] provide great tips for safe C++ programming. Advanced features of the C++ language itself are discussed in [2], [4], [7], and [14]. A collection of answers to frequently asked C++ questions is provided in [1]. The C++ I/O library is described in great detail in [6]. Good references for the STL include [10] and [11], as well as the 1,000-page gorrillas. The classic reference for the C programming language is [3].

1. M. Cline, G. Lomow, and M. Girou, *C++ FAQs*, 2d ed., Addison-Wesley, Reading, Mass., 1999.
2. J. O. Coplien, *Advanced C++*, Addison-Wesley, Reading, Mass., 1992.
3. B. W. Kernighan and D. M. Ritchie, *The C Programming Language*, 2d ed., Prentice-Hall, Englewood Cliffs, N.J., 1997.
4. A. Koening and B. Moo, *Ruminations on C++*, Addison-Wesley, Reading, Mass., 1997.
5. J. Lajoie and S. Lippman, *C++ Primer*, 3d ed., Addison-Wesley, Reading, Mass., 1998.
6. A Langer and K. Kreft, *Standard C++ IOStreams and Locales: Advanced Programmer's Guide and Reference*, Addison-Wesley, Reading, Mass., 2000.
7. S. Lippman, *Essential C++*, Addison-Wesley, Reading, Mass., 2000.
8. S. Meyers, *Effective C++*, 2d ed., Addison-Wesley, Reading, Mass., 1998.
9. S. Meyers, *More Effective C++*, Addison-Wesley, Reading, Mass., 1996.
10. S. Meyers, *Effective STL*, Addison-Wesley, Reading, Mass., 2001.
11. D. R. Musser and A. Saini, *C++ Programming with the Standard Template Library*, Addison-Wesley, Reading, Mass., 1996.

273

12. B. Stroustrop, *The C++ Programming Language*, 3d ed., Addison-Wesley, Reading, Mass., 1997.

13. B. Stroustrop, *The Design and Evolution of C++*, Addison-Wesley, Reading, Mass., 1994.

14. H. Sutter, *Exceptional C++*, Addison-Wesley, Reading, Mass., 2000.

15. C. L. Tondo and B. P. Leung, *C++ Primer Answer Book*, Addison-Wesley, Reading, Mass., 1999.

Index